DEAF IN JAPAN

D1246583

DEAF IN JAPAN

Signing and the Politics of Identity

KAREN NAKAMURA

CORNELL UNIVERSITY PRESS

ITHACA AND LONDON

Copyright © 2006 by Cornell University

All rights reserved. Except for brief quotations in a review, this book, or parts thereof, must not be reproduced in any form without permission in writing from the publisher. For information, address Cornell University Press, Sage House, 512 East State Street, Ithaca, New York 14850.

First published 2006 by Cornell University Press

First Printing, Cornell Paperbacks, 2006
Printed in the United States of America

Library of Congress Cataloging-in-Publication Data
Nakamura, Karen, 1970–
    Deaf in Japan : signing and the politics of identity / Karen Nakamura.
        p. cm.
    Includes bibliographical references and index.
    ISBN-13: 978-0-8014-4350-3 (cloth : alk. paper)
    ISBN-10: 0-8014-4350-4 (cloth : alk. paper)
    ISBN-13: 978-0-8014-7356-2 (pbk. : alk. paper)
    ISBN-10: 0-8014-7356-X (pbk. : alk. paper)
    1. Deaf—Japan—History. 2. Japanese Sign Language—History.
  3. Group identity—Japan—History. I. Title
    HV2883.N35 2006
305.9'0920952—dc22
2006007159

Cornell University Press strives to use environmentally responsible suppliers and materials to the fullest extent possible in the publishing of its books. Such materials include vegetable-based, low-VOC inks and acid-free papers that are recycled, totally chlorine-free, or partly composed of nonwood fibers. For further information, visit our website at www.cornellpress.cornell.edu.

Cloth printing   10 9 8 7 6 5 4 3 2 1

Paperback printing   10 9 8 7 6 5 4 3 2 1

This book is dedicated to my mother and father,
who probably never dreamed that their child
would follow in their footsteps.

Contents

~

Illustrations

xi

Note on Transliterations
and Translations

I have romanized Japanese words using a modified Hepburn system, and given local terms in the text in italics when clarification is useful: *rōa* (deaf) or *shuwa* (signing). For names and words that have entered common use in the United States, the English spelling is used: Tokyo, Showa.

Japanese names are given in the culturally appropriate order, family name first, except when I am discussing a person who has published in English or is otherwise known to Americans: for example, Suzuki Tarō and Yamada Hanako, but Prime Minister Yasuhiro Nakasone. When referring to informants who are not public figures, I use the –san honorific as a sign of respect. Politicians, movement leaders, authors, and other public figures are referred to by family name only, as is standard in academic practice.

All translations are mine unless otherwise identified. Japanese Sign translations were verified with native signers where possible. Names of government ministries are those used prior to the January 6, 2001, reorganization. The former names of current political parties (for example, Japanese Socialist Party) are also used, reflecting the time period in which the research was conducted.

In accord with customary Deaf Studies transliteration practice in the United States, signing is glossed in UPPER CASE. The reader should note that while signers often use grammatical markers such as facial movements or speed or direction of signs, these are not included in glosses. A gloss such as CAR-BUY can seem ungrammatical, but the subject–object relationship is indicated in sign through placement of the

CAR noun and direction of the BUY verb hand movement. Depending on these factors, CAR-BUY could be: I bought a car; she bought my car; he bought many cars; or he bought her car. I avoid glosses except where they are absolutely necessary to clarify meaning or when they have entered colloquial usage.

Preface

After a long day of rather boring meetings, the dinner party was a welcome af-
fair. The Tochigi Prefectural Deaf Association had rented one of the larger ban-
quet halls at a hotel in the Kinugawa hot springs resort northeast of Tokyo,
where they were hosting the regional deaf conference. A short table for the five
honored guests was at the front of the room with two long tables extended down
the center, seating about fifty people. The conference participants sat quietly
during the formal speeches, but as soon as the food and drinks were brought in,
the room exploded with laughter and sound. People chatted in sign. One by one,
the various conference members shuffled to the front of the room with large sake
bottles to honor and fill the cups of the dignitaries, who were slowly but surely
becoming very, very drunk. The man next to me was trying to teach me the
signs for some words that I would not normally encounter in polite conversa-
tion. We were constantly interrupted by a steady stream of table banging, hand
waving, and shouts of "oi, oi!" (hey! hey!) around us, as people tried to get the
attention of their friends across the room. Someone was at the front of the room,
doing a sign improvisation skit.

I FIRST began studying Japanese deaf identity, politics, and sign language in the mid-nineties. Although I am hearing, I was attracted to this
topic for two reasons. The first was the intellectual challenge. We do not
think of Japan as a hotbed of minority identity, yet deaf groups there are
vibrant and politically active. As an anthropologist, I had been interested
in minority politics and social mobilization, and studying the deaf
seemed to present a novel case.

I was also attracted to the deaf for personal reasons. Their liminal position in Japanese society mirrors my own experiences as a "returnee Japanese" (*kikokushijo*), a Japanese national who was raised abroad as a child and returned in late adolescence. Many returnees face social discrimination because of their linguistic and cultural difference from the mainstream (cf. Goodman 1990). Like returnees, the deaf men and women in this book are Japanese by birth and blood, but are a marginalized minority. Deaf people are linguistically different, culturally different, and politically different from the mainstream, and yet, unlike many other excluded minority groups in Japan, they have managed to argue for a place in Japan *as* Japanese. I had a vested interest in understanding what it was about the deaf community that allowed it to succeed in such a hostile climate.

THE common impression that hearing people have of the existence of the deaf is that of the "silent world," a world bereft of all sound, thankfully void of TV commercials and cars honking, but also lacking laughter, the sound of music, or your mother's voice. This image of silence, an absence of sound, is perhaps the one that is least apt for describing the deaf, either from an external, "objective" hearing person's standpoint or from the perspective of deaf persons themselves.

Gatherings of deaf people are rarely silent. The deaf parties that I attended were just as raucous as any hearing gathering of Japanese people. Their only saving grace was the absence of drunken renditions of country music songs on the *karaoke*, but there were often impromptu comic acts and storytelling instead. Deaf people often vocalize while signing; when they laugh or cry or express feeling, they use their vocal cords as well as their hands. Foot stomping and table banging are common ways to get someone's attention. While it is possible to sign in absolute silence, many doing so find it about as comfortable as a hearing person would trying to speak without using his hands or facial gestures for embellishment. Some amount of sound is part of normal signing, from claps of the hands or snaps of the fingers to vocalizing words or exclamations.

From a deaf person's perspective, the world is hardly silent either. Very few have total hearing loss; most will pick up some degree of environmental sounds even if speech is unintelligible or only moderately intelligible with a very powerful hearing aid. Some have tinnitus or ringing in the ears. Even for those who are profoundly deaf, the world is a noisy place in terms of vibrations. There is a story of a student at Gallaudet University in Washington, DC (the only four-year college for the deaf in the world), who could not study in her dorm room because the vibrations of people running up and down her hallway always made her want to poke her head out to see what was going on. While deaf people do not gain a "sixth sense," they often pay more attention to things that hearing people ignore or that are washed away in the rush of other senses, such as vibrations and movement in their peripheral vision.

Given the perceptual and cultural gulf between hearing and deaf people, what does it mean to be a hearing anthropologist working with deaf communities? Although ethnographic writing attempts to get into the shoes (or sandals) of native informants, there are limitations to even the deepest of ethnographies or thickest of descriptions. Can one really understand what it means to be in a different culture, to grow up with a different language and belief system, or to occupy a different type of body? As both authors and readers of ethnographies, we are limited by our language, culture, gender, age, religion, and, in my own case, my status as hearing (or, more accurately, not-deaf).

Given this, do I personally know what it is like to be deaf? After a decade of working on the topic of deafness in Japan, I have an inkling of some aspects, mostly the positive social ones. For example, I have sensed what it means to be part of the community, to share a common language among friends, but I do not know how itchy hearing aids get in the humid summers or how annoying they can be when they feedback. Although I have on occasion traveled in Southeast Asia where I did not understand the local language, this experience pales in comparison with the experiences of my deaf friends in their own country. As a native English and Japanese speaker and listener, I rest on centuries of linguistic colonialism and a "rational" biomedical view of the body that sees impairment as loss. When communication breaks down in a foreign country, I can blame the Other in a way that deaf people in their own country cannot, since they themselves are constructed as not only biologically lacking, but also as intellectually inferior owing to the perception that they lack (spoken) language.

Outside the disability community, able-bodied persons' temporary experiences with disability—a week where they had to use crutches, or visual sensitivity from a migraine—might lead many to believe that surely anyone would leap at any technology, any innovation, any chance to become "normal." Disability for the non-disabled often means loss. For the most part, though, people who were born with physical impairments do not talk about their lives in terms of loss, and those in the deaf community in Japan are no different.

Instead of the ways that their bodies have betrayed them, deaf people talk about the different opportunities their life courses have given them, the friendships made, the loves won and lost. Some people talk about their deafness as a gift or opportunity and would not want it taken away. If there is a sense of loss and frustration, it is directed toward those who are able-bodied but closed-minded: the parents who did not learn how to sign, the schoolteachers who could not communicate well enough to convey a full education, or the media that remain inaccessible. For in their conception, disability is a social issue—it is society that disables them, not their bodies. They might emphasize the cultural aspects of the deaf community—the development of sign language and deaf culture. However, there is considerable variation in attitudes and opinions within the deaf community, and some would disagree with this cultural framing of deafness and focus more on the politics of hearing impairment.

Intertwined in this book are many stories and one story. At its heart, it is a biography of a community going through generational changes. Deaf identities as well as the way people sign have changed in Japan over the last one hundred years. By tracing archival records, life histories, and institutional politics, I give several accounts of how the deaf community has been able to achieve important political gains and positive social acceptance when other minorities have not. Although I have tried to show multiple perspectives, ultimately this book is also one story, woven by one researcher. American Deaf readers may find that this book leans too much to the side of assimilation, social welfare, and disability politics while hearing readers may find my advocacy for vibrant cultural deafness to be slanted in the opposite direction. I hope this will mean that I have struck the right balance as well as opened space for further discussion of the issues involved.

KAREN NAKAMURA

New Haven, Connecticut
http://disabilitystudies.jp

Acknowledgments

THIS book is based on more than fourteen months of participant observation and archival research conducted in Japan between 1996 and 2001. First and foremost, I must thank the Japanese Federation of the Deaf (JFD) for granting me remarkably open and frank access to the organization. In 1998, I was allowed to work for a year as an intern in the Tokyo head office of the JFD. The number of persons within the organization to whom I owe thanks easily exceeds the bounds of this acknowledgment, but I want especially to express my gratitude to the then-JFD president, Takada Eiichi; the then-head of the Tokyo office, Ohtsuki Yoshiko; and the then-president of the Tochigi Federation of the Deaf, Inagaki Seiichi. Individuals in the JFD who provided special help far beyond the call of duty include Mori Soya, Ōya Susumu, Akima Hiroko, Miyamoto Ichiro, Shigihara Michie, Ishizawa Haruhiko, and Suzuki Etsuko. I am indebted to my sign language transcriber/translator, Ogi Asako, without whom the chapters on the life narratives would have never been finished.

From the bottom of my heart I thank the countless deaf persons who opened their hearts and homes to me. When I began my research project ten years ago as a new and naive ethnographer, I never could have imagined the amount of trust and openness I would encounter. Now I can never imagine being able to fully return this gift in kind. I have tried hard to ensure that in this book I have stayed true to the lives entrusted to me.

Intellectually, I owe my existence to the teachers who have guided me through my academic career. William Kelly has been my *sensei* in every aspect of the word; one could never hope for a wiser adviser, more brilliant and meticulous scholar, or kinder friend. Sonia Ryang and John Campbell have been both role models and shadow advisers.

My research in Japan was made possible by a Small Grant for Dissertation Research from the Wenner-Gren Foundation (#6144); a Yale Council on East Asian Studies Charles Kao Research Grant; the Yale Prize Fellowship; and a Mellon Grant from the Department of Anthropology at Yale University.

I wish to thank the Japanese Federation of the Deaf for kind permission to reproduce various photographs, sign language drawings, and diagrams (figures 4.1, 5.1, 7.1, 8.1, 11.1, 11.2, and 11.3) in this book. I would also like to thank Okamoto Inamaru for his kind permission to reproduce a screen painting (figure 3.1). Yazawa Kuniteru granted me the use of his diagram (figure 2.1), Hattori Akiko illustrated the many ways to be deaf (figure 2.2), and Mizuno Matsutaro of the Alumni Association of the Tsukuba University School for the Deaf granted permission for use of a photograph from their alumni records (figure 3.3).

Roger Haydon at Cornell University Press guided me through the labyrinthine process of book publishing and one could not hope for a better copyeditor than Kay Scheuer. Final revisions of the manuscript were possible because of the help of a small army of friends and colleagues. I thank Robert Pekkanen, Suzanne Kamata, the anonymous reviewers for the Press, and countless others for their time, patience, and critical comments. Leila Monaghan gave up her Thanksgiving holiday to rework the manuscript into a much more coherent narrative. I will ever be in her debt.

Matsuo Hisako has been an integral part of my life for the past four years. Her constant support and encouragement made the book writing process bearable, even enjoyable at times.

PORTIONS of chapter 8 will be published in "No Voice in the Courtroom?: Deaf Legal Cases in Japan during the 1960s," in *Going to Court to Change Japan: Social Movements and the Law*, ed. Patricia Steinhoff. University of Michigan Center for Japanese Studies series.

Portions of chapter 9 were previously published in "Resistance and Co-optation: The Japanese Federation of the Deaf and Its Relations with State Power," *Social Science Japan Journal* 5 (1)(2003):17–35.

Portions of chapter 11 appear in a forthcoming article titled "Creating and Contesting Signs in Contemporary Japan: Language Ideologies, Identity, and Community in Flux" in the journal *Sign Language Studies*.

DEAF IN JAPAN

CHAPTER ONE

Introduction

The staff of the Japanese Federation of the Deaf (JFD) was unwinding at the end of a long workday. The headquarters of the largest association of the deaf in Japan had about fifteen employees crammed into the eighth floor of a small office building in central Tokyo. The majority of the senior staff was deaf, while about half of the junior and part-time staff members and interns (including myself) were hearing. The chief of the Tokyo office, Ohtsuki Yoshiko, had been a long-time activist in the JFD's women's division. In her sixties, she was known, loved, and feared for her forthrightness and spunk. Although she herself was deaf, Ohtsuki-san often vocalized while she signed to make it easier for her hearing employees to understand what she was saying.

One of the JFD members from the outer metropolitan area had dropped by with some snacks, and we were enjoying them while he told us stories about what was going on in his local association. He had recently gone to a lecture organized by a new deaf organization called D-Pro, which had a core group of young activists. In a series of talks and publications, D-Pro was insisting on a separatist deaf identity with a unique sign language and cultural orientation different from mainstream (hearing) Japanese. They were promulgating a notion of a pure Japanese Sign Language (JSL)—an exclusionary position counter to the one espoused by the JFD, which was arguing at the time that Japanese Sign was any sign form used by any deaf person in Japan.

Under the D-Pro model (and the American cultural Deaf model, which D-Pro drew from), deafness was a quasi-ethnic status. The purest deaf were those who were born to deaf parents and for whom signing was their first language. The next purest were those who were born deaf and attended schools for the deaf at an early age. Those who were late-deafened or had not gone to schools for the deaf were not truly deaf in this model, but only "hard of hearing." At the lecture, the D-Pro speaker apparently disparaged the JFD as a "hard-of-hearing organization (nanchōsha dantai)" and the signing used by JFD members as an impure form of sign mixed with spoken Japanese.

Ohtsuki-san listened to this narrative with visibly growing irritation. Finally, in anger at D-Pro's attempt to disqualify both her identity and her signing, she blurted out in sign, "THAT'S SIGN FASCISM!"

As usual, Ohtsuki-san spoke out loud at the same time she signed this, so according to D-Pro, even in her moment of ultimate exasperation she was not signing pure JSL; further proving she was not really deaf, but one of those "hard-of-hearing" masqueraders.

THIS book is the story of three generations of deaf people in Japan and how the shifting political, social, and educational environment of the last century shaped their lives. The development of schools for the deaf and the birth of politically active organizations of the deaf during this period profoundly affected the types of friendships, social networking, jobs, political outlooks, and marriages possible for each cohort.

My central thesis is that the social and institutional history of postwar deaf communities in Japan enabled an unusual form of personal and mass organizational identity politics to emerge in the 1970s and 1980s. Articulating signing as a different mode of communication and not a fundamentally different language from spoken Japanese, the center-left Japanese Federation of the Deaf co-opted discourse surrounding social welfare policies in Japan for the benefit of its members. However, just as certain historical forces created a generational cohort that accepted this assimilationist message, subsequent changes in deaf education and etiology have caused a new, more radical separatist generation to emerge in the late 1990s.

We cannot assume that identities based on biological categories such as disability are any more stable than those based on ethnic categories. All such categories are socially constructed and historically specific. For example, unlike many of the ethnic minorities in Japan (Ainu, resident Koreans, and Chinese, for example), the JFD argues for a fundamental Japaneseness. In this regard, they are similar to *kikokushijo* (returnee Japanese, the group to which I belong); some *nikkeijin* (Brazilian-Japanese); and the more assimilationist front of the Burakumin former outcaste movement. But all of this must be set against the context of generational changes within the deaf community. The younger generation represented by D-Pro argues that they are profoundly non-Japanese in language and culture and instead are members of a global Deaf culture and community. In this way, they are similar to factions of the Ainu native movement who argue that they are part of a global First People's struggle and are not ethnically Japanese.

This book takes us through the various shifts in the deaf community over the past hundred years. While there has been great interest in the history of minority social movements, much of it has unwittingly become hagiography (literally, the lives of saints), as authors tend to focus on the elite leadership of the groups and not the general membership. I have tried to avoid this by balancing the history of deaf schools, political organizations, and movement leaders with the life stories of five rural deaf women whose experiences span almost the entire twentieth century.

The first woman is "Nakano Shizuyo," who was born in 1913 in the northern edge of Kyoto Prefecture. We explore her story in chapter 4. Because her family was poor, Nakano-san was able to attend only a year of informal education at a local "temple school." Her parents forbade her from marrying, she never had any children, and she was largely secluded from the outside world until her forties, when Japan was in the process of recovering economically from the Pacific War. At about the same time, the nascent JFD was gaining prominence as the representative organization of the deaf in Japan. It was at this point that Nakano-san began to see more of the world outside of her small village through her local deaf association, an affiliate of the JFD.

Regional associations of the deaf such as the one she belonged to in northern Kyoto Prefecture sprang up in the 1950s and provided many essential community functions. By hosting drinking parties, hikes, picnics, barbeques, hot spring tours, and other social events, the local associations created a separate, parallel version of mainstream Japanese society for their members. Participating in this parallel society helped sustain the feeling within the deaf community that while they might be socially isolated from the mainstream, they were still Japanese at heart.

It is in this complex postwar environment that the second cohort of postwar deaf women emerged. Three life stories from this generation are presented in chapter 6. The first, Sano Hiroe, was born in 1926. As compulsory education for the deaf was only instituted in 1948, Sano-san had a bare few years of schooling, but even then her life course was much different from that of Nakano-san. Sano-san was able to work freely outside the home, marry a deaf man, and have children. These are experiences she shares with the other women in this group, such as Horikawa Hiro (born in 1946), who went on to lead the Women's Section of her local prefectural association of the deaf. The youngest woman in this cohort, Funata Hatsuko (born in 1951), attended school for twelve full years, but her hopes for college were dashed when her high school counselor told her that no college would accept a deaf applicant and that she should become a hairdresser instead. Struggling against social discrimination such as this, she managed to get a factory job, marry, and raise a son.

The director of the Tokyo office of the JFD who blurted out, "that's sign fascism," comes from this middle generation, as do most of the senior staff and leadership at the JFD. The movement she grew up in profoundly shaped the worldview of the director, Ohtsuki-san. Her deaf politics are inclusive—to her anyone who is hearing-impaired is deaf—and her sign language politics are equally encompassing. She has no tolerance for those who would criticize other deaf persons because their signing is too much like spoken Japanese. That is because in her mind being deaf and being Japanese are not contradictions.

This brings us to the youngest and most recent cohort of deaf people. Starting in the 1970s, deaf children in Japan were encouraged to mainstream, attending their regular local schools rather than residential schools for the deaf. They were taught to speechread and speak orally rather than to sign. This resulted in a generation of children who grew up not identifying as deaf and not using sign as their primary communication method. Ironically, in college many of these students became attracted to the notion of a cultural deaf identity and vibrant deaf culture espoused by American Deaf activists. The more radical ones formed groups such as D-Pro and sought to wrest control of Japanese Sign Language away from the JFD.

The subject of my final biographical chapter grew up in this mixed environment. Born in 1980, Yamashita Mayumi went to a kindergarten for the deaf, but was mainstreamed from first grade until she graduated from high school. Although like many in her generation, she did not have a strong sense of herself as deaf and could not sign, she ended up choosing to go to the only college for the deaf in Japan. There she learned how to sign and gradually became more aware of her identity as a deaf person. After graduation, she returned to the deaf community, this time as a teacher at a school for the deaf in Tokyo.

Postwar Deaf Political Activism

Up through the end of the 1970s, deaf people in Japan had few legal rights and little social recognition. They were classified as legal minors or mentally deficient. They were unable to obtain driver's licenses, sign contracts, or write wills. Many deaf men and women worked in factories or as beauticians, printers, shoe-shines, or dental technicians, or were simply unemployed. Schools for the deaf in Japan taught a difficult regimen of speechreading and oral speech methods and vocational skills. Very few graduates were able to attend college. Even by the mid-eighties, deaf persons were rarely seen signing in public. The dominant social/legal attitude toward the deaf dictated that—like other minorities in Japan—deaf people should try as hard as possible to assimilate even if societal discrimination in employment and marriage made such homogenization difficult.

The 1980s was a decade of much political mobilization behind the scenes. The United Nations declared 1981 as the first International Year of Disabled Persons. Many nations, including Japan, enacted legislation in response to this. After that, the UN realized that a single year for disabled persons would not yield the results they wanted, so they declared 1983–1993 as the International Decade for Disabled Persons. This prompted further political mobilization from the disability lobby in Japan, responses by politicians, and legislative activity. For the most part, however, the largely political and legal changes that occurred in the 1980s were not visible to those who were not part of the politically active disability community.

Through this period, the Japanese Federation of the Deaf was the leading national political and social organization for the deaf in Japan. It mobilized the protests, lobbied the politicians, organized the petition drives, oversaw the interpreter-training programs, published sign dictionaries, and even built a nursing home for elderly deaf residents. Infused with a new leadership who had come of age in the postwar period, the JFD adopted a collaborative approach to working with the Japanese government.

Called "participatory welfare" (*sanka fukushi*) by one JFD leader, their strategy involved working *with* the government in providing resources to the deaf community through grants and contracts. Their politics deemphasized the linguistic differences between Japanese Sign and spoken Japanese and highlighted the social responsibility of well-bodied Japanese to help their own (that is, disabled Japanese) through increased social welfare services and local volunteerism. These inclusive and as-

similationist politics derived from the experiences of the middle generation of deaf described above.

The past decade and a half alone has seen much change. In 1989, after
the death of Emperor Hirohito and the end of the Showa era (1926–1989),
the Japanese scholar Kanda Kazuyuki presciently wrote, "this year, the
first year of the Heisei era, has the potential to be the first year of rapid
[deaf] social change (1989:30)." That prediction turned out to be true.
During the 1990s, the public television network NHK regularly broadcast a Japanese sign–interpreted news hour and hosted a weekly educational program named *Signing for Everyone*. There have been at least
three hit mini-series on television with deaf characters. Instructional sign
courses and seminars became very popular with housewives eager to
become volunteer sign interpreters.

Comic books that taught signing became trendy among (hearing) Japanese students. Companies began slowly hiring deaf people in nonman-
ual labor positions and holding workshops for their hearing co-workers
to ease the transition. The World Federation of the Deaf held a massive
international congress of the deaf in Tokyo in 1991. These visible changes
were accompanied by other social and legal shifts. In 1993, a major revision of disability law in Japan was passed. Several schools for the deaf
began openly experimenting with signing in the classrooms. By the end
of the 1990s and the beginning of the new millennium, the deaf community was in the public spotlight.

The JFD was a major force behind this transformation, and we need to
understand how they pushed for it. Political arguments for social change
can take several different forms: human rights (rights that accrue to us on
the basis of being human); civil rights (rights that accrue to us on the basis
of being a citizen of a particular nation); ethnic diversity rights (recognition of the linguistic or cultural needs of minorities); and so forth.

The model that the postwar JFD leaders promulgated was a mixture of
civil and disability rights. First, they stressed that deaf people in Japan
were quintessentially Japanese with all of the linguistic, ethnic, and cultural markers of mainstream Japanese. They argued that because of a
physical impairment as well as ensuing social discrimination, Japanese
deaf persons were not able to achieve full parity with the mainstream in
education, employment, or social integration. Thus, it was the responsibility of other Japanese, via the government, to ameliorate the difference
through social welfare benefits, hiring quotas, and awareness education.

In many ways, we can view the JFD-led deaf movement as one of the
few successful minority social and political movements in Japan. In the
mid-1990s, however, a new generation of deaf activists emerged who re-

lied on a very different model of social change, based on American minority identity politics and linguistic separatism.

Minority politics in the United States is unique because of the availability of the powerful and articulate frame of ethnic multiculturalism. In America, new groups such as "Somali-Americans" or "Hmong-Americans" are immediately recognized as being part of the same domain as Hispanic-Americans, African-Americans, and Japanese-Americans. Members of new immigrant groups are understood as being entitled to bilingual language support in the classroom, minority civil rights, or protection under anti-discrimination laws without having to argue for this status. In Japan by contrast, it has been very difficult to argue for a "Korean-Japanese" identity since there is no general recognition of the existence of ethnic minorities.[1] In sociological terms, there is no *frame* for ethnic minorities in Japan. Within recent years, various social scientists in anthropology, political science, and sociology have begun to look at the intersection of language, identity, and politics in contemporary social and political movements and the role that these framing narratives play.[2]

Once frames such as ethnic multiculturalism are established, it is easy to extend them to include other nonethnic categories. For example, the American gay/lesbian movement has articulated itself as part of the multiculturalism frame. The rainbow flag of the gay and lesbian movement mirrors the rainbow colors of ethnic diversity. Gay bashing is a federal offense under the Hate Crimes Statistic Act of 1990, along with other violent crimes motivated by race, religion, national origin, and ethnicity. In other cultural contexts, it is not obvious that being attracted to people of the same sex or gender has anything in common with being a member of a minority ethnic group. Nor should it be. These types of frames are created and extended by social activists, not discovered.

The deaf political movement in America has leveraged the multiculturalism frame to great effect. Founded in 1864, Gallaudet University in Washington, DC, is the world's first and only four-year college for the deaf, but up until 1988 it had never been led by a deaf president. Students during the 1988 *Deaf President Now* protests at Gallaudet argued that they

1. Legacies of Japan's colonial expansion in East Asia during the Pacific War, ethnic Koreans in Japan are referred to as *zainichi* Koreans, or resident Koreans. Volumes have been written on this; see Ryang (1997) or Fukuoka (2000).
2. Erving Goffman's original formulation of a frame as an "interpretive schemata that simplifies and condenses the 'world out there' by selectively punctuating and encoding objects, situations, events, experiences, and sequences of actions within one's present or past environment" (Snow and Benford 1992:137) has been extended into the field of mass social movements by a number of scholars (Gitlin 1980; Melucci 1980; McAdam 1994; Morris and Mueller 1992; Laraña, Johnston, and Gusfield 1994).

were entitled to a deaf president just as historically black colleges or colleges for women were led by their own. Many television viewers at the time were struck by the sight of deaf protesters carrying banners stating, "We still have a dream," or declarations that "This is the Selma of the Deaf." The deaf students succeeded in forcing the hearing president of Gallaudet to resign, and a deaf man was chosen to replace her. Signed into law two years after the Gallaudet protests, the Americans with Disabilities Act (1990) was presented as a new civil rights law, extending anti-discrimination protections to people with disabilities. These examples show the power of the ethnic minority frame in the United States.

In Japan, for many reasons, it has been difficult to establish a similar type of powerful ethnic minority frame.[3] As a result, groups such as the JFD have had to use other frames in order to leverage political power: human rights, an appeal to the commonality (and thus mutual responsibility) of all Japanese, neighborhood volunteerism, and perhaps most powerfully with the government, a sense of falling behind the West. And as a result, disability social welfare in and of itself has now become a powerful frame in its own right.

The disability frame impacts the community differently from an ethnic minority frame. For example, men and women in the deaf middle generation in Japan unhesitatingly and unequivocally argue that they are Japanese first and deaf second. This inclusivity allowed the movement to expand rapidly during this period and accomplish real political change. Arguing that signing (*shuwa*) was a different mode of spoken Japanese and not a separate and unique language permitted its use in public schools for the deaf without raising the ire of the Ministry of Education. But when the youngest generation of deaf activists emerged in the 1990s, they introduced a totally new frame, one that advocated a cultural deaf identity and recognition of a Japanese sign *language*.

In 1995, several forceful articles by the leaders of D-Pro, a radical new Deaf political and cultural activist group, appeared in the mainstream intellectual journal *Gendai Shisō*. This represented a break from the politics of the previous JFD-led generation. One of the articles begins:

> *A Declaration of Deaf Culture*: We Deaf people take this as a (basic) definition: "Deaf people are a linguistic minority who converse using Japanese

---

3. Lacking the multiculturalism frame, gay and lesbian politics in Japan have struggled to come up with a suitable strategy. Somewhat ironically, the disability frame in Japan has become so powerful in its own right that groups such as transsexual activists have been calling themselves "gender identity disabled" (*seidōitsusei shōgai*) rather than embedding themselves in the gay and lesbian movement. That itself is a subject for another book.

Sign Language, a language that is distinct from the Japanese language."
The previous perspective was that "Deaf people" equaled "People who
can't hear"—a biomedical disease model that focuses on impairment.
This is changing to a new perspective of "Deaf people" equal "People
who use Japanese Sign Language as their daily/normal language"—
namely, a social-cultural one. (Kimura and Ichida 1995:354)

This manifesto highlights the differences between Deaf culture and
hearing culture in Japan. It stresses the importance of language within
the Japanese deaf community and the development of a separate "Deaf
culture" (*rō bunka*), drawing on ethnic minority positions espoused by
American Deaf activists (cf. Padden 1980; Padden and Humphries 1988).

D-Pro's Declaration borrows American deaf studies scholar Harlan
Lane's concept of the Deaf as a colonized people without a country. The
capital D in Deaf here symbolizes a strong cultural minority identity and
primary relationship with signing.[4] But while the plight of deaf students
in Japanese schools is comparable to those of other linguistic minorities
in Japan, no mention was made in the D-Pro Declaration of resident Koreans, Chinese, Okinawans, or Ainu. Instead, an early article in their
newsletter *D* compared deaf discrimination to the oppression of left-
handed individuals (May 1, 1992).

Here, the leaders of D-Pro had a problem. As mentioned before, a
broadly successful, identity-based "new social movement" (Melucci 1980:
1994) using an ethnic minority frame is nonexistent in Japan or at least invisible. There are certainly many minority groups: the Burakumin, a former outcaste group; the Koreans who were brought over as forced laborers
during the colonial period (1910–1945); the Ryukyuans/Okinawans who
were forcibly annexed by Japan; and the Ainu, who are the aboriginal residents of northern Japan whose lands were occupied and colonized by the
Japanese beginning in the eighteenth century. But there is no extant notion
of an active "Burakumin culture"; there is no emergent Korean-Japanese
culture discussed positively in the mainstream press;[5] Okinawan nationalism is largely ignored by mainland media; and the Ainu native culture

4. Following standard notation in American Deaf studies (Woodward 1972; Padden
1980), "Deaf" (with a capital D) indicates people who identify with "Deaf culture" and
"Deaf politics" and who use sign language as their primary language; lower-case "deaf"
indicates individuals who are audiologically deaf. Neither implies the other, and so one
can be "deaf" without being "Deaf"; for example, elderly people who become late-
deafened are not usually considered Deaf.

5. This has changed slightly in the past few years with the emergence of a new generation of resident Koreans. The "Korea boom" (*hanryū*) in Japan with the popularity of dramas such as *The Winter Sonata* starring Bae Yong Jun—who is known in Japan as *Yon-sama*
or "Lord Yong"—may yet prove to be more than just another short-lived fad.

(while still alive) has been encased behind museum glass in the popular consciousness. This underscores the powerlessness of the ethnic minority frame in Japan, not the lack of minority groups in general.

Former Japanese prime minister Yasuhiro Nakasone infamously declared in September 1986 that the United States was a "less intelligent society" with its "blacks, Puerto Ricans, and Mexicans" compared to mono-ethnic Japan (Wetherall 1993:3). Although Nakasone was not the brightest politician Japan ever produced, most Japanese on the street would blink uncomprehendingly if asked about Japan's ethnic minorities *(shōsū minzoku)*. The absence of a prevalent ethnic model has existed in large part because the Japanese government has actively subdued ethnic identities since the turn of the nineteenth century in the name of national unity. For example, early in Japan's colonial phase, the Ainu had been forced, under such laws as the Hokkaido Former Aborigines Protection Act (1899), to adopt Japanese names and to abandon the Ainu language and customs. This same pattern emerges for Okinawans and resident Koreans as well. This suppression of minorities was not unique to Japan; in many ways Japan borrowed both the concept and implementation details from the United States and European colonial powers.

This unrelenting pressure to assimilate resulted in many second- and third-generation Koreans, Okinawans, and Ainu no longer identifying as such or not even aware of their ancestry. In a 1995 nationwide poll, 99 percent of respondents (regardless of nationality) considered themselves to be of Japanese ethnicity.[6]

If D-Pro framed itself as an ethnic and linguistic minority and used that as the basis for political rights, they would have difficulty leveraging the relatively weak local concepts of ethnic diversity and multiculturalism. The leaders seem to recognize this. In the Declaration they

---

6. Source: NHK Broadcasting Culture Research Department, January 6, 1995. "The data utilized in this publication/presentation was originally collected by NHK Broadcasting Culture Research Department. The data was obtained from the Japan Public Opinion Location Library, JPOLL, Roper Center for Public Opinion Research, University of Connecticut. Neither the original collectors of the data, nor the Roper Center, bear any responsibility for the analyses or interpretations presented here."

There were approximately 1.4 million legal foreigners in Japan in 2001, which is 1.1 percent of the total population (MHLW 2003:184). Thus, the 1 percent of respondents who answered with a non-Japanese ethnicity could easily be just the resident foreign population. Resident Koreans are legally considered foreigners unless they naturalize. The Statistics and Information Department (SID) of the Ministry of Health, Labor, and Welfare does not keep any official statistics on the number of ethnic minorities with Japanese citizenship in Japan (personal communication, SID staff member, November 10, 2004).

write: "perhaps some people will find some resistance to the term 'ethnic group'; instead we could say that the Deaf are a 'linguistic minority.' " The authors lead their readers away from the problematic discourse on native ethnic minorities in Japan and instead tried to draw authority from the American multicultural frame.

The Physicality of Deafness and Deaf Identity

Although deaf politics in Japan are embedded within larger disability politics, this book mainly focuses on the deaf community and only intermittently talks about broader disabilities. For although JFD leaders in Japan often use the mantra of disability rights in making claims to the State, actual interaction between the deaf leadership and other disability groups (with the exception of those who are deaf-blind, deaf-wheelchair-users or otherwise multiply disabled) has been limited until recently. The same communication barriers that separate the deaf community from the non-signing mainstream also separate them from the non-signing disability community.[7]

Deafness has been called a hidden disability because you cannot tell from looking at someone that she is deaf unless she is wearing a hearing aid. The main social handicap caused by deafness is communication with hearing people since so much of mainstream cultural, social, and business life is conveyed through speech. The blind-deaf writer Helen Keller is said to have once remarked that while blindness cuts you off from the world, deafness cuts you off from other human beings, by which she meant the majority who do not know how to sign. Being deaf is a hybrid and intersectional identity. You are who you are—Japanese, a Christian, a painter, photographer, architect—but the language barrier places you out of the mainstream of all those categories.

With deafness, as with physical gender,[8] many people believe that there is a clear physicality that underlies deaf identity—a biology of deafness. Many people think there is an essential quality to deafness, for example that all deaf everywhere in the world must surely understand each other using a universal sign. They see a deaf person as physically

7. This has changed with the creation of the Japan Disability Forum in October 2004, which integrates activists across multiple disabilities including deafness.

8. See Anne Fausto-Sterling's (1993) article "The five sexes: why male and female are not enough" for a critique of the prevalent view that there are two and only two sexes bound into our biologies.

deficient, or at least tangibly different from a hearing person. In this book, I argue instead that while the causes of deafness may be similar across cultures and times (illness, genes, and so on), the sociohistorical construction of what it means to be deaf varies considerably.

Although all deaf communities have discovered manual signs as a primary means of communication (perhaps pointing to the neurological, inherent adaptability of the brain), the forms of signing and relationship with spoken language within these communities are highly variant, and the politics of deafness are also multitudinous. British Sign Language is distinct from and mutually unintelligible with American Sign Language, which is distinct from Japanese Sign Language. Meetings at the World Federation of the Deaf are just as much a Tower of Babel as those at the United Nations.[9]

At the Gallaudet Deaf Prez Now demonstrations in the United States, deaf student protesters carried placards stating, "Deaf can do everything but hear." Perhaps that is the most (and least) one could say about deafness and identity. The diverse identities created by the product of a physical impairment, social institutions, family, history, and individuality all contradict an essentialized, unitary, and mandatory nature to deaf existence.

In many ways, because deaf communities across the globe have each created their own sense of (deaf) identity, (sign) language, and (visual) culture, it is easy to imagine them as types of ethnic minorities. However, deafness is very different from other ethnic identities (such as being Black or Hispanic) in that very few deaf children are born to deaf parents, only 10 percent in most estimates. That means that rather than through their families, the majority of deaf people arrive at their identity as deaf through social institutions such as schools for the deaf in childhood or deaf associations as adults. Because the deaf community represents a unique type of non-family-based, nonethnic, cultural, and linguistic minority, we need to approach the study of deaf identity through different channels from those for traditional ethnic minorities. In the next chapters, we will first look at the demographics of deafness and linguistics of signing before exploring the early history of deafness in Japan.

9. In 1973, the World Federation of the Deaf constructed Gestuno as an international communication tool. But like Esperanto, Gestuno is criticized for being both artificial and Eurocentric in both derivation and use.

CHAPTER TWO

The Politics of Japanese Sign Language

Language choice is identity choice.
—CAROL PADDEN, American Deaf Studies scholar

As any linguist will tell you, all language claims are political. When people in the street argue that their language is distinct from another language, that someone speaks the national language correctly or incorrectly, or that this language is simply a dialect or creole of that language, they are making fundamentally political statements, not descriptive or scientific ones. Languages are part and parcel of the national borders (both physical and ethnic) of the "imagined nations" that separate us (cf. Anderson 1991)—"imagined" not because there might be tangible cultural and ethnic boundaries between two nations, but because the differences that seem so clearly defined on a map become a swirling mix of pointillistic variation on the ground. Although "French" people might carry French passports and speak French, when they try to precisely delineate what constitutes being French or French-ness (as being opposed to being Belgian or Swiss or part of the EU), they are committing political acts, not scientific ones.

The *Declaration of Deaf Culture* reproduced in the introduction was written by two of the leaders of D-Pro, the group that advocates a Deaf culture perspective. For many Americans, especially those who are liberal and educated, the declaration is framed so completely within the American discourse on ethnic and linguistic diversity that its political nature is largely invisible. Unfortunately for D-Pro, many Japanese disagree with the declaration, calling it "radical" and disputing the existence of a separate "Deaf culture." That many of those in disagreement with D-Pro are in fact deaf themselves adds some mystery to the situation.

13

Part of the cognitive power of D-Pro's declaration is its deft use of a seemingly linguistic argument, namely that Japanese Sign Language (JSL) is an independent, autochthonous, natural language;[1] that it is the native language of deaf persons in Japan; and, furthermore, that JSL's lexicon, morphology, syntax, and pragmatics differ from spoken Japanese because they are separate language systems. Since this premise is apparently grounded in linguistic fact (that is, the language claim appears neutrally based in science), we are less apt to deconstruct it in the same way we might other, more political aspects of D-Pro's position, such as its stance against cochlear implants, for example.

The goal of this chapter is to explore, analyze, and ultimately deconstruct this entity known as *Japanese Sign Language (Nihon Shuwa)*. However, as Japanese sign language scholar Kanda Kazuyuki has written, the linguistic situation in Japan is far from simple:

> It is commonly thought that deaf people are able to understand each other using sign. That is certainly true; however, deaf people [in Japan] use a variety of different languages based on individual differences, and we cannot say that they all use the same method of communication. For example, a deaf person may be very fluent in Japanese Sign[2] but may be unable to communicate in spoken Japanese. Another deaf person may use both speech and sign simultaneously. And yet another deaf person may use speech as well as converse using pen and paper (i.e., swapping notes). The source of that difference lies in each individual's particular language environment, especially the type of deaf education they received. (Kanda 1989:30)

While most people involved in the deaf community in Japan do not normally divide Japanese sign into "JSL" and "Manually Coded Japanese," at least two terms have emerged to describe the wide variation. There is *dentōteki shuwa* (traditional signing) and *Nihongo-taiō-shuwa* (literally "signing that corresponds to the Japanese language"). No one really warms to the phrase *dentōteki-shuwa* (Traditional Signing) because it

---

1. "Natural language" is used here in the linguistic sense, as opposed to an artificial language such as Esperanto, Gestuno, or Manually Coded English (developed as a pedagogic aid).

2. Here, Kanda adds a footnote regarding his use of the term "Japanese Sign," as many scholars were differentiating between variant forms of sign extant in Japan, especially in regard to the younger generation who were signing while speaking at the same time: "I'm aware of the phrase Traditional Sign (*dentōteki-shuwa*); however that was coined in opposition to Simultaneous Signing (*dōjihōteki-shuwa*). I believe that the term *Japanese Sign* (as in *Nihon shuwa*) is the most appropriate one when referring to the still-changing form of sign [being used today]" (Kanda 1989:43)."

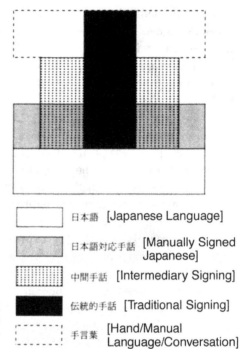

日本語	[Japanese Language]
日本語対応手話	[Manually Signed Japanese]
中間手話	[Intermediary Signing]
伝統的手話	[Traditional Signing]
手言葉	[Hand/Manual Language/Conversation]

Figure 2.1. Yazawa Kuniteru's model of Japanese sign variations. Source: Yazawa (1996:29). Used with permission.

makes it sound as if the language should be in a museum, but it is the common term for the type of signing used by the older generation deaf as well as some of the younger generation who are trying to recover their traditions.

Yazawa Kuniteru, a veteran (hearing) educator in schools for the deaf, has come up with the model in Figure 2.1 to describe the various sign systems in Japan.

Here, Yazawa is making a political statement (again, statements about the coherence of languages are usually political). In his model, "traditional signing" covers a broad range from purely gestural communication to manually signed Japanese. This is a broader definition than the one given above, and is somewhat controversial. The effect of his statement is that traditional signing is the central element of the deaf community, shared by all who participate in it, regardless of the exact way they sign. This is a sentiment shared by many leaders in the JFD.

I would like to emphasize that even more than "cultures," "languages" do not exist singularly, as there are no physical bounds that constitute a language system. By nature, languages are gregarious beasts. Every language varies at the individual, familial, local, and regional levels. Even single speakers/signers can and will vary their register or styles depending on the situation. An individual signer might mix the two styles when signing to different people, or even within the same conversation. The notion of linguistic homogeneity is deceptive, since languages are in constant contact with one another and will intermingle, borrow, and blend. We are always already constantly speaking creoles of a sort. The old sociolinguist's quip that a "language is a dialect with an army and navy" applies here.

In this chapter, I am primarily concerned about language as practiced. As we shall see in later chapters, language use is intimately related to identity issues. Although the general public generally speaks of language as a static and bounded entity (so the idea of an English Only Movement in the United States has some political support), the reality is that language is dynamic and amorphous. If there was an English Only constitutional amendment, which dialects of English would be considered authoritative? The Midwestern dialect spoken by Minnesotan public radio hosts? The speech of Boston Brahmins? Texan oil tycoons? Immigrant New York City taxi cab drivers? Bilingual Hispanic schoolgirls? The English Only movement is premised on the belief that there is a pure English at the center and impure dialects around the periphery. On close examination, language purity is a purely political concept.

Sign languages are similarly messy, with many regional dialects and idiolects. Signers will change how they sign depending on whom they sign with. This does not mean that signing is not a natural language, but it does complicate pinning down *exactly* what Japanese Sign Language might be. The five women whom we will meet later in this book all sign with very distinct differences, and I would be hesitant to call any single variety Japanese Sign Language in fear that that would mean the others would be considered *not* JSL.

Who gets to determine language orthodoxy is fundamentally what is at stake in Japan. This is a topic we will return to in chapter 11. However, since it is difficult to talk about a subject without first describing it, even if we go on further to deconstruct our own creations, let us assume that there is something named Japanese Sign Language that is internally consistent and coherent and elide these political considerations for the moment so that we can return to a fuller deconstruction in the later chapters.[3]

---

3. In a sense, thinking mono-linguistically about Japanese signing reduces all of the interesting differences that drive this book: among them age cohorts, power, regionality, and access to formal education.

Sign Language Variation

A common misconception among many hearing people is that sign languages are universal or mutually intelligible among signers from different countries.[4] Nothing could be further from the truth. Sign languages vary as much as other natural languages, or even more, as there has traditionally been less state activism in unifying sign language dialects within nations. Sign languages with different lineages such as American Sign Language and Japanese Sign Language are of course mutually unintelligible; a JSL signer would be unable to immediately understand what an ASL signer is saying in conversation.

Although the United Kingdom and the United States share a spoken language called English, British Sign Language and American Sign Language are mutually unintelligible. Even when fingerspelling English loan words, the deaf people in the two countries use different systems— the British use a two-handed system while the Americans borrow the one-handed fingerspelling style used in France, Spain, and other continental European countries.

Because sign languages often form around schools for the deaf, students at different schools for the deaf in the same city may even use different forms. The anthropologist Barbara Le Master (2003) provides an excellent example in Ireland, where two Catholic schools for the deaf in the same city developed different signing forms. Because the schools were segregated by gender, the language variation also carried over to the adult population, with men signing differently from women. Other scholars have found variance among older Black and white signers in the U.S. South where schools for the deaf were segregated by race until the middle of the twentieth century (Aramburo 1995; Hairston and Smith 1983).

Even within the same language community, there can be wide variation. Signers can have "accents" or idiolects—that is, they may sign particular words using slightly different (or totally different) forms; their grammar may follow different use patterns; pacing may be rapid and clipped or slow and drawling; their gesturing may be broader or larger, or smaller and more compact. These accents can vary across gender boundaries (one sweeping generalization being, for example, that deaf

---

4. Another common myth is that sign languages are invented by "someone." That same *someone* is often referred to when people argue: "Why couldn't *they* make it [sign language] universal?"

women in the United States tend to sign more compactly than men do), age, or geographic region. Astute native signers can often look at another signer and tell what region he or she is from, or even what school for the deaf he or she might have attended. Hearing people who learn sign in adulthood often have particular accents that mark them as non-deaf,[5] but hearing children of deaf adults (so-called CODAs) can sign so fluently that they are considered culturally Deaf. Deaf children of deaf parents sign differently from their peers born of hearing parents, and these "deaf of deaf" are often the center of American deaf communities.

Donald Grushkin writes poignantly about the dilemma faced by the "hard of hearing" in the United States, who find themselves alienated from both hearing and deaf communities. Being hard of hearing is less a statement of audiological ability than one about language choice and community identity. Signing ASL without voicing places you with the American cultural Deaf community; using oral speech and speechreading places you within the hearing community. True biculturalism/bilingualism is difficult. Grushkin writes of the "Deaf militancy . . . [that] asserts that some aspects of being hard of hearing are proof of nonmembership within the Deaf culture" (2003:114).

The Demographics of Deafness

Genetic deafness can be found in all countries and all times although it has rarely been the predominant cause of deafness. In remote villages or islands, an isolated gene pool can cause the normally recessive gene to express at a higher rate than usual. Nora Groce analyzed the case of the population on Martha's Vineyard in the late nineteenth and early twentieth century in the United States (Groce 1985). More recently, a team of medical researchers has found an isolated village in Indonesia with similar characteristics (Winata et al. 1995; Morell et al. 1995; Friedman et al. 1995).

Except in such anomalous cases, it is estimated that only about 10 percent of deaf children are born to deaf parents. This also means that 90

---

5. We could stereotype a "hearing accent" in both Japanese Sign and ASL as including: following the spoken grammar form rather than making use of the gestural/spatial potential; clumsier transitions between signs; greater focus on discrete words, adjectives, and adverbs rather than sign classifiers and gestural/facial markings of size, speed, or distance; chronological discontinuities in storytelling; less repetition and less use of chaining.

percent of the deaf community are born to hearing parents and usually have limited access to sign language until they enter the school system.[6] Thus, schools for the deaf play an essential role in identity construction. Just being physically deaf does not imply that you will sign or that you will identify as part of the deaf community. Biology is truly not destiny here.

Just how many physically deaf persons are there in Japan? According to the latest government report (Cabinet Office 2003), there were 346,000 registered people in 2002 with hearing impairments sufficient to receive social welfare benefits. Japan has different classes of registered disabilities. Class 5, the lowest level, involves hearing loss of 80 dB in both ears, while a Class 1 or 2 severe disability is complete hearing loss in both ears with concomitant communication impairment. The total population of Japan in 2003 was 126,139,000; thus, "hearing-impaired" persons represent 0.27 percent of the populace. The way the government structures this part of the welfare system, elderly persons who lose their hearing primarily for age-related reasons do not generally register as hearing impaired.

During my field period, everyone I met who had a severe enough hearing impairment to cause communication issues with hearing people carried the government disability ID (*shōgaisha techō*). Registering as hearing impaired with the local welfare office and receiving the ID card makes you eligible to receive a large range of social benefits including a significant disability pension (over $1,700 per month for people with severe disabilities in Tokyo); discounted medical equipment; free municipal transportation; discounted travel on national and municipal railways and national highways; and discounts on a broad variety of public and private services. Even the most adamantly culturally Deaf leader of D-Pro, when I interviewed her in 1997, admitted that she was registered, carried the *techō*, and received the monthly pension.

The opposite is not true. Just because you carry the *techō* disability ID card does not mean that you sign or that you are part of the deaf community. It only means that you are classified as having a significant hearing impairment or other disability. Compared with governmental or organizational statistics, the number of "native" signers is much less clear. This is because we cannot precisely define the boundaries of Japanese

---

6. Even if the school is strictly oral and forbids sign language, the children almost always use some form of signing when communicating with each other. In oral schools, this is seen as a matter of grave concern.

Sign, and whether those who are hard of hearing or late-deafened, for example, can be said to be using it. As of 2001, approximately 20,000 hearing people passed the JFD affiliate-run sign training courses and there were over 6,000 registered interpreters for the deaf in Japan.[7]

The number of members in the Japanese Federation of the Deaf (which allows only people who are deaf to join) was 25,518 in 2003 (JFD 2004:113). While we can make the assumption that nearly all members of the JFD can sign, not everyone in the JFD signs the same way; some sign while at the same time simultaneously speaking in Japanese, using a temporal/sequential grammar; others turn their "voices off" and sign without voicing, using a signing form that makes heavy use of spatial/simultaneous grammar forms. There is no precise division between these two forms, and for the most part they are mutually intelligible. I will resist, for the most part, the tendency to label the latter form "true JSL" (*hontō no Nihon shuwa*) and the other just "Signed Japanese" (*Nihongo-taiō shuwa*) as this is precisely the topic of later chapters. The most I can say is that more than 25,000 and perhaps less than 400,000 people use sign communication in some form in their daily life activities in Japan.

Sign Linguistics and the History of ASL

The American scholar William Stokoe is often referred to as the founding father of sign *linguistics* (it must be stressed, not sign *language*). A professor at Gallaudet University in the 1950s and '60s, he noticed an apparent structure to the sign communication among his deaf students. At that time, signing was thought to be merely a form of miming or a derivative/broken form of English. Stokoe brought linguistic analysis to bear on signing and, to his astonishment (and that of the rest of the hearing world), discovered that sign communication was a natural language system with a very different structure from spoken English. He gave it the appellation "American Sign Language" to make it clear to other linguists that a language system was involved (Stokoe 1960).

Stokoe set up the basics of sign linguistics. He noticed that in sign languages there were parallel analogues to phonemes, morphemes, lex-

---

7. For an explanation of the procedures by which interpreters are examined and licensed, see the report by the Culture and Information Center for Hearing-Impaired Persons (1998).

emes, grammar, and pragmatics. For example, in ASL there are basic handshapes (phonemes) that make up component, meaningful parts of words (morphemes) such as the word ending –PERSON used to sign things such as TEACHER or WAITER. Stokoe discovered that morphemes also have a spatial dimension; for example, the temple area of the head signifies MALE while the cheek area signifies FEMALE in ASL morphology. Other researchers continued his analysis of the syntax and pragmatics of sign languages. It quickly became apparent that this was a totally new and unexplored area of linguistics.

ASL is an amalgam of French Sign Language (brought by the Deaf educator Laurent Clerc), modified French initialized sign forms (what we would call today Manually Coded French/English), and the native, local, and home sign language systems used by deaf children in the United States before Thomas Gallaudet founded the first school for the deaf in Hartford, Connecticut, in 1817. The graduates of Gallaudet's school went on to become educators of the deaf themselves, spreading across the country. This development is often cited as the reason why ASL is relatively uniform across the United States, and indeed we do see relatively little regional variation. However, we have to remind ourselves that this is a constructed story line that centers a pure and unchanging ASL in the narrative. Owen Wrigley puts it as follows in the preface to his *Politics of deafness:*

> Rather than search for the origins of Deaf culture and the fall from grace of sign language, which is the hagiographic frame of Harlan Lane's dominant study, Foucault would have us recognize that "History teaches how to laugh at the solemnities of the origin." He calls on Nietzsche in reminding us that the "lofty origins is no more than 'a metaphysical extension which arises from the belief that things are most precious and essential at the moment of their birth.'" (Wrigley 1996, xvi)

Wrigley is referring to the American deaf studies historian Harlan Lane's singular focus on the contributions of particular American and European educators and leaders: Thomas Gallaudet, Laurent Clerc, Abbé de L'Epée, Abbé Siccard, and others. Traced this way, American deaf history gains a particularly singular teleological course: from L'Epée, to Siccard, to Clerc, to Gallaudet, in a manner reminiscent of the Catholic lives of the saints. This hagiographic method ignores the widespread political, social, and linguistic variation in the community as well as the contributions of many other people who were not in leadership positions.

We can read elements of the contemporary cultural Deaf movement in the United States as resistance to this hagiography of elite, well-educated men. The recent blooming of the cultural Deaf movement has centered the "deaf-of-deaf"—the deaf children of deaf parents—as the core elements of Deaf culture, the bearers of the purest and most beautiful ASL, the sign poets, the storytellers, the leaders, and the political activists. In this counternarrative, the deaf-of-deaf served as the protectors of Deaf culture in the United States during the long period when it was pushed underground, between the Milan Congress of 1888 and the rediscovery of Deaf culture and ASL in the late 1960s (cf. Lane, Hoffmeister, and Bahan 1996; Preston 1994).[8] ASL and cultural Deaf values are passed down, mother to child. This version foregrounds the contributions of working-class deaf people against Lane's hagiographic frame that centers on the educated and privileged. Read this way, the story of the purity of the ASL lineage is also one of class struggle (Monaghan 2004).

The language mythology of a singular ASL is sustained in part by the American construction of cultural Deafness that excludes the hard of hearing, orally deaf (that is, deaf people whose primary form of communication is speech and speechreading), and late-deafened. These deaf persons, while they may use ASL-related sign communication forms, are specifically excluded from inclusion as "Deaf" or the recognition of their signing as "ASL"—for example, Heather Whitestone, a former Miss America who is orally deaf (she does not sign except on stage), and I. King Jordan, the first deaf president of Gallaudet University (installed after the DPN movement in 1988), are both late-deafened. Neither is considered real "Deaf" by the "Deaf militants," to borrow Grushkin's (2003) phrase, nor are they said to sign ASL. Instead they are somewhat dismissively said to use "pidgin sign English" (PSE) or "Manually Coded English" (MCE). It is easy to claim language and ethnic/cultural homogeneity when one is willing to exclude outliers.

In Japan, there has been no similar veneration of the deaf-of-deaf until very recently with the D-Pro generation. None of the leaders within the JFD, famous sign poets, or *rakugo* storytellers have been deaf of deaf until the last decade. As the story of the deaf community in Japan develops, we will see that the struggle between the JFD and D-Pro is not only

8. Conversely, the "oral deaf" (those taught speech/speechreading skills over sign language) or "hard of hearing" have been seen as on the periphery of deaf culture and politics in the United States. This has not always been the case. A stigma used to be attached to the "low verbal," but this later developed into a pride in being an "oral failure."

generational but also linguistically bound with similar but different aspects of class distinction.[9]

The Origins of Japanese Signing

Unlike the American case, no one is quite sure where Japanese signing came from.[10] Japanese Sign is unrelated to sign language forms used in the United States, Europe, or China. There are some similarities between Korean and Taiwanese Sign Languages and Japanese Sign, but this has been attributed to the colonial period rather than pre-modern language transport.[11] There are no founding language fathers such as Thomas Gallaudet or Laurent Clerc within the Japanese deaf community. There are some important contributors, such as the founder of the first school for the deaf in Japan, Furukawa Tashirō. But they are not credited with creating Japanese Sign or even standardizing it. For the most part, signing in Japan is best described (and is seen by deaf persons there) as an autochthonous language. The title of the JFD's series of sign books sums up this perspective nicely: *Watashi-tachi no Shuwa* or *Our signs*.

What we can deduce is that before the Meiji period began, a hundred and forty years ago, there was very little sense of a unified Japanese sign language (Kanda 1989:31).[12] Natural sign languages typically form around schools for the deaf, as these provide the ideal conditions of communities of deaf children. Sociolinguistic research done in Nicaragua (Senghas and Kegl 1994; Senghas 2003), for example, has shown that a

9. Judy Kegl writes in the production notes for BBC TV's *Silent Children, New Language* (BBC TV 1997) that there were *no* deaf-of-deaf and very little genetic deafness in Nicaragua until the advent of schools for the deaf. This is because deaf individuals were sequestered in their houses and not allowed to marry—very similar to the situation in Japan until the advent of compulsory education.

10. Okamoto (2000) has an innovative foundation theory based on a correlation between sign handshapes and Kanji. This has not yet been broadly accepted by other sign scholars. The cultural critic Donald Richie writing informally in a 1980 essay published in his 1992 collection, *A Lateral View*, notes how culturally embedded Japanese gestures are, then gives as examples a series of gestures familiar to any Japanese signer (thumbs referring to men, little fingers as women, and others). Japanese culture is certainly rich in its gestural vocabulary, especially within its many niche segments (fishermen, sushi chefs, gangsters, and the like). I am not aware of any studies that have yet explored these specialized gestural systems and their impact or influence on Japanese signing.

11. For more information, see JFD (1994). This report notes that although the older generation uses a sign form that is still reminiscent of Japanese signing, the authors cannot see that same influence in the new generation of younger signers.

12. Scholars interested in the genealogy and transformations of Japanese Sign would do well to read Kanda's (1989) short monograph (in Japanese).

natural sign language (that is, one complete with its own syntax and morphology) appeared within a few decades of the founding of a school for the deaf. Before that time, there were only home signs, incomplete sign language systems used in the homes of families with deaf children.

Unless there is a genetic disposition toward deafness within a closely bounded community, the natural level of hearing impairment within a population (often less than 0.5 percent) is not a sufficiently critical mass for a language community to form in rural areas. The process of modernization, with its shift toward great population densities, greater incidence of epidemic influxes, and improved infant mortality (the diseases that used to kill children now are survivable, though sometimes with deafness as a result) bring larger numbers of deaf children together and help create deaf communities. Thus industrialization and urbanization are necessary components for a deaf social identity to develop.

The first school for the deaf in Japan was founded in 1875 in Kyoto by the aforementioned Furukawa Tashirō. Prior to founding the school, Furukawa saw deaf children signing outside the window of the prison cell where he was temporarily detained for forging documents related to a peasant protest. This was one of his inspirations for using signing in the classroom when he founded his school. His observation provides some evidence for the early existence of signing in Kyoto. Unfortunately, soon after it opened in 1875, the Kyoto School switched to an oral form owing to the global effects of what is called the Milan Conference (1880), an international meeting in which hearing teachers at schools for the deaf unilaterally decided that oralism was to be the main method of deaf education. Deaf teachers were not invited to attend (Van Cleve and Crouch 1989).

Looking at elderly deaf who grew up in Japan before the Pacific War, we see only limited evidence of a unified national sign language system prior to the 1940s. Teachers of the deaf had founded a few regional schools, but only a small portion of the deaf population was able to attend. For example, Nakano-san, whom we will meet in chapter 4, went to school only for a year. She is fairly typical. As a result, she and many other deaf persons born before the war tend to use a sign language composed of an amalgam of home signs, local signs, greater use of classifiers, and otherwise nonstandard sign forms.[13] Their sign grammar departs even further from spoken Japanese than current signing. As a result,

---

13. Jill Morford (1996) has an excellent review essay on home signs and language acquisition.

very few people (mostly deaf adults who are in daily contact with these individuals) can communicate smoothly with them.

That the older deaf people do not use a standard signing is not surprising, because there was little social or political pressure for a single national sign language before the war. The Japanese government was not a unifying factor, as it did not recognize the use of sign in schoolrooms until the 1990s.[14] The Japanese Federation of the Deaf, which encouraged social activities among local and regional deaf groups, had much more impact on language unification in the postwar period. It is through these social activities as well as movement of people from rural to urban areas that the various types of signing in Japan begin to consolidate.

After the end of the Pacific War the American Occupation Forces mandated compulsory education for all Japanese, including the deaf and blind. Schools for the deaf sprang up all over Japan, at least one in each prefecture. While signing was officially not permitted in these schools, ancillary effects happened. First was the conglomeration of children who had never met other deaf children before. It has been well documented in sign linguistics that natural (sign) languages emerge in this type of situation. After the first cohort graduated, they created alumni groups, centering deaf community life around the schools.

The Japanese Federation of the Deaf drew much of its strength from these alumni associations.[15] Although it was not very politically active until the 1960s, the nascent JFD served a crucial socializing role. The annual Deaf Meeting was a huge attraction (and continues to be so), drawing members from all across Japan. The location of the meeting rotates among the 47 prefectural organizations and usually draws 2,000–4,000 people. For many, it is a time to reconnect with friends, travel, and see Japan. This central purpose has not changed over its fifty-year history.

Nevertheless, there was no central institution that served to homogenize Japanese signs for most of the modern period. There was no Gallaudet University churning out deaf teachers and professionals, serving as the ivory tower from which new knowledge and new signs could disseminate; nor was signing broadcast widely on TV until the 1990s. The

14. The Ministry of Education still does not recognize sign language as a valid form of educational communication in elementary schools. It has not developed any special curricula for schools for the deaf at any grade level. The ministry has, however, "accepted" that use of sign language may be necessary at the middle and high school levels.

15. The first national deaf meeting was held in 1906; the first deaf association was formed in 1914 as the Tokyo Deaf Club. The Japanese Association of the Deaf formed in 1916. A large cadre of the original members came from the alumni groups of the Kyoto and Tokyo Schools for the Deaf, the two oldest schools in Japan.

only homogenizing forces were the school systems, which could standardize signing only at the local level, and the admixture of individuals at JFD meetings. This changed starting in the 1960s, as the JFD became more interested in codifying the lexicon, teaching interpreters, and otherwise standardizing the vocabulary of Japanese Sign.

But even now, Japanese Sign is a relatively diverse language system. Despite the JFD's best efforts, the lexicon is not standardized. Even relatively basic words such as STUDENT and NAME differ from Sapporo to Tokyo to Kyoto and among signers. There are at least three main variant ways to sign "Deaf": one brings the open palm from the ear to the mouth; a second uses the index finger (much like the ASL "DEAF"), and the third has the dominant palm cover the ear while the non-dominant palm covers the mouth.[16] There are also synonyms in use such as *mimi ga kikoenai ("ears can't hear"),* which has the dominant palm waving toward the ear.

The hard of hearing or *nanchōsha* are given a particularly descriptive sign: an open palm splits the face in two. This is similar to the sign for *half,* referring to Japanese with mixed ancestry. Although deaf politics are constructed differently in the United States and Japan, the liminal position of the non-signing hard of hearing is the same.

In addition to the variations in the actual signs used, there are also visible regional differences in grammar and syntax. Although the various strains of sign remain mutually intelligible, I have noticed that two signers from different regions will often drop down into a register that more closely approximates spoken Japanese grammar concomitant with verbal mouthing, in order to facilitate the use of speechreading to aid the sign communication.

For example, Tochigi Prefecture just north of Tokyo is often cited as having a very different sign language than the rest of Japan. The lexicon used there is relatively consistent with other regions, but the grammar system is different. Twenty-odd years ago, Tanokami Takashi, a hearing teacher at the Tochigi Prefectural School for the Deaf (the only school for the deaf in Tochigi) introduced *dōjihō,* simultaneous signing while speaking. He borrowed this system from Britain in order to improve the understanding of spoken Japanese among the students at the Tochigi

16. For right-handed signers, the dominant hand is the right hand and the non-dominant hand is the left. The reverse is true for left-handed signers (although many will sign "right handed"). However, many signers will switch hands in various circumstances, for example, when text messaging with a cell phone or driving.

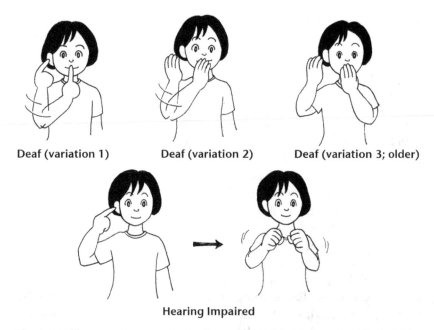

Deaf (variation 1)　　**Deaf (variation 2)**　　**Deaf (variation 3; older)**

Hearing Impaired

Figure 2.2. There are many ways to sign the word DEAF in Japanese sign. Illustrated by Hattori Akiko.

School. Several generations later, the Tochigi students, now adults, still sign with a strong Japanese grammatical influence.

Unlike signers in other areas, Tochigi deaf people in their forties and fifties use a sequential syntax (words have meaning because of their word-order placement), and they use sign words or fingerspelling conjunctions, prepositions, and topic particles ("*ha*" in "*kore ha pen desu:* this [topic] is a pen)." Signers from outside Tochigi, in contrast, tend to drop both prepositions and pronouns, either relying on the pragmatics of the conversation to carry the meaning or using a spatial/gestural indexical relationship (pointing to an object, and signing "PEN" to indicate that *this* is a pen).

Other Japanese deaf persons complain that they cannot understand Tochigi dialect signers. This perhaps has more to do with politics than with reality. The signing used in Tochigi is indeed different in that it follows Japanese spoken grammar and syntactical structures more closely than other dialect forms, but within the grand scheme of dialects of Japanese Sign it certainly does not seem different enough to render it mutually unintelligible. Instead, Tochigi Prefecture is engaged in complex language politics. Tokyo residents see Tochigi as a rural backwater, and the Tochigi dialect of spoken Japanese is considered country bumpkinish. This metropolitan snootiness carries over to Tochigi signing, which is considered awkward and strange.[17]

LANGUAGE codification requires political power. In the case of the deaf this would mean either the establishment of schools that all use the same sign language, or the development of deaf cultural institutions that have the power to define the bounds of sign language. Neither of these exists yet in Japan. Only in the last ten years has a unified sign dictionary emerged (Yonekawa 1997), and preliminary attempts are just being made at codifying the syntax (Matsumoto 2001).[18] There is a wide variance of vocabularies in local dialects as well as different syntactic systems in use, ranging from those in perfect alignment with spoken Japanese to those that use a spatial-temporal grammar.

Unfortunately, the main Japanese Sign lexicon remains relatively small. The aforementioned comprehensive sign dictionary published by the JFD in 1997 has only 4,800 individual signs. One major reason for this remains that signing is not widely used in classrooms. While many high schools for the deaf use sign informally, there is no formal usage at the secondary school level. Signing is not used at the college level either, and there is no central institution such as Gallaudet University where seminars are conducted at the undergraduate and graduate level, a situation in which new signs and specialized vocabularies are created by necessity.

One method of compensating has been the use of Kanji signs, signs representing Chinese characters for technical terms. For example, anthropology (*jinruigaku*) is signed using its three component Kanji signs: HUMAN-VARIATION-STUDY. However, unless the listener is conversant in spoken Japanese, can speechread the pronunciation, or has encountered the term before, this string of Kanji signs is incomprehensible.

In her (1995) ethnography *Do you see what I mean?*, Brenda Farnell

17. Non-deaf (hearing) Japanese play the same language games. Much is made of Japan's cultural homogeneity, which ostensibly includes language. Yet at the same time, language is used to reinforce difference and centrality, for example, during NHK (public television) documentaries about the northern regions of Japan. The dialogue of residents is often open-captioned (subtitled) because their speech differs from standard (Tokyo) dialect. The U.S. equivalent of this would be PBS subtitling remarks made by an older Southerner because Northerners would not understand. In the 1996 movie *Trainspotting*, Scottish brogue was subtitled and (mis)translated, to comic effect.

18. In contrast, the Gallaudet "Green Book" series (Baker-Shenk and Cokely 1980) has long served as a technical description of ASL and a teacher's guide to teaching the grammar.

poses questions about the narrowness of Western concepts of language by expanding the definition of language to include gestural and performative aspects. In Japan, the question of Japanese signing's *language* status has been ignored by all except D-Pro, who are using it toward the particular political goal of redefining deafness into cultural Deafness. They are doing this by codifying Japanese Sign Language grammars and attempting to create a "pure JSL," which would de-center the late-deafened and hard-of-hearing college-educated elites who dominate the leadership of the JFD.

The JFD's official position has been that "Japanese Sign (*Nihon shuwa*) is . . . the type of signing used by deaf persons living in various parts of Japan" (JFD 1998b:2)." In other words, if you are a deaf person living in Japan and you sign, you are using Japanese Sign by definition. There has been resistance in the JFD leadership and membership to narrowing this tautological definition any further. In a pivotal essay, in contrast to a specific definition of Japanese Sign as only those forms of signing that do not involve synchronous mouthing, JFD leader Matsumoto Masayuki writes:

> Establishing a definition for the term Japanese Sign (*Nihon shuwa*) is difficult because of the linguistic and social problems relating to the question of what the Japanese language (*Nihongo*) itself is. If you characterize the Japanese language as "the forms of language (*kotoba*) used in Japan (both past and present)," then Japanese Sign could also be conceived as part of the Japanese language (with the spoken language consisting of one form and signing another form of the Japanese language as a whole). . . . Defining Japanese Sign as "only the type of signing that does not involve mouth movements," is based on the same principle as establishing the Tokyo dialect as the common language (standard Japanese [*hyōjungo*]), in contrast with other regional dialects. . . . It all boils down to how you want to define the term "Japanese Sign." (1997b:4)

Here, Matsumoto underscores the JFD policy of blurring the difference both between the Japanese language and Japanese Sign and between the variations of Japanese Sign that are closer to or further from spoken Japanese grammar (in that they use mouth movements or not). In line with this, the main focus of the JFD's linguistic efforts in the 1980s and 1990s was to codify the lexicon and to introduce new vocabulary words to match new or existing terms in spoken Japanese. Almost no effort was made in syntactic analysis until the end of the twentieth century.

The avoidance of syntax is deliberate; *syntax*, more than anything else, is divisive. It divides both Japanese Sign from spoken Japanese and traditional signing from manually coded Japanese. It splits the deaf community from the hearing, and the hard of hearing from the deaf of deaf. That is why the JFD avoided focusing on grammar and syntax in order to build their mass movement and why D-Pro seized on it as central to their notion of cultural Deafness and pure JSL in order to differentiate themselves from the previous generation.

To get to the roots of this emerging language war between the JFD and D-Pro, we must start at the very beginning. The next several chapters examine the history of the deaf in Japan and explore the lives of five deaf women through their own words. Then we will return to the issue of Japanese Sign Language.

CHAPTER THREE

The Early History of the Deaf in Japan

We know very little about deaf lives before the twentieth century, especially outside of Western Europe. People with hearing impairments certainly existed prior to the modern era, and we can find scattered references to them in historical material, but historians and other writers took little note of them at the time. Before the last century, deaf people largely were not educated and rarely left memoirs or other texts. Thus we can learn about what their lives might have been only from secondary sources written by non-deaf persons.

In this chapter, I summarize early attitudes toward the deaf in Japan, noting the first references to deafness and disability in Japanese history/mythology as well as briefly covering the early teachings of the three major religious systems in Japan (Buddhism, Confucianism, and Shinto). Then we move to the late Meiji period, where written historical records provide some of the social and institutional background for Nakano-san's story in the next chapter.

The Establishment of the Japanese State and Religious Systems

Around 400 C.E., various clans were brought together by the Yamato dynasty to constitute a more or less unified nation-state centered around the town of Naniwa (contemporary Osaka) and extending from the western island of Kyushu to the Kinai plains in the east. As Japan traded with its neighbors to the west, various influences came across the Korea Strait. Two major religious systems, Confucianism and Buddhism, entered Japan during the fifth and sixth centuries. In response, in 550 C.E. the imperial household introduced the word "Shinto" to describe the native folk beliefs of Japan and thus the three major religious systems were defined: Confucianism, Buddhism, and Shinto.

There was considerable inter-clan warfare and confusion on the main island of Japan until 593 when Prince Shōtoku became the regent of the imperial court. Prince Shōtoku immediately began a number of reforms: he established Buddhism and Confucianism as the official religions of the state; formed strong diplomatic relations with the kingdoms of Korea and China; and wrote the first national constitution (604 C.E.) based on Confucian and Buddhist principles. Each of the three major religious systems established by the eighth century understood the causes of disability differently.

Early Shinto

Shinto, or the *Way of the Kami* (Gods), is an animistic belief system involving hundreds, if not thousands, of local deities or *kami* who reside in natural objects such as large trees, mountains, streams, or rivers. Shinto is concerned with maintaining harmony, balance, and purity with humans and the universe. Humans are naturally good, but evil can be caused by a lack of harmony or balance or through impurity (physical or mental defilement). Compiled in 712 C.E., the *Kojiki* ("Ancient Chronicles") is one of oldest literary works in Japan as well as one of the central texts in Shinto. However, it is more a collection of myths and quasi-historical tales than it is religious canon. In the early stories is the first literary appearance of a person who might be described as being disabled.

The first chapter of the *Kojiki* describes the creation of the cosmos, the world, and the Japanese islands. The male god Izanagi meets the female god Izanami, and together they create the first island in the ocean of chaos. They build a house on the island and marry. Out of their relationship, a "leech child" (*hiruko*) is born. The stories vary as to his disability: some say he had no arms or legs at birth, others that he had no bones. Bearing the disgrace of his parents, the leech child was put out to sea at the age of three in a reed boat (he subsequently returns to become the god of fishermen, Ebisu). After ritual purification, Izanami goes on to give birth to the islands of Japan as well as the full pantheon of (able-bodied) Japanese deities.

There are two alternate readings as to the nature of the impurity that caused the leech child to be born. Many authors suggest it was because Izanami greeted her husband first when they met and that violated a taboo against women speaking before men (NCDLM 1998:7). Another interpretation is that Izanagi and Izanami were brother and sister, and thus it was an incestuous and impure relationship (Ninomiya 1986:202). In either case, a violation of the laws of nature caused the birth of the leech child.

Shinto attitudes toward disability seem mixed. On the one hand, disability is associated with the spiritual impurity of parents. On the other, author Ninomiya mentions that the deity "Fukusuke is also regarded as good luck for merchants. . . . He is intellectually disabled and has hydrocephalus; his appearance is a chubby man with a huge head and short build. Until recently, many merchants kept intellectually disabled people and Fukusuke dolls in their shops, believing that they would bring happiness" (1986:203). These dolls bear a striking resemblance to people with Down Syndrome. Itō also cites several sources that suggest evidence that the deity Ebisu (the grown-up version of the leech child) is also hard of hearing, perhaps deaf, as various local customs have supplicants bang the door to his shrine loudly to attract his attention (1998:20). The god of fishermen, merchants, and wealth and fortune, Ebisu is often portrayed with very large ears, as well as a large stomach. Thus it difficult to argue that disability only has negative connotations within Shinto belief systems.

By the Heian period, the Shinto notion of *kegare*, or spiritual pollution became widespread among the nobility and then down through the social classes. Avoidance of death, blood, illness, and other spiritually polluted material was necessary. Shinto priests (with the emperor as chief priest of the Japanese nation) performed *yakubarai* or purification ceremonies. This emphasis on purity would contribute to the increasingly class-based social structure as well as the creation of outcaste groups such as the *eta* and *hinin*. These outcaste groups, which after the social reformations of the Meiji Revolution would become labeled with the euphemism *burakumin* or "people of the village," were responsible for meat butchering, leather tanning, executions, and other tasks that were considered ritually impure under Shinto. We will return to the burakumin again in the contemporary period as their political mobilization makes for an interesting comparison with the deaf, but there is no direct relationship in Shinto between burakumin and disability.

Several chapters later in the *Kojiki*, contained within the legend of the Emperor Sui'nin (roughly first century B.C.E.–first century C.E.), the figure Homuchiwake-miko is a priestess (*miko*) who is mute or cannot speak. One author (Itō 1998:23) cites her as an early example of someone with speech or linguistic disabilities, possibly deaf. The presence of early historical figures with various disabilities gives some indication that the disabilities were not unknown in early Japan and that they were not all associated with the lower classes.

Buddhism

Buddhism officially entered Japan from Korea in 538 C.E., although it was not formally recognized as a state religion until the time of Prince Shōtoku in 593. While it may have been a religion of the imperial court, it took many centuries before Buddhism became a religion of the masses. The teachings of many Buddhist sects in Japan suggest that physical impairment in this lifetime may have been the result of bad karma (*on*) in a previous lifetime. Pronouncements included, "Karma from a past life will cause one to be born mute in this life," "Those who violate the Lotus Sutra will become deaf and mute," "The wife of the man who violates the Lotus Sutra shall bear a child who is mute; if a woman violates [the Lotus Sutra], her child will follow a similar fate" (Itō 1998:35). In a collection of Buddhist tales collected by the monk Keikai, twelve of the stories mention individuals who are deaf, blind, or otherwise disabled; all twelve stories also associate this disability with past sins (Ninomiya 1986:204).

This negative attitude toward disabilities was, on the other hand, balanced by the Buddhist philosophy of compassion. The eighth-century monk Saint Gyōki is credited with founding *fuseya* or sanctuaries within temple grounds all across Japan that served in part as refuges for orphans, elderly, sick, destitute, and disabled (Itō 1998:37). These would later provide the template for the *terakoya* or temple schools that were the first precursor of public education in Japan and the only type of school that my informant Nakano-san in the next chapter was able to attend.

Confucianism

Based on the writings of the Chinese scholar Confucius, Confucianism has been called a moral philosophy as well as a religion. Emphasis is placed on the maintenance of hierarchical social order and social relationships. In 701, a Japanese legal system based on Confucianist belief called the *Asukano Kiyomihara Ritsuryō* was enacted, establishing the emperor's power and the *koseki* family registry system. Itō (1998:27–31) notes that among its declarations, the *Ritsuryō* categorizes individuals into various ranks or social statuses, including those who are disabled. This was an early example of the bureaucratization and formularization of disability in Japan.

Within the *Ritsuryō* system, people who are deaf in both ears are considered *zan'shichi*, the most minor form of disability, which included those who were blind in one eye, had no thumbs, or only three toes. The term, which literally means "uncured illness," is still used in contemporary mainland China to refer to people with disabilities (pronounced *canji* in Mandarin Chinese).

The moderate category of *hai'shichi* included those who were mute, dwarfs, those without use of an arm or leg, and those with intellectual disabilities. The most serious category, *toku'shichi*, included those blind in both eyes, without both arms or without both legs, with dangerous contagious illnesses, mental illness, and similarly severe disabilities. An analysis by Itō (1998) of the *koseki* records of one village of 2,372 people in the eighth century revealed 32 disabled individuals, including one who was totally deaf and one totally blind.

Why were the deaf categorized as the least disabled? Taking a position that draws from social constructionist and historical materialist perspectives, Itō argues that society and social frameworks create disability. In the mostly agrarian Nara period (710–794 C.E.), deaf peasants experienced few problems because farming required little hearing or communicative skills; thus they were considered to be only lightly disabled because they could work. Being blind or having no arms or no legs would render someone unable to contribute labor on a farm; thus such people were classified as having the severest form of disability.

The rationale behind government measures in the Nara period toward disabled persons lay in the Confucian beliefs that upheld the emperor system. Natural disasters were seen as the result of the emperor not following the law of the heavens; thus the victims of such natural disasters were in part the responsibility of the emperor and his administration. This philosophy, the *tenkenron*, was expanded to include the elderly, physically weak, and handicapped as the direct responsibility of the emperor (Itō 1998:26–27). This contrasts with Buddhism, where disability was considered the result of individual or family action or inaction.

Buddhism and Disability in the Middle Ages and Tokugawa Period

In the middle ages, we know that Buddhist monks such as Eison (1201–1290) and Ninshō (1217–1303) were active in the creation of temples and hospitals that housed the disabled and the destitute, including facilities for those with leprosy. There are depictions of people who are disabled, walking with wooden *geta* clogs on their hands because they have no legs, and so forth, on scrolls and paintings of that era (NCDLM 1998:8).

During this period, blind people were able to learn musical instruments such as the shamisen and koto as well as medical practices such as massage and acupuncture. They formed self-sufficient associations or guilds where they would train younger members in the skills of their arts. The famous *biwa-hōshi* or itinerant blind minstrels emerged during this time. Rather than being a peripheral part of Japanese society in the middle ages, the blind musicians and blind massage therapists and acupuncturists were central to social functioning.

The peak of Japanese feudal society, the Tokugawa period (1600–1868), was a time of great social stability, which made possible the development of vibrant merchant culture and the creation of urban centers such as Osaka and Edo (modern Tokyo). The growing importance of education coupled with industrialization pulled people out of their farming communities and toward the cities in growing numbers. This affected deaf persons at the time in two ways. First, although they were able to farm alongside their hearing family members within the rural environment, it must have been more difficult to achieve social integration with hearing people in the cities. Second, while deaf may have been isolated from other deaf in the countryside due to the low population density, within urban centers there were more opportunities to meet, congregate, and develop social communication methods with other deaf people and thus establish the beginnings of a unified signed language.

Tokugawa Japan was a rigid caste-based society. People belonged in separate social castes (warrior, peasant, merchant, craftsman, and the outcaste Burakumin), and intermingling of the castes was forbidden. During this period, the blind musicians were able to appeal to the Tokugawa government and have their guild system, called the *Tōdōza*, formally recognized (NCDLM 1998:9). The creation of the guilds and occupational specialization, however, appears to be unique to the blind community. There were no parallels in communities of people who were deaf or physically impaired.

Okamoto Inamaru, a researcher of deaf history in Japan, finds the first visual representation of the deaf in a screen painting done in 1604. In the top left corner, there is a group of beggars who appear to be gesturing to each other (Okamoto 1999a:35). From the positioning of the hands of the main "signer" and the attentiveness of his "listeners," Okamoto postulates that the painting depicts a group of deaf individuals, perhaps a roving troupe of deaf beggars (this is speculative, as there is no definitive caption or other indication).

By the mid-Edo period (early 1700s), the association of beggars (*kojiki*, literally, "to beg for food") with deafness seems to have solidified. In 1713, a doctor living in Osaka by the name of Terajima Ryōan published the *Wa-kan Sansai Zue*, the first illustrated encyclopedia of Japan.[1] The entry for *ofushi* (the archaic term for "mute") reads:

> *Ofushi* [gives spelling in Chinese Kanji and pronunciation in Japanese]. The term mute (*ofushi*) refers to those who have no [ability to communicate in] words. There are those who are not only mute, but are also deaf (*rō*), and they have become that which is to be pitied. There are also those who, after maturing, gradually gain the ability for language. The child of the Emperor Sui'nin, Homuchiwake no Miko, grew up without saying a single word. When she was 30 years old, she saw a swan and gained the first use of language. (Terajima 1713, cited in Itō 1998:100)

第 1 図　慶長 9 年（1604）秀吉七回忌の豊国臨時祭礼図屏風（徳川黎明会蔵）
左隻施餓鬼部分

Figure 3.1. Screen painting from 1604 with deaf beggars. Source: Okamoto (1999a:21). Used with permission.

1. *Wa-Kan* = Japanese and Chinese. *Sansai* = the Heavens, the Earth, the People.

Figure 3.2. Deaf beggar in *Wa-kan Sansai Zue* (Terajima 1712).

There is also an entry in the *Wa-kan* for deaf (*rō/tsumbo*) that reads:

> *Tsumbo.* Commonly referred to as tsu-n-bo. Because the ears of the deaf are unable to hear, the deaf are ignorant, trapped inside a cage [basket] of ignorance. They have the ears of a dragon, unable to hear. (Ibid)

Parenthetically, according to legend, dragons have no ears and are deaf. The ears of the dragons fell into the ocean, where they became seahorses, which is not-so-coincidentally the mascot animal and logo of the Japanese Federation of the Deaf.

What is curious about the *Wa-kan Sansai Zue* is that the entries for people with other physical disabilities are largely positive (or not nearly as negative as the deaf examples). For example, there is a drawing of a person with no arms writing Kanji with his brush held by his feet. One possible explanation is that in the Edo period, deaf beggars were a visible presence in the streets and it is likely that Terajima had actually seen them, while people with other physical disabilities tended to be secluded by their families and he resorted to his imagination when describing them.

Pre-Meiji Schooling of the Deaf

We know from case studies in other countries such as Ireland (Le Master 2003), Nicaragua (Senghas 2003) and Nigeria (Schmaling 2003) that schools for the deaf are an essential ingredient in the formation of deaf communities and coherent sign languages. However, there is no evidence of systematic schooling in Japan for the deaf before the Meiji period (1868–1912). There were small private "temple schools" (*terakoya;* literally: temple huts), some of which had deaf pupils. In her life narrative in the next chapter, Nakano-san, a deaf woman born in 1913, refers to her brief encounter with one of these schools in a neighboring town. But unless their parents were rich and did not depend on their labor in the fields, most people who were deaf remained uneducated, kept at home, and were not allowed by their families the opportunity to interact widely with other deaf persons. The government itself did not engage in the business of operating schools for the deaf until the Meiji period, and widespread compulsory education for the deaf did not occur until after the end of the Pacific War in 1945.

The temple schools originated out of the tradition of Buddhist monks teaching neighborhood children how to read and write during the Muromachi era (fourteenth century). They became popular in the late Edo period (1850s) up until the turn of the century, when compulsory education for all able-bodied children was enacted by the Meiji government. Between 1854 and 1868, between 300 and 400 new temple schools were opened each year. Although the original *terakoya* were affiliated with temples, the term became a generic name for a privately run (non-government) elementary school with students staying on average three to four years, although some were known to spend seven to eight years. These schools taught children basics of reading, writing, and arithmetic, with popular ones attracting over a hundred students, although many had only two or three students (Itō 1998:134–135).

The Japanese scholar Ototake Iwazō interviewed 3,090 elderly Japanese men and women who had attended temple schools during the Edo period. This research, published in 1929 as *The history of the education of the masses in Japan*, indicates that 8.6 percent of the 3,090 temple schools reported had students with some form of disability. This included students who were deaf, blind, intellectually disabled, or physically disabled; however, according to Ototake, the majority were deaf. As the first subject taught was Chinese calligraphy, these deaf students had an advantage over their blind classmates.

Meiji Revolution of 1868 and the Modernization of Japan

In the decades before the Meiji Revolution in 1868, progressive thinkers and scholars looked beyond the borders of Japan and realized that their country was in danger of becoming yet another victim of the European colonial rampage in East Asia. These scholars traveled to Europe, determined to learn how to create the social and industrial frameworks needed to modernize (at once Westernize, militarize, and industrialize) the nation. Fukuzawa Yukichi was one of this group, focusing his attention mainly on education. In 1862, he traveled to the West and commented on the London School for the Deaf, noting that they used fingerspelling and oral methods (speech training and speechreading) to educate the deaf in England. He also visited France and the Netherlands, which also used the oral method. In 1866, two years before the Revolution, he published his findings in his "The Situation of the West (*Seiyō Jijō*)" (Itō 1998:187–192).

In 1863, another young politician/scholar named Yamao Yōzō was sent to learn more about British shipbuilding techniques. He traveled as part of an expedition including the future Meiji leader Itō Hirobumi and others. After returning to Japan, Yamao entered the new Ministry of Construction, which was responsible for the physical infrastructure of the rapidly industrializing Japan. While in the United Kingdom, Yamao visited the shipyards at Glasgow and marveled at how they were using deaf workers alongside hearing. In 1871, Yamao wrote a petition to the new Meiji government titled, "A White Paper on the Creation of a School for the Blind and Mute." He argued that through education the deaf (and blind) could learn a profession that would allow them a life of their own, free from the condescension and pity of the non-disabled (Tsukuba 1991:4). His argument was that Japan, as a *modern* nation, must involve all of its citizens. The argument was inherently competitive, pitting Japan against England and other Western powers.

The First School for the Deaf in Japan

With the support of the new Meiji government, the first school for the deaf was opened in Kyoto in 1878 by Furukawa Tashirō,the young teacher mentioned in the previous chapter.[2] He was the fourth son of the head of one of the most prominent *terakoya* in the Kyoto area, if not the whole nation. In his twenties, he was arrested for forging some documents in his attempt to aid peasants in a dispute over farmland, one of the many peasant revolts fermenting during that period caused by tax hikes, growth in tenant farming, crop failures, and starvation (in roughly that temporal order). While he was in jail, Furukawa looked out of his prison window and saw two deaf children being teased. He writes in his prison notes:

> There is nothing as unfortunate in life as the deaf-mute. For not only is their physical condition miserable, but by the very movement of their body they cause normal people to despise and make fun of them. Treated as the unwanted waste of human kind, theirs is truly a sad situation that compels our deepest concern. I contemplate, with some resentment, why the Creator would do such an unjust thing as this. Possessing human bodies, the highest form of life on this world, all humans must live as such and be able to receive the fruits of such an existence. To not be able to receive an education and fully live their lives as human beings must be the cruelest punishment of all. And it is a crime for us to withhold such an education from them. If the deaf were able to do the same things as normal people, then they would not face the discrimination and shame that they do now. Furukawa Tashirō, *Tesshin-roku*, cited in Itō (1998:225)

Furukawa established his school, initially called the Kyoto Blind-Mute Institute (*Kyōto Mōa'in*), in 1878, the eleventh year of the new Meiji period. The timing was not coincidental. He was able to establish his school with government help because the Japanese government was pushing to create more modern social institutions after the Revolution, spurred by the scholars returning from abroad such as Fukuzawa and Yamao.

The Kyoto school was followed two years later by the Tokyo School for

---

2. Furukawa actually started teaching deaf children in 1876 (Meiji 9) on a limited scale at the Kyoto Jōkyōku #19 Elementary School (Tsukuba 1991:10). Remarkably, within two years, he developed his own pedagogical method for teaching deaf children, including the invention of his own fingerspelling system, which was later abandoned, and then much later replaced with a system based on ASL fingerspelling (ibid.). Okamoto Inamaru has written extensively in Japanese on Furukawa's life and career.

the Deaf and the Blind (1880), and slowly other larger prefectures built their own institutions. Although these schools received some government backing, students still had to pay for their own expenses (room, board, schoolbooks, and supplies[3]) and attendance was not mandatory. As many parents did not see any occupational future for their deaf children, they considered the schools a waste of money and did not send their children to them. Rural peasant families were especially loath to send their deaf children, who were a valuable labor source. Only very rich urban residents could afford to send their deaf children to be educated.

Regardless, the schools grew rather quickly. The *100-Year History of Blind-Deaf Education in Kyoto Prefecture* (Editorial Board for the 100th Anniversary of Deaf and Blind Education 1978) provides us with detailed enrollment numbers from 1892 to 1977. From a mere 47 students in 1892, the (renamed) Kyoto School for the Blind and Deaf took less than a decade to double its number of students and break a hundred pupils. Growth continued to be rapid with only a small dip during 1912–1920. In the 1930s, there were around 200 deaf students attending the Kyoto school in all grade levels. With about fifteen grade levels (K–12), that meant an average of approximately thirteen students per class. In reality, most children attended only a few years of elementary school and were not allowed to progress (for various reasons) to a secondary education.

While this rapid increase in the number of students may appear a possible result of the growing popularity of the school, we must put it in the context of a rapidly expanding Japan. The general population almost doubled from 43.4 million in 1899 to 72.8 million by 1944. Japan was quickly modernizing, but that did not extend to all of its social institutions equally quickly. For the most part, rural deaf children were kept in their family homes to perform manual labor, even as they grew into adults.

The First Deaf Associations

The Tokyo School for the Deaf opened in 1880 and the first alumni association was formed in 1891 (Tsukuba 1991:8). The slightly older Kyoto School for the Deaf also boasted a very strong alumni association, and

3. Early school documents indicate that the prefecture paid 80 percent of the tuition. In the fourth year of the school's operation, the student contribution to tuition was ¥10.4 yearly with ¥13 for food. (Editorial Board for the 100th Anniversary of Deaf and Blind Education 1978:60)

these associations became a central core around which communities developed. In turn, graduates of other schools also started to create their own local alumni associations.

In 1906, the first national conference of the deaf was held in Tokyo, sponsored by the Tokyo School for the Deaf Alumni Association. The primitive transportation networks made national conferences difficult, but people continued to meet to work on issues such as deaf education. In 1915, leaders from the various alumni associations met in Tokyo and decided that a national association was needed. Later that same year, Japan declared war against Germany and entered the First World War.

The next year, at a meeting hosted by the Kyoto School for the Deaf Alumni Association, the Japan Association of the Deaf was formally created with its headquarters in Tokyo and branch offices in Osaka and other major cities. Yamao Yōzō, the same hearing politician who wrote the white paper advocating the creation of schools for the deaf, was elected its first president. Konishi Shinpachi, a former principal of the Tokyo School for the Deaf, was elected chairman. The JAD continued to host annual meetings right through the middle of the Pacific War.

The Japanese Association of the Deaf published a monthly newsletter, the *Rōa Geppō* (Deaf Monthly Report), starting in 1931. The first issue was

Figure 3.3. Deaf schoolgirls dancing for a military audience (1940). Source: *Tsukuba University School for the Deaf 100-Year History* (1991:40). Used with permission.

indicative of the state of the organization: the lead article concerned new genetic research at Kyushu University which found that deafness could not be inherited if one parent was "normal." Other pages reported human-interest stories and association meetings. On page 4, the *News* reported that after enduring many years of domestic violence, a sixty-eight-year-old farmer murdered his twenty-six-year-old "mute" son. The court sentenced him to only three years imprisonment with hard labor (*JDN*, June 15, 1931).

By 1939, the JAD had 1,816 members. A picture in the issue of March 3, 1940, shows students from the Tokyo School for the Deaf[4] performing for injured soldiers on leave from the Sino-Japanese War (1937–1945), with a sign behind them that reads, "Thank you dear soldiers!" That the deaf were considered part of the nation-state is not itself that remarkable; colonized Koreans and Taiwanese were also considered second-tier citizens in the Japanese empire. The Imperial Army screened its soldiers carefully, rejecting those with physical disabilities or diseases such as leprosy. After Japan attacked the United States in 1941, the JAD came under government pressure to become a registered social welfare association. The JAD closed its doors in 1944 on the eve of defeat by America.

4. The Tokyo School for the Deaf has undergone many name changes. It is currently the Tsukuba University School for the Deaf, attached to the prestigious national Tsukuba University.

CHAPTER FOUR

Life History: Nakano Shizuyo

A Prewar-Generation Deaf Woman

1913

I was born on April 30th of Taisho 2 [1913]. I could not hear at all. I had lots of brothers and sisters. I was the third child. We kids would scrounge around for food to put in our mouths, but it was often rotten, we'd spit it out. So my sisters and brothers would all want to suckle at my mom's breasts. Her breast milk was better than any of the food that was available.

I was so skinny [from malnutrition] when I was four years old, I couldn't even walk straight. We scrounged around for things to eat. When I was four years old, I couldn't speak or hear.[1] Four years old. It was very difficult.

What follows is the reconstructed life history of "Nakano Shizuyo," a deaf woman who grew up in Miyazu, a small town located on the far northern side of Japan, near the Sea of Japan.[2] Told in her own words, Nakano-san's story paints a moving portrait of the limited educational and social opportunities available to rural deaf men and women in her generation. Her family sent her to only a single year of schooling at a local *terakoya*. She spent much of her life taking care of her siblings' children and working in the fields and factories of rural Kyoto. Her life, and

---

1. This is confusing and could possibly also be interpreted as "It was difficult to be deaf."

2. I have used a pseudonym for her: despite her obvious intelligence, because Nakano-san was quite elderly and not well educated, there was a question of whether I was able to provide her with everything she needed to give full informed consent. Even though she signed the standard interview forms that I gave her, the request was translated through the head of the nursing home. Because of this, I decided unilaterally to use a pseudonym in her case to protect her privacy.

the others that follow, are intended to ground the larger-scale social and institutional histories that frame this book.

Nakano-san was born in a Japan that was rapidly modernizing. The Meiji Restoration in 1868 marked the beginning of a rapid industrialization initiative by the new government as it sought to catch up to the Western colonial powers. However, modernization was still of limited impact in the agrarian countryside where Nakano-san grew up in the 1920s. Famine caused by poor crops and overtaxation had been a hallmark of the earlier Tokugawa era and continued in the Meiji and Taisho periods. The situation improved slowly. As her life story progresses through to the postwar period, we begin to see increasing technological encroachment into her village life, from factory looms to industrial sewing machines.

Interview Notes

Nakano-san was eighty-five years old when I interviewed her in 1998. Her signing style was extremely difficult to understand by those who did not share her daily routines. Her signing grammar was almost totally spatial—using the space in front of her and the position of her hands to indicate the relationship between subjects, verbs, and objects in her sentences—rather than linear sequencing, which is what spoken languages such as Japanese and English use. Native ASL signers would find this visual grammar familiar, but it was not the style used by the middle-generation deaf people with whom I normally signed. Nakano-san also used many signs that were not part of the standard Japanese Sign vocabulary. Some of them may have been from a regional or generational dialect or her own idiolect.

Most interpreters and deaf people younger than sixty know only the postwar form of signing, which borrows heavily from spoken Japanese for its structure and is much more linear. Like me, they have problems understanding elderly signers such as Nakano-san. This is one reason for the social isolation of the elderly deaf in Japan. Interpreters trained for middle-generation deaf, who make up the bulk of the community, are usually not competent enough to translate for the older generation, and this means that elderly deaf have difficulty receiving adequate medical care at hospitals and clinics.

The director of the residential nursing home, Ōya Susumu, served as my interpreter during the interview. Deaf himself and part of the middle generation, he had known Nakano-san since she had arrived at the facility and was able to communicate fairly smoothly with her. Unfortunately, even with his help, the translation of Nakano-san's interview was difficult. There was no way that I could have understood her narrative by myself, and I was greatly aided by his skill as an interviewer.

Nakano-san is in many ways a remarkable and unusual deaf woman. Unlike many rural deaf, she was fortunate enough to receive a year of basic schooling, which allowed her to read and write Kanji and kana characters. Although she never learned to speak or speechread and was never much in contact with the greater hearing world outside of her family, she was energetic and intelligent. The difficulties she faced growing up in rural Japan were probably common to many deaf persons of the time, as was the discrimination she experienced, most notably from her own family, who for reasons unknown never allowed her to marry or to have children. Let us start at the beginning of her story.

The Early Years (1920s and 1930s)

Nakano-san notes that her early family life was difficult:

> *I had lots of siblings. The oldest was a girl, the second was my brother. My elder sister died. My older brother died a while ago. I was the third. The fourth was my brother, he's away in Kyoto [City]. The fifth was my sister who lives nearby in Iwataku City, here in Kyoto Prefecture.*
>
> *My younger brother used to work in television repair, but he got a disease in the chest. He threw up a lot of blood and died. It smelled horribly. I gathered up [all of the clothes and sheets] and burned them in a fire. I hosed down the room. It was a disease of the chest. My younger sister went to Kyoto as a bride.*
>
> *The youngest child was my brother. He worked in road construction. He drove a dump truck. He made a lot of money and built a house right next to mine and lived there for a long time. A big house with two stories. My house was so small, so cramped. His house was huge, a first floor and a second floor, two stories. His bride came from so far away, from a small mountain village, to marry him. She signs "marriage" by imitating the headdress and walk of a traditional Japanese bride.*

Nakano-san came from a very poor rural family with eight children. Her narrative style is nonlinear and her story jumps around in places—the first black and white televisions were not introduced in Japan until the 1950s—but it is clear from the context that her family was not one with many resources. The "disease of the chest" that her brother died of was most probably tuberculosis.[3]

When she was eight years old, the rest of her siblings went to elementary school, but Nakano-san had to stay home. Elementary education was technically compulsory for all citizens, but school supplies cost money, and attendance was never checked, especially in rural areas. It was also easy to receive waivers for disabled children "freeing" them from compulsory education.

> When I was eight years old, in the morning everyone would line up [in front of the house] at eight o'clock to go to school. I was so envious (urayamashikatta[4]). Sigh. I stood there with my finger in my mouth. I wanted to play with them. I cried. I went to my mother and cried and cried. My mother told me, "We don't have any money." I was so envious of everyone.
>
> Everyone would line up and I would wave good-bye, good-bye, smiling. But they would leave and I would start crying, tears streaming down my face. I couldn't go to school because I was deaf.

Instead, she took care of the local neighborhood children.

> The neighbors, the people living next door, I got money from them for babysitting. I was friends with them. They fed me many things, it was so tasty! All of the little neighborhood kids, I took care of them, I carried them on my back.
>
> If I was playing by myself, [my parents] would come and yell at me, angry and pointing their finger at me. They would tell me to go take care of the children. I carried them on my back. Oh my shoulders hurt . . . oh they hurt. . . .
>
> My little brother, he was such a crybaby. I fed him and he grew so tall. Then he married and set up his new house right next to mine. She smiles at the thought.
>
> When my nephew was just a little baby, I carried him on my back (onbu-suru) [that is, raised him]. Oh he was so, so cute. She looks at the photo of her nephew as a boy and pats it as if patting him on the head. I bought him a bicycle. He was so happy. He would go tearing around the neighborhood on it. I bought it for him. He was so cute.
>
> I saved up all my money and bought him a bicycle. He was so happy. When he got big, he wanted a guitar, he wanted to play the guitar. He was very good. I took good care of him. It took lots of money. His mother and father wouldn't buy it so he came to me and I bought it for him. All of their needs and wishes, I answered (amaete ageta).

3. Ōya-san provided the elucidation that it was tuberculosis. Nakano-san signed "chest disease," but that is not a known translation for tuberculosis in modern JSL. It isn't listed in standard JSL dictionaries as such.

4. This is signed by biting on the index finger of one hand, in a pensive gesture. It is part of Japanese body language. So the next sentence (I stuck my index finger in my mouth) is actually part of the single gesture.

Nakano-san and her mother were not able to communicate well. Her memories of her mother mostly involve her getting beaten with a bamboo cane or being thrown in the shed. She remembers her mother yelling often, her mouth moving fanatically, rages falling on deaf ears but scared eyes. With her siblings, she was able to communicate in home signs, gesturing and miming to get her meaning across.

As well as her use of visual grammar, one of the prominent things about Nakano-san's signing is the lack of fingerspelling. Although there was a prewar form used at the Kyoto School for the Deaf, current Japanese fingerspelling was introduced after the war. Nakano-san writes words such as place-names on the palm of her hand with her finger using Chinese characters. Her fingernumbering system is also nonstandard. She counts numbers above 5 by adding 5 of one hand to the number on the other (5+3=8), numbers above ten by clapping both hands and then indicating the number (5+5+3=13) and so forth. This differs from the current one-handed numbering system in JSL.

Early Adolescence (1925)

When I was ten + two [twelve] years old, a teacher came by my house a teacher came to talk with my mother. I went to a school. There were bald men who prayed there. There were five students. . . . The first was deaf. . . . the second . . . hold on . . . all together . . . The first three were boys, and there were two girls, including me. And then there was another child who was blind. She mimes not being able to see, arms outstretched in front of her like a Japanese ghost.

There were four children who were blind. And 10+2 children who were deaf. . . . hold on . . . she counts on her fingers. *Eight children who were deaf, we used our hands to talk. We learned how to read. We had to rest our hands on our legs. The teachers taught us how to write, "A I U E O."* She writes the five vowels of the Japanese language on her hand in hiragana characters. *It was tough!*

I had six friends. Myself, another girl, another girl, two boys, and one other. We spoke to each other using our hands [signed]. The teacher also talked with his hands, he signed well.

Oh . . . I forgot . . . the two boys, their names were . . . She traces the names in Chinese characters on her pant leg with her finger. *Hanamoto-san.*

Oh I can't, I forgot already. She picks up a pen and paper. She writes MIYAZU . . . MŌA . . . TERA (Miyazu Temple for the Blind and Mute).

Nakano-san recalls signing with the other students. She learned how to write hiragana and Kanji (Chinese ideographs), remembering the Kanji characters for her classmates even seventy years later. Unfortunately, this happy period in her life ended when, a year after she entered, the school was destroyed by an earthquake. It is likely that her school was located at Chigenji, a prominent Buddhist temple in Miyazu City.

> *There was a terrible earthquake, and the temple, it crashed to the ground. I was 10+3 years old. There was no money.*
> *I wanted to go to Kyoto [to the Kyoto School for the Deaf], but there was no money. No money. The school in Kyoto was so expensive!* She looks angry.

Nakano-san had heard about the Kyoto School for the Deaf, but her parents refused to let her go. She lived (now, as then) on the northern side of Kyoto Prefecture; the train fare to Kyoto City and her boarding costs would have been exorbitant. She was too valuable working for the family to be sent away to residential school in a distant city.

As noted in the previous chapters, temple schools were very popular in the late part of the nineteenth century. Archival research reveals that there was indeed a school for the deaf named the *Miyazu Mōa Gakkō* (Miyazu School for the Blind and Mute). There are very few records remaining for this school, but in the *100-Year History of Blind-Deaf Education in Kyoto Prefecture*, we find the following information:

> The Miyazu Blind and Mute School opened on September 28th, 1925 . . . in Miyazu City. The founder was Nakamura Tokijirō. Nakamura was born in 1895 in . . . Yamanashi Prefecture and in 1923, he was with the normal division (*futsūka*) of the Tokyo School for the Blind. . . . In 1925, he came to Miyazu. It is said that deaf students lived in the same building with him and his wife. . . .
> The school soon moved to the grounds of the Chigenji Temple. . . . The students came from all the surrounding areas and spent their days there. Instead of a teacher-student relationship, it was more like father-children. The school later moved to Iwayamura village and there it was destroyed in the Okutan Earthquake. (Editorial Board for the 100th Anniversary of Deaf and Blind Education 1978:133)

Nakano-san remembers the monks praying in the building where she took classes, so she must have entered after the school moved to the temple grounds. It is remarkable that there were as many as twelve disabled students (eight blind and four deaf) at a rural temple school, although Miyazu is one of the larger towns in northern Kyoto Prefecture.[5] Nakano-san does not indicate who the teacher was; however, if it was

---

5. In 1993, the population was still only 25,000.

Nakamura Tokijirō (no relation to this author), then we begin to see glimpses of how Japanese Sign Language began to unify. Schoolteachers and principals were moving between the various blind and deaf schools, taking their knowledge of local sign languages with them. Although Nakano-san signs things such as numbers differently from younger Japanese signers (and she conspicuously does not use fingerspelling or any Kanji signs), there is a core element of her signing which is recognizably "Japanese."

A class portrait was taken at the Miyazu School, but her mother refused to give her any money so that she could buy one of the copies. Thus, there are no pictures of Nakano-san during her childhood years. However, we have a photo of the Miyazu School taken in 1925. The priest with his robes is visible front and center. Perhaps one of the young girls on the sides is Nakano-san, who would have been twelve at the time it was taken. She recalled a photographer coming to take a formal school picture:[6]

> *At the temple, they had us stand in a row, and they took a photo with a big flash.* Her signing is so descriptive, she even shows the shutter button pushed by a remote cable release, as professionals are wont to do. *But it was so expensive. [She/I?] became so angry![7]*

After the Miyazu School was destroyed, Nakano-san went back to working at home.

> *When I was 10+2 years old, I was still small. When the snow would fall, my mother would stay indoors and make sandals. I would look over her shoulder and memorize what she did, and copy it. There was a big stone mortar.* She stretches her arms out to show how large it is, almost a full span in diameter. *I would grind against it. Grind and grind and grind.[8]* Grinding the straw rushes softened them for weaving.
>
> *For the children, we'd make these tiny sandals, only a few centimeters long. [And for adults], these big ones.*
>
> *My mother didn't teach me. When it would snow, I would watch her from the corner of the room, stealing glances[9] at her doing it, and learned that way. I made many and I became very good at it.*

6. This photograph was located well after my interview, and I did not have the opportunity to verify it with her.

7. No subject was attached to this verb phrase.

8. According to Ooms (1996:261), making footgear was the occupation of the lowest socioeconomic rank. The fact that Nakano-san then had to go sell them door-to-door, beggar-style, is another indicator that they were not financially well off.

9. The JSL sign for "stealing glances" is quite literally stealing a look.

宮津盲唖学校創立一周年記念写真 大正十五年九月頃、宮津市智源寺、教室には写真の本堂の左前にある禅堂が用いられたという（盲学校教諭白畠庸氏提供）

Figure 4.1. Miyazu School for the Deaf, 1925. Source: *100-Year History of Blind-Deaf Education in Kyoto Prefecture* (1978:262). Used with permission.

> *I made a whole bunch of the sandals, tied them all up in a big string, carried them on my back. . . . Slung over my shoulder, I would walk all the way to town by myself.* She mimes marching, slapping her shoes against the floor so it makes a stomping sound. *And I would sell them.* She spreads her hands out, as if displaying her wares on a straw mat thrown on the ground.
>
> *I was strong.* She flexes her biceps. It seems a happy memory, she smiles.
>
> *I was, 10+2 years old. 10+3, 4, 5. Then I stopped. Then I went to work at Ishikawa.*

Although her family was initially very impoverished and the children suffered greatly from malnutrition, the opportunities for Nakano-san's family improved as her brothers and sisters began attending local primary schools. By the end of the decade her family was able to obtain a cow.

She fondly remembered the family cow. She recalled when it gave birth, the calf popping right out of its rear end. The family was so proud of its new acquisition that the earliest photo in Nakano-san's possession is of her entire family in front of their home, posing with their cow. Nakano-san herself is not in the picture. She was working in the factory when the photograph was taken; they did not see it necessary to call her back to include her.

1930s: Factory Work

When she was sixteen, Nakano-san started to work at a local textile factory. She enjoyed this freedom from her family; fondly remembering the cook who would serve up large bowls of lunch every day.

> *I worked at a factory. They had looms with spools and threads. I worked on the looms. I used to commute between the factory and my home every day.*
>
> *At the textile factory, they would make these great meals. The cook was very good at cooking. We would all sit down in a row, she would put the bowls it front of us, and we would eat. The cook would call me over. She was cooking a whole big huge pot of food. Everyone would come to eat together. It was so delicious. Everyone who was weaving cloth, they would come to eat. The food was very good.*

By this time, industrialization was starting to reach the backwaters of Kyoto Prefecture. Even now, sixty years later her fingers recalled the deft movements she needed to make for the machines. The factory was a family business, and sometime during her mid-late twenties, she and the owner's son became amorously involved.

> *He was a good man.*
>
> KN: Was he hearing?
>
> *Yes, he was hearing. He lived in Ishikawa.* She writes the place name on the palm of her hand.
>
> *At night, he would come to my house, around 6:30 p.m., he would come to visit me, to take me away. [He told me] I was so thin and beautiful! My parents were so angry!* She signs "angry" by sticking her fingers up like horns on her head, like the Japanese oni devil.

Her boyfriend was hearing but did not mind that she was deaf. Her parents, however, forbade their relationship. Her father beat her over the head with a bamboo cane that they used to stoke the flames of the boiler. He locked her in the storage shed outside the house every night so that she could not continue their evening meetings.

> *No, no, I couldn't see anyone. My parents would yell at me and hit me.[10] They would take a bamboo rod and hit me with it. They would yell and yell at me. They would hit*

---

10. She is using the Japanese sign *gami-gami-iu*, which means to "scold vehemently." It is signed by the fingers flapping in front of the mouth, clearly derived from the deaf experience of having hearing people yell at them, lips wagging incomprehensibly.

me on the arm with the bamboo rod. At night, they would open the front door, throw me out of the house,[11] and close it in my face.

She pulls out the photo of her family with the cow in front of the house. *See that shed on the side? That's where they threw me in and locked the door. They would open the door and throw me in. The door could be locked [from the outside]. It had a latch. [They would lock me in and] I would bang and bang and cry and cry.*

[My mother told me] it was impossible [for me to marry anyone]! She yelled at me and hit me. [Because I was] deaf. I can't get married. She hit me with the bamboo rod. My father yelled at me and hit me with the rod. And at night, they would throw me in the shed and lock the key. All night long.[12] For six hours, all night long.

Her boyfriend was persistent in wanting to visit her. Nakano-san's parents called her boyfriend's house to talk to him and his parents.

They called up [my boyfriend's house in] Ishikawa and told [my boyfriend]. . . . They were angry and in the morning they called him up and yelled at him. In the old days, the telephones hung on the wall and had these two huge bells on them, you had to spin a crank on the side to call, and you spoke into the wall. [They told him on the telephone] they were angry. That he couldn't [see me].

That night, [my boyfriend from] Ishikawa was nowhere to be seen, he never showed up. I wondered what happened to him. I waited and waited for so long, and he never showed up.

Not giving up, however, her boyfriend somehow arranged for her to escape and live in his house, with his parents. It was quite a distance between the two households, but she packed her bags and went willingly with him. Soon afterwards, her mother made the same trek to Ishikawa and forced her daughter to return with her. This is the last we hear of this boyfriend.

My mother [went to Ishikawa] and she and his mother talked and talked and talked. My mother was angry and brought me back forcibly. I gathered up all my things and said good-bye. I bowed good-bye [to him]. I was crying.

My mother gathered up all my things, wrapped them up in a huge bundle, and tied it all up with rope so you could carry it on your back. My mother. Put it all in a wicker suitcase. She wrapped them up in a huge bundle. She gathered everything up. Weeping. Weeping. I was crying.

We walked. And then caught a bus. Paid the bus fare. I went with her, the two of us. She carried everything on her back. We walked. Paid the bus fare and got

11. Whereas American children are grounded in the house for punishment, being locked out of the house is standard punishment for many Japanese children.

12. Ōya translates her sign as *zūtto* (English: "for the entire time/duration"). She signs it using an index finger going in a crescent shape up to down, a non-standard Japanese sign. The modern form is to hold the two index fingers parallel horizontally, delineating a span of time.

*on. Allllllll the wayyyyy far away. One whole hour. We walked for a whole hour.
Up the mountain. And got on the bus. We had to wait [on the bus] for a long
time. We went back to town.* She writes "town" on her hand.

After that, they made me work in the fields, hoeing all day long. Her face
shows the strain as she imitates hoeing the fields. *I got all of these calluses
on my hands.* She points them out.

*I was so beautiful. See this photo of me? See I was so feminine and slender, I
was so beautiful, it was nice. Many men were attracted to me, they always surrounded me.*

She sighs and looks depressed.

If I think about this . . . I feel like crying.

It is difficult to understand why her family was so much against her
relationship with the factory owner's son. We might speculate that her
family did not think the relationship would be accepted by the parents
of the boy (because of either social class or disability issues), which
meant that their child could be left pregnant and unwedded. Another
more likely reason could have been that the family did not want to suffer
the economic loss of their daughter if she married out. In traditional Japanese marriages, daughters leave the natal family and become members
of their husband's family lines. Even at that time, Nakano-san served an
important economic function, bringing back a paycheck from the factory
as well as providing free labor in rearing her siblings' children.

1940s: The Postwar Years

In her thirties and after the close of the Pacific War, Nakano-san took a
new job at a factory much closer to home. On weekends, she made bamboo brooms. She was not allowed any rest time or personal time, with
her evenings occupied by taking care of her siblings' children. She doted
on her nieces and nephews, buying them toys out of the savings she had
accumulated. Although she was extremely pretty and many men were
attracted to her, her family refused all suitors. She was never allowed to
marry and never had any children of her own.

*After the war, I started working on the silk looms. On Sundays, I made brooms.
I'd go stomping off in the morning.* She stomps her feet against the ground
as if she's marching. *Off, off, off into the mountains. I'd chop down the bamboo
until I had a big huge bundle as big as this.* She puts out her arms as if in a
big bear hug. *And then I'd put them all on my back and carry them down [to
the market].* She stoops over from the weight as she puts the pile on her
back. *Twice [in one day]! I was strong.* She flexes her biceps.

> *I would find the short ones, about this high. I would cut the branches off, one by one, one by one.*
> *I wasn't allowed any of my own time because I'm so stupid!* She suddenly hides her face in embarrassment. *I'm so stupid. I didn't go to school.*

She was not often allowed out of the house for personal visits even when she was in her thirties. She worked, took care of her siblings' children, and worked even more. There was no mention of the Pacific War in her narrative. She was too remote from any of the bombing and from the subsequent occupation forces. Although other cities were ruthless fire-bombed, Kyoto was not targeted by American bombers because of its cultural treasures, and rural non-industrial areas were also left alone.

She had two or three deaf friends who lived in the same area. One of them was an old woman:

> *She would come to our house. I would greet her at the door and bow. Then she would comb, comb, comb my hair. And put oil in it and make it all beautiful and coifed. It was very nice!*[13]

Another of her friends was the former president of the local deaf association, who was a few years younger than she was. We know that she attended some of the local deaf association meetings. She showed me a group photo of the founding of her local deaf association in 1947 in which she is present. Most of the members have stayed in the area, although many have passed away by now.

Even into her thirties, her family exerted a tremendous amount of control. Other conversations with elderly deaf have made plain that this was not unusual, especially in the case of women. One elderly woman in Hokkaido told me that her ovaries were surgically removed when she was a teenager—ostensibly because of painful menstruation cramps.[14] Her parents also forced this woman to marry against her will. She talked about how she suffered under her hearing husband, much as Nakano-san suffered under her parents. Both talked about being liberated after their oppressors passed on to the next life.

13. Up to the 1970s, hair styling remained a main occupational category for deaf persons in Japan. Most schools for the deaf in the postwar period had limited options for senior high school students: sewing, carpentry, hair styling, printing, and dental work.
14. In the United States, many countries in Europe, and elsewhere, forced sterilization or other measures to prevent intermarriage of deaf and other disabled individuals was common in the early twentieth century as part of the widespread eugenics movement (Monaghan 2003a). I cannot confirm that forced sterilization of disabled people was common during this period in Japan, but the anecdotal evidence is strong.

1950s: Self-Enterprise

Nakano-san's father died at the age of seventy-five in 1954. She was forty-one at the time and gained considerably more freedom by his death. She had mentioned that when she was in her thirties, people would occasionally come to visit, but this became much more prevalent when she was in her forties, and she would go out more often as well. She had many photos of herself on trips or drinking parties with her deaf friends. It is clear that the local association of the deaf played a central role in her social activities.

After her father's death, Nakano-san bought a small shed in the neighborhood and moved out of her family home. She started a small textile workshop and operated the machines by herself. We do not know much about what she did during the postwar boom years. I assume her small business venture was successful since she made enough to support herself.

In the immediate postwar period, the local deaf associations were very loosely organized and served primarily a social function. Most of them had developed out of the alumni associations of prefectural schools for the deaf. The Japanese Federation of the Deaf brought them together under a single umbrella in 1947, but the difficulties of transportation and communication limited their ability to unite politically. For the most part, the main function of the postwar local associations was to provide a safe social space for interaction between deaf individuals. Nakano-san and her friends went on group outings, visited various tourist spots across the country, and enjoyed banquet parties.

1960s–1980s: Local Deaf Associations

It is not clear what happened in the thirty-seven years between Nakano-san's father's death in 1954 and her own retirement in 1991, because her narrative trails off. The photos she showed us made it apparent that she was active in her local deaf association. The relationships were strong enough that she still vividly remembered a woman she hated in the association. Her face was scratched out in all of her photographs. And defacement was not enough; Nakano-san continued to hit her mutilated photo with her fist while she talked about her.

Although she bought the shed with her own savings and gained financial independence with her textile workshop, the machinery in it was leased from a larger business. When her eyesight started failing in her early seventies (the mid-1980s), she was fired as a subcontractor and the equipment was taken away from her. She gave the shed to her nephew and retired.

In her narrative, we do not see much interaction with the hearing world outside of her immediate family. She worked for herself and because of her brief period of schooling, was able to communicate with pen and paper at a basic level. The first group of interpreters for the deaf was formed in Kyoto City in 1963, but even by the late 1990s, there was still a dearth of qualified interpreters in rural areas such as Miyazu. So she may not have interacted much with the people outside of her small community of friends.

What is remarkable about her tale is the degree in which she was part of the broader socioeconomic changes that were sweeping Japan. It was very much the work of small subcontractors like Nakano-san that helped drive the rapid economic reconstruction. But as with many in her generation, her own physical decline coincided with the beginning of the end of Japan's "bubble" period.

1990s: Ikoinomura Nursing Home

Nakano-san entered the Ikoinomura deaf nursing home in 1992 at the age of seventy-nine. Since then, she has been active in their workshop, making straw and cloth sandals, which the facility sells at bazaars and conferences. She also participated in the home's deaf theater troupe, which traveled across Japan giving performances. In 1995, she accompanied a group from the facility on their "Dream Vacation to Hawai'i," paid for by the funds accumulated from workshop and theater sales. She also went to schools, sign language circles, and local deaf associations giving demonstrations on how to make straw sandals.

It is fortunate that Nakano-san was able to enter the Ikoinomura facility where she was able to thrive in a safe environment with peers and staff who were able to communicate with her (although her idiosyncratic form of signing did make things difficult). There are many elderly deaf who are not so lucky. In Japan much more than in the United States, it is expected that elderly parents will live with their adult children after retirement. Nursing homes are not as common, and the ones that do exist often expect that the adult children will continue to provide supplementary care such as laundry and holiday coverage. Because Nakano-san has no children like many elderly deaf of her generation, there is no one who can contribute care for her.

But Nakano-san's future remains murky. Funding for the nursing home currently comes from a mixture of prefectural social welfare grants, national health insurance, and private donations. Recent changes to the elderly care social insurance (*kaigo-hoken*) means that she will have to contribute a larger co-pay. It is conceivable that unless more private donations make up for the increase in consumer payments required by the new system, many of the elderly deaf in the Ikoinomura facility could find themselves homeless. The new system is very confusing and has caused much concern in even the middle-aged cohort, who know they will be entering retirement in the next couple of decades. They are the focus of the next section.

CHAPTER FIVE

Middle-Generation Deaf in the
Postwar Period

Japan's defeat and the end of the Pacific War in 1945 brought massive and mostly positive changes to Japanese society. The last few years of the war had placed enormous burdens on the social system, and the large majority of deaf persons as well as the general populace benefited from the cessation of hostilities, the more democratic government order, and restoration of the economy. By far, however, the greatest change for the deaf community was the institution of compulsory education for all citizens (disabled or otherwise) by the Supreme Commander of the Allied Powers (SCAP, General MacArthur) effective April 1, 1948.[1] I use this date to mark the beginning of a middle period of deaf history that extends until 1970, the advent of mainstreaming practices in Japan.

While government-sponsored schools for the deaf and blind such as the Kyoto School for the Deaf had existed in Japan since 1878 and general education was technically compulsory, children with disabilities were not required to attend. Because schools for the deaf were few and far between, the cost of room and board was enough to discourage most parents. As a result, unless their parents were rich or they lived close

---

1. April 1 is the beginning of the fiscal and academic year in Japan. The *JDN* was quick to report new information coming from the United States. In its March 15, 1949, issue, it introduced the "American Manual Alphabet" (spelled out in English) and noted that it was being used as a *"sign language"* among ordinary people as well" [emphasis mine]." The American fingerspelling was quickly adopted in Japan, and the very next issue (*JDN* April 15, 1949) introduced the new Japanese fingerspelling format, based on the American Manual Alphabet.

enough to a school to commute, most persons with disabilities were unable to gain a formal education.

The government mandate in 1948 for equal education access[2] greatly boosted enrollment at schools for the deaf. This effect was multiplied by two other demographic factors. The first was the postwar baby boom in Japan. The considerable growth in the birthrate alone guaranteed a growth in the number of deaf children. However, there was also a massive movement of families from rural areas into the cities, seeking jobs and new opportunities. This huge population migration caused stress on the still-devastated municipal sanitation and medical systems. It was an epidemiological nightmare.

Streptomycin, or *sutomai* as it is called in Japanese, is an antibiotic that was developed in 1943 by American scientists. Effective against pneumonia, tuberculosis, spinal meningitis, and typhoid fever, it was used widely in the postwar period in Japan. For the brief few decades until bacteria developed a resistance to it, streptomycin was a wonder drug, a shining sword in the doctor's bag that could cure most bacterial infections. And in the tumultuous postwar period, these types of infections were rampant and deadly, especially for children.

Unfortunately, this shining sword cut both ways (as miracles are often wont to). Streptomycin belongs to a family of antibiotic drugs known as aminoglycides. The margin of error between a therapeutic dose and a toxic dose is very small, especially in children. One of the principal hazards of this drug family is ototoxicity—it damages the eighth cranial nerve, which is responsible for hearing and balance. Until better antibiotics were developed in the 1960s, a whole generation of children in Japan were saved from death by infection, but deafened consequently.[3]

---

2. Unfortunately, the mandate also included a clause that permitted parents of severely disabled children to be "allowed" to let their children stay at home and not be educated. While the number of severely mentally and physically disabled who stayed at home is unknown, this only became a visible social problem when the media began reporting on *hikikomori* or children who decide to stay at home for whatever reason. Even now, these *hikikomori*, who are often depressed, suffer from learning disabilities, or are anti-social, can refuse to go to school without repercussion. The children are socially promoted and can graduate from middle school and finish their compulsory education without ever having stepped into a classroom. Compulsory education in Japan means that the government is compelled to provide everyone with the opportunity for an education, but does not mean that everyone is compelled to take it.

3. Judy Kegl notes that the United States imposed a trade embargo on Nicaragua during the Contra War which prevented modern antibiotics from reaching the country. As a result, many children were deafened by ototoxic drugs (BBC TV 1997).

Because children were deafened by streptomycin treatment for an infection (caused by everything from TB and typhoid fever to nasty cuts), they could (and did) become deaf at a variety of different ages, but most frequently between the ages of two to eight. Perhaps it is the nature of children in that age bracket, old enough to get into trouble, too young to have fully developed immune and nervous systems. The streptomycin-treated children were unique in that they were post-lingually deaf. That is, they were able to hear and speak at the time that they became deaf. Spoken Japanese was already their primary language.

In contrast, in other industrialized countries many of the modern deaf "bubbles" (anomalously large cohorts of deaf individuals in the same age group) have been caused by outbreaks of rubella (German measles).[4] If a woman catches rubella in the first three months of pregnancy, damage to the auditory nerves of her developing fetus can occur. We can demographically trace the deaf bubbles in New Zealand and the United States to rubella outbreaks in those countries in the 1940s and 1960s (Monaghan 1996, 2003b). These rubella children are prenatally or prelingually deaf and, for those who attended schools for the deaf, signing is the primary language. There is thus a critical difference in the centrality of signing between the Japanese and the American or New Zealand cases.

For example, it has been argued that the 1988 "Deaf President Now" cultural deaf revolution at Gallaudet University was created in part by a unified cohort of prenatally deaf, rubella children who used ASL as their primary language. The year 1969 was particularly bad; there were 57,686 reported cases of rubella in the United States. Nineteen years later, this cohort attended Gallaudet University in the late eighties, and this critical mass was a factor in the Deaf President Now movement. After 1969, an effective vaccine for rubella was approved for use in the United States and the number of cases dwindled. There are now currently less than 200 domestic cases of rubella each year and only a small fraction involve pregnant women (Yazbak and Lang-Radosh 2001).

In postwar Japan, by contrast, streptomycin caused a large group of formerly hearing children to become deaf after having learned how to speak Japanese. They may have attended a hearing school for several years before transferring to a school for the deaf. In any case, postwar

---

4. Cf. the rubella epidemic in 1965 in Okinawa, discussed below. I am calling the cohort produced by that epidemic *dankai no sedai* as well.

schools for the deaf saw a huge increase in their student numbers as well as students with more diverse audiological backgrounds.

Schools for the deaf then (as now) shared the same basic curriculum as their hearing counterparts. Or, to put it another way, the Ministry of Education was loath for a multitude of reasons having to do with nationalism and language ideology to create a separate curriculum for deaf children. Schools for the deaf were run with exactly the same course plans and textbooks as regular schools. Until recently, signing was not even recognized by the Ministry of Education as a valid pedagogic form of communication. Spoken and written Japanese for the most part is still the only recognized language for compulsory education in Japan.[5]

In both hearing and deaf schools in the immediate postwar period, students used the same textbooks, educators came out of exactly the same teacher-training programs with exactly the same (lack of) qualifications,[6] wrote the same things on the blackboards, and gave the same lectures. The only difference was that in schools for the deaf, no one could hear the teacher speaking. When the teachers had their backs to their classes, writing on the blackboards, no one could read their lips. Then, as now, teachers at schools for the deaf were not required to have any special training in speech therapy or deaf pedagogy, let alone signing. Most were regular graduates of teachers' colleges who just happened to be placed in a school for the deaf.

In this environment, post-lingually deafened students had a tremendous advantage over their pre-lingually deaf classmates. These children already had a base of Japanese on which they could build their speechreading and

5. For example, international schools that use any other language than Japanese as a primary educational medium are not recognized as full schools. This is the problem I faced when I graduated from my English-speaking international high school in Tokyo. Under the Ministry of Education rules, technically, I was not a high school graduate. If I had wanted to apply to Tokyo University, for example, I would have had to first pass the *Daiken,* the Japanese equivalent of the GED, or apply as an international student. Korean students graduating from Korean schools in Japan face the same problem; often their only university option is to go to North or South Korea (or the United States or United Kingdom; cf. Ryang 1997). We can read much about language ideology and nationalism in this refusal of the Ministry of Education to conceive of a curriculum independent of language. Very recently (2004), the ministry has approved a few foreign-language schools such as the Kyoto Korean School (see footnote 11 below on their baseball team) as full-fledged schools.

6. Although there is now a special teacher-training program for those entering schools for the deaf, it focuses mainly on biomedical issues such as auditory impairment and hearing aid tuning. It does not contain any training in signing. It is also not mandatory; many teachers in schools for the deaf have not undergone even this meager amount of special education.

speech skills, as well as stronger academic skills such as reading and writing. Signing was common in the school grounds and in the dorms at night (and some teachers took the time to learn it), but unlike in the United States a strong dormitory culture based around signing did not have an opportunity to develop. The schools had been created in a rush to meet the law, and the alumni and intra-dormitory relations that usually thrive in these environments had not yet congealed.[7] The students with the strongest base in the Japanese language rose to the top of the school system. After graduating, they formed the core leadership of the Japanese Federation of the Deaf after the mid-1960s.

The Middle-Generation Deaf and the Rebirth of the JFD

Dankai no sedai is a term that has been applied to the baby boomers in Japan (Sakaiya 1980). *Dankai* means a mass or clump of dirt and describes the group-centered mentality of this cohort. The *dankai no sedai* grew up during the incredible economic growth of postwar Japan. The mythos is that they are the salary-men and housewives who rebuilt Japan. The men were stoic and utterly dedicated to their lifetime careers. The women were the "good wife/wise mother" (*ryōsai kenbō*) and the "education moms" (*kyōiku mama*) who pushed their kids through cram-schools to get into the top universities. Everyone worked hard, and success was borne of those efforts. This meritocratic sentiment can be seen as almost a Japanese Calvinism.

The deaf *dankai no sedai* middle generation shared the same postwar boom euphoria and work ethic. As children, they were crammed into school buildings that were not designed to handle their large numbers. They too had a sense of a common spirit, a common goal. But at the same time, they felt the social prejudice that ostracized them from mainstream Japanese society. The rhetoric of a shared nation-building had reached them, and they wanted to be part of it. At the same time, the social/political milieu of Japan was in ferment. Other groups such as the former Burakumin were reasserting their status as full Japanese citizens as well. Communist and socialist groups spread among labor unions, teachers,

7. As Richard Senghas (2003) notes, the irony of nascent deaf dormitory cultures is that younger deaf children are often more competent in signing than their older peers, by virtue of earlier exposure to sign and their greater linguistic flexibility in language acquisition.

Figure 5.1. The Japanese Federation of the Deaf was founded on June 25, 1947, at the Ikaho hot springs. Source: JFD archives. Used with permission.

and students. All were working toward new models of an egalitarian Japan, although the various groups clashed mightily on both theoretical and practical fronts.

The Japanese Federation of the Deaf was founded from the ashes of the defunct Japanese Association of the Deaf in 1947. The leadership in the early years drew from the prewar generation and were politically inactive. The JFD calls the immediate postwar period their "Era of Pleading" (*onegai jidai*) because if they needed anything the leaders had to go to the government offices, hat in hand, to plead for resources or services. The deaf as such were not a political constituency and relied on the pity of government bureaucrats and administrators. This changed when a new group of radical young leaders came of age within the JFD in the 1960s. Strongly influenced by the turbulent political milieu of the times, these leftist leaders brought the JFD into a new era of social activism.

Operating within the Youth Section of the JFD, these activists from the middle generation spread the mantra of social inclusion. Everyone was considered deaf (*rōa*) and questions about just how *well* you heard and how *much* you signed (vs. using speech) in your everyday life were elided for the general goals of the *undō*—the political social deaf movement.[8] This is the same middle generation that Ohtsuki-san, the deaf leader described in the introduction who talked about "sign fascism," emerged from. The movement also directly and indirectly shaped the lives of the three women (Horikawa-san, Sano-san and Funata-san) whom we will meet in the next chapter.

The "Rubella Children" of Okinawa

Let me briefly diverge from the main narrative to explore an odd phenomenon that occurred in the mid-1960s in Okinawa, which is the southernmost island group in Japan. Okinawa is famous for its golden beaches but also for the deaths of tens of thousands of civilians in the Pacific War, and the American military bases that are still there. Some people also remember it for a deaf baseball team that almost made it to the high school nationals.

In 1964, there was a massive epidemic of rubella in Okinawa Prefecture. There had been an earlier epidemic of rubella in the United States in 1963 and 1964, and it was most likely transmitted to the islanders through the American military personnel on the island (Ono 1991:13). The Vietnam War was in full gear, and Okinawa was a major staging area for the B-52 bombers. American troops mingled freely with the islanders.

Approximately 500 "rubella children" (*fūshinji*) were born between the fall of 1964 and the spring of 1965 in Okinawa Prefecture. Of that, an estimated 300 had severe or multiple disabilities, and the great majority were deaf or hard of hearing. The students were initially mainstreamed in local kindergarten and elementary programs, but the prefectural school board found that many of them were slipping academically and made the decision to build a special school that could accommodate them during their middle school and high school years (grades 7–12; or 1977–1983). Thus, the Kitashiro School for the Deaf was created.[9] After

8. Although the JFD would shrink from the comparison, we can draw some parallels in membership structure with the Buraku Liberation League (more fully discussed in chapter 7). The BLL uses residence and attendance at meetings as the criteria for former Burakumin status, not lineage.

9. According to Ono, the parents of the rubella children were split 50:50 in favor of and

1983 it would be demolished. The majority of the 146 students lived in the dorms (Ono 1991:12–15).

When the deaf students entered high school in 1980, they formed a baseball team with sixteen boys playing and five girls as managers. Baseball was then, as now, a very popular Japanese high school sport. Many of the students had played on their elementary school teams when they were part of the regular school system, and many looked forward to entering the national summer competition. They were then very surprised when they found out that, as students at a school for the deaf, they were not able to play in the prefectural intermurals against other schools. Paragraph 16 of section 3 of the Student Baseball Bylaws stated that "only schools that are incorporated under section 4 of the School Education Law" were allowed to participate in the intermurals. Section 4 included only regular schools and excluded special schools for the deaf, blind, or those with intellectual or physical disabilities; schools on American military bases; international schools; and some other categories.

The deaf students filed a formal complaint with the prefectural high school baseball commission in May 1981. The following November (that is, after the season had already ended), the baseball commission reluctantly agreed to allow them to play in the local tournament. The next season, the deaf team reached the prefectural intermurals, but did not make it to the nationals—which are played in the famous *Kōshien* baseball stadium in Hyogo Prefecture, near Osaka (*JDN* November 1, 1981:1). In emotional terms, Koshien is the Japanese equivalent of Chicago's hallowed Wrigley Field.

The baseball commissioners were ostensibly concerned that the deaf students might be struck on the head by a baseball because they could not hear the ball in play.[10] My own interpretation is that *Kōshien* baseball

---

against the Kitashiro School for the Deaf. The parents against it wanted their children to continue to be mainstreamed. Those for it recognized their children were falling behind in the mainstream programs and wanted an educational environment that recognized the special needs of their children as *deaf* children (1991:49).

10. I.e., the sound of the ball striking the bat, the ball whooshing through the air toward a player, etc. However, I can state from ample personal experience in middle school that being hearing does not prevent getting hit by a baseball if you are not looking in the right direction. These fears are really imagined/projected fears.

Even now, when Japanese adult deaf baseball teams play against each other, they use the regulation "soft" ball (*nankyū*) which is the same size as a "hard" ball (*kōkyū*) but is made out of rubber, like an oversized Spalding. In the U.S.-Japan Deaf Friendship Baseball tournament of 1999, this was a point of much irritation to the American players, who felt insulted by having to play with a soft rubber ball.

has commonly been seen as the epitome of national purity and pride in Japan.[11] In the summer, it seems as if every television set is turned to the national high school championships. The baseball commission most probably thought a group of deaf kids would sully the sport in the same way as Jackie Robinson was seen as a threat to "good ol' American baseball" in 1947 when he became the first African-American player in the major leagues.[12]

The story of their struggle was almost lost. While the *Japanese Deaf News* and some sports newspapers followed the story as it occurred, it was not pulled together into a single narrative until baseball writer Tobe Yoshinari published his (1987) *Harukanaru Kōshien* (roughly, *Kōshien [Stadium] ever so far away*). The story gained much broader appeal when it was serialized by comic book artist Yamamoto Osamu in *Weekly Manga Action* as *Harukanaru Kōshien* between 1988 and 1990. There was also a (1990) live action film of the same name by director Osawa Yutaka. Ono Takushi's (1991) *Haikō no Natsu (The summer that school closed)* is the most detailed account, although lesser known.

Since the high school baseball commission's decision in late 1981 to allow deaf students to play in the prefectural intermurals, none of the deaf high schools in Japan have made it to the national semifinals. It will be interesting to see if and when one does, although this is unlikely as mainstreaming has meant that few high schools for the deaf have even the requisite nine boys to form a team. It was the unusual nature of the rubella epidemic in Okinawa that allowed for this one-time phenomenon.

Born just a year after the Tokyo Olympics, the Okinawan deaf cohort was the last large cohort of deaf children in Japan. When they graduated in 1983, the school board closed the doors of the Kitashiro School for the Deaf permanently. After that, all the deaf children in Okinawa were educated inside the regular school system. Educationally, the Okinawa

---

11. In 1999, the Kyoto Kankoku Gakuen (Kyoto Korean School), a school for resident Koreans, was allowed to play in the national championships. In 2003, the captain of the Kyoto Kankoku Gakuen team opened the 85th National Summer High School Baseball with the Athlete's Oath given in both Korean and Japanese.

12. In the major leagues in Japan, there has not (yet) been an equivalent to William Ellsworth "Dummy" Hoy (1862–1961), who was a deaf player in the major leagues in the United States. Hoy was a graduate of the Ohio School for the Deaf and is said to have taught his teammates how to sign. It took almost a hundred years from the time William Hoy last played in 1902 for another deaf major leaguer to emerge in America. Curtis Pride debuted in 1993 with the Montreal Expos and has played for a number of teams since then. Ryan Ketchner, who pitches in the Class A team affiliated with the Seattle Mariners, is also a likely candidate for the major leagues.

rubella children share much with the next generation in that they were mainstreamed and then later returned to schools for the deaf. But because there were so many of them and because they all went to the Kitashiro School for the Deaf during their middle and high school years, they have a shared experience of deafness and deaf identity that would be lost in the generations that followed them. From this they drew their strength.

Indeed, it was this last characteristic that led to the uncharacteristic action of petitioning the high school baseball commission for the right to play. The students had grown up in a period of radical deaf politics in Japan. The year they raised their protest, 1981, was also the United Nations International Year of Disabled Persons (IYDP) with the slogan "Full Participation and Equality," which encouraged the students to see their situation in the frame of human rights politics. According to Ono (1991), the captain of the team was particularly incensed since he would have been allowed to play had he stayed in the regular school system instead of being forced to transfer to the school for the deaf.

The deaf *dankai no sedai* generation spans the years from those who attended school starting with the advent of compulsory education in 1948 up to this last generation of Okinawan deaf children. These individuals, now aged from mid-thirties to mid-fifties, have a cohesion as deaf (*rōa*) and location within the national body politic that we do not see in previous or succeeding generations. In the next chapter, we look at three women whose lives were shaped by these changes in the postwar generations and how they situate themselves as deaf Japanese.

CHAPTER SIX

Three Postwar Women's Lives: Sano Hiroe, Horikawa Hiro, and Funata Hatsuko

As we saw in the previous chapter, the conclusion of the Pacific War in 1945 brought about a great number of mostly positive changes in Japanese society and the deaf community. The economy recovered dramatically, the population exploded, military production shifted to industrial production, schools for the deaf were established nationwide, and the Japanese Federation of the Deaf reconstituted itself both socially and politically. But how did these many extraordinary events affect the lives of ordinary deaf people growing up in this period?

Scholars and the popular press have attempted to bracket the individuals emerging out of the postwar period as belonging to two particular groups: the Showa-Single-Digiters (*shōwa hitoketa sedai*), those born between 1926 and 1935 (Showa 1–9 using the Japanese imperial calendar); and the Group Generation (*dankai no sedai*), the baby boomers born in the immediate postwar 1947–1949 described in the previous chapter.

The unfortunate difficulty of fieldwork is that real lives do not always fit into the sociological categories that we create. The three women who are the subject of this chapter are a case in point: Sano-san was born in 1937, Horikawa-san in 1946, and Funata-san in 1951. None of these women are technically Single-Digiters or the *dankai* generation, but they all share the postwar reconstruction experience. We clearly see in their lives the social and individual transitions that accompany the postwar period as well as the shared deaf group identity that characterizes their generation.

A tremendous degree of social change occurs in the scant fourteen years that separates the birth of the first woman from the last. Born in 1937, Sano-san received only a few years of formal education at a residential school for the deaf before the intense destruction of the final part of the war prevented her from continuing further. Compulsory education for all disabled children was introduced several years after the Allied occupation, but Sano-san never returned to school because her family was too poor to afford it. Compared with the schooling of Nakano-san, the subject of chapter 4, the two or three years of formal education that Sano-san received shaped her life choices considerably. She was much more involved with the local deaf community and met her husband (also deaf) through her school's alumni association.

By the time the youngest woman, Funata-san, moved through the system, schools for the deaf were well established. She attended school for the full twelve years and yearned for college, but was denied entry. Although her experiences were very different from Sano-san's, she is still a product of this generation. She had a strong affiliation with the local association of the deaf, and most of her friends came from the middle age bracket.

Interview Notes

I was introduced to the two other Ibaraki Prefecture women through Horikawa Hiro, who is a leading figure in the Deaf Women's Division of the Ibaraki Prefectural Deaf Association. I first met Horikawa-san at an *onsen* ("hot spring"). I was attending a Regional Association of Deaf Women meeting. As was typical of these meetings, it was held at a conference center in a hot spring resort town. After a long day of rather boring meetings, we ate a sumptuous dinner, drank too much beer and *sake*, and sneaked off to the hotel's famed mineral baths. While we were soaking in one of the large tubs, one of my friends introduced me to Horikawa-san. She was in her early fifties and seemed to be a fascinating woman. Although steam was interfering with our ability to see each other and have a sign conversation, we promised to meet at a future point.

Horikawa-san later invited me up to her house in Ibaraki Prefecture (about a hundred kilometers northeast of Tokyo). I rode one of the express trains, which took about two hours to arrive. Horikawa-san met me at the station, and we drove back to her house in her car. She lived in perhaps the largest Japanese home that I have ever been to. It was a huge, traditional wooden structure in a very rural surrounding. The

wood detailing was meticulous. As we walked in, we saw a small workshop to the side of the house with kimonos neatly piled. The Horikawas
were engaged in the small and traditional but very lucrative home business of sewing family crests onto silk kimonos. They were among the
few artisans who are still able to do this by hand. They had a three-
generation household, with Mr. and Mrs. Horikawa, their son and
daughter-in-law, and their new baby. We sat on their back porch and
chatted in the sunlight while we waited for Sano-san and Funata-san to
arrive.

Finally, all the participants had come together. We bundled into a
minivan together with a sign interpreter (kindly arranged by Horikawa-
san, but we never used her help much beyond asking her to chop veg-
etables), and took off. Horikawa-san had gone to the trouble of renting a
small "mountain cabin." About half an hour away, on the top of a mountain was a resort development of about forty log cabins, mainly designed
for Tokyo residents trying to escape the hot and humid summers. It was
the off-season, so there were not many people around. Horikawa-san
said that she did this often with her (deaf) friends; they could come here
and drink, eat, and not be bothered by their husbands or children.

We cooked a delicious dinner and had a couple of beers while watching the sunset. After dinner, I conducted the first round of interviews
with Horikawa-san, Sano-san, and Funata-san. Although my original in-
tent was to have a round-table discussion, it ended up that most of the
interviews were structured serially. Part of this was the logistics of
videotaping the interviews since it was difficult to pan the camera from
signer to signer if the conversation shifted. We went late into the night,
slept soundly, and continued the following morning.

I chose this cohort of three women because of the strength of their stories and the way that their lives have interwoven over the past four
decades. But they also reveal many of the major themes that I found in
the stories presented by other deaf individuals born between 1935 and
1970—the tumultuous postwar period, the introduction of mass schooling for deaf students, the difficulty of classrooms where the primary instruction was spoken Japanese, and the strength they found in becoming
part of a deaf community. What is unique about these three individuals
is that they represent a major moment of transition in Japan and the
phases of transition can be clearly seen in each.

For example, they signed using the same system of signs, but each was
influenced by her education in formal Japanese and oralism. The older
Sano-san used a grammar system that was primarily visual-spatial and

with very little fingerspelling, but the younger Funata-san used a grammar much closer to spoken Japanese. Yet they belonged within the same cohort, associating with each other, but not with the older generation (prewar) or with the younger (post-1970s mainstreamed youth).

Sano-san: Transitioning between *Hitoketa* and *Dankai*

1937

Good evening. My name is Sa-no. It is nice to meet you. A long time ago, I was born in Yokosuka—do you know where that is?—it's in Yo-ko-ha-ma. My mother died giving birth to my sister. I lost my hearing when I was three years old.

Sano Hiroe was born in 1937, just as Japan was flexing its imperial power. Korea, Taiwan, and the Ryukyus (Okinawa) had already been annexed. There were open hostilities with China. By the time her hearing impairment was discovered, Japan had entered Indochina and had its eyes on the natural resources in the Dutch East Indies and Malaya. It would be interesting to know whether her father was conscripted; she does not mention it in the interview. Sano-san was old enough to remember much of the war and its aftermath, though she was also the beneficiary of the postwar reformations.

Sano-san mentions that her younger sister was also deaf, but this sister does not appear in her narrative. Given that her sister was deaf, perhaps their mother carried a recessive gene for it. Sano-san does not give a (medical or folk) reason why she became deaf, and she might have in fact been born deaf and was only discovered to be so at the age of three. After Sano-san's mother died giving birth to her younger sister, her father remarried and had a hearing son with his second wife. Sano-san refers to her stepmother as "Mother" in this narrative.

1942–1944

When I was seven, my family moved to Ibaraki Prefecture, which is about 100 kilometers northeast of Tokyo. We rented a house. My father went into the hills to look for somewhere to build a house. In between some trees, he built a house without asking anyone's permission,[1] and we moved there.

Unlike Nakano-san's parents, Sano-san's father was actively involved in her education. Even before the war was over, she was able to go to school for a year.

---

1. That is, he was a squatter.

My father saw me playing idly around the house without going to school and was worried. My father didn't know of any schools for me. My father asked, "Where are the schools for deaf people?" No one knew. He asked at the city office and no one knew. I was about seven years old. . . .

My father asked around and there was a school that used to be an old military school before the Showa period (mid-1920s). Although she stayed in the dorms during the week, like most residential students, she went home on the weekends. *He rented a room [in the dorm] there and placed me there. I commuted from home by steam train. My father tried to teach me the timetable for when the train would come and go. I was still very young and couldn't hear a thing, so I didn't understand. I would often mistake the time, so when the train came, I would go running for the train station and jumped on the train as it left, crying in tears. This happened all the time. I couldn't read anything so I didn't understand what time the train would come, I couldn't read the timetable.*

When I was small, I wasn't able to communicate with the other hearing kids. I wasn't able to tell them I was deaf, so they used to tease me. Around me, everyone was talking with their mouths. They laughed at me. When my mother said, "Everyone here's hearing, you're deaf," everyone laughed. I couldn't hear anything, I didn't understand a word.

Life at the school for the deaf was strict. Signing was forbidden.

At the deaf school, the teachers would rap our hands with canes. They forced us to sit on our hands. It was an oral-method school and very strict. The boys were hit on the cheeks with a cane, which often caused them to bleed. The girls were hit on their fingers.

After class, we would go outside during recess time to play. When it was time for the next class to begin, we children didn't know what time it was and so instead the teachers used a big drum. We'd feel the vibrations and know to return to the classrooms.

In the dorms, they use a large bell to signal us to get out of bed or to come to dinner. The school used a big drum. The huge sound going "DONG" "DONG" would vibrate through our bodies, letting us know to come back to class.

Many of the same themes of familial oppression that came up in Nakano-san's life story repeat themselves with Sano-san, although as we shall see, her parents lighten up considerably after the war. This could be attributed to the changing economic situation in Japan as a whole as well as in their family, the changing cultural attitude toward deafness and disability (in Japan as a whole and their family), or more simply her growing independence from her family.

When I was small, I didn't understand anything my mother said [in spoken Japanese]. When I tried to write something on a piece of paper and hand it to her, she'd say things like: "Say it out loud," "All of you deaf people are no good," or "Hearing people are good."

When I walked to school, I couldn't hear anything. One day, someone threw a rock at me from behind on my way to school. In the old days, the roads weren't asphalt and concrete but dirt roads and there were many rocks on the side of the roads. When I walked back from school, I was afraid someone would throw another rock at me so I walked along the railroad line. When I tried to tell my mother what happened, it was hard to communicate with her in sign. She nodded her head said, "Oh, I see, I see." She wasn't even looking at me at all, which was painful for me.

My mother didn't understand at all, so I had to learn to suppress my feelings. My father said, "Deaf people shouldn't be walking on the rail tracks. I'll take you to school." But my father had a job, so I knew he couldn't take me.

There was that kind of teasing when I walked to school. But one day [when some kids were teasing me], this man on a horse came thundering by. He yelled, "Hey you kids, stop it!" All the hearing kids saw the horse and ran away. I started crying. The man took me up on his horse. I was so relieved that he rescued me. The horseman was one of my father's friends. The next day, I was worried that the boys who teased me would exact their revenge, so terrified, I walked along the railroad tracks back home, a very circuitous route.

1945

Sano-san was able to go to school only for two to three years because of the war. The Allied bombing of civilians began in earnest after March 1945, after most of the military and industrial targets had been flattened. The nation girded itself for an invasion by the Americans. It is notable that one of the things that Sano-san does not mention during this period was the mass starvation that was sweeping through the country. People were literally eating the bark off the trees.

After a while, the war started. One day, my parents told me: "In the skies, a lot of planes will come and drop bombs. When you see that, you have to run into the shelter and cover your head." I could see the planes in the distance dropping bombs, but I didn't understand what they were doing.

The next day, I was playing outside when the planes suddenly came and started dropping bombs. The surrounding houses all heard [the planes? the air-raid sirens?] and ran into the shelters, closed the doors, and hid. I couldn't hear the planes above me so I was walking in the streets without a single worry. I was looking at all of the people hiding inside their doors and wondering what they were up to. The people inside the shelters waved their hands telling me to come in quickly, quickly! They pointed up in the sky. Later on, several bombs fell in that area where I was walking.

Although war is often seen as a great equalizer, the reality is that the richer families in Japan were able to send their children and other loved

ones to safer areas in the countryside, while the poorer families remained in the cities near their jobs and the factories, which were being
heavily bombed. Sano-san's vignette vividly portrays the difficulties suffered by the deaf because of inadequate means of communications. The
lack of effective visual public warning systems (for floods, typhoons,
volcanoes, earthquakes, and nuclear power station disasters) continues
to vex the deaf community even now.

After the war ended, life did not go on normally for her family because of rampant rural poverty:

> *After the war was lost [1945], I went into the mountains to search for and pick
> up undetonated bombs [for scrap metal]. After the war was lost, I thought of
> going back to school, but our family didn't have enough money for me to take the
> train, so I couldn't resume school. Instead, I worked in the mountain fields along
> side my parents.*
>
> *At that time, I was wearing wooden clogs (geta). Since I was running around
> in them all day long, the bottoms of them wore thin and they finally broke. Unfor-
> tunately, we were so poor that my mother said we couldn't buy new ones for me.*
>
> *We were still very poor, so my parents made brooms, you know, for sweeping
> up dust. My father took a great big bag of them and carried them on the train all
> the way to Tokyo to sell at the market. On his way back, a great earthquake
> struck the Kanto area[2] and the train stopped. My father was terrified and ran out
> of the train and hid in the trees. He saw all the houses and buildings all fall to the
> ground. In the evening, the train got going again and my father got on it and re-
> turned back to Ibaraki Station.*

Sano-san was the only one of these three women who did not vocalize
or mouth while she signed, nor did she sign using a grammar influenced
by spoken Japanese. Her signing is much less spatial and gestural than
Nakano-san's, however, and is recognizably within the mainstream of
current Japanese signing. As Sano-san mentioned, the lack of effective
hearing aids or classroom headphone systems made it very difficult for
her to pick up oral or speech skills, and she went to school for only a
short while. The theme of not being able to understand recurs at numerous times throughout her interview.

1946–1950s

After the war, invitations for events and festivals would arrive at Sano-
san's house from the local school for the deaf. Her parents strictly for-

---

2. The Great Kanto Earthquake struck in 1923. It is unclear whether this is a temporal
discontinuity in her narrative or whether she is talking about a smaller earthquake that
struck the Kanto area.

bade her from attending such things. When she asked why, they told her it was better that she hid her deafness and to try to assimilate. It was better to be hearing. In her interview, she said:

> *I thought my parents should just abandon that way of thinking [forced assimilation]. But my father was worried that as a deaf person, I would have trouble communicating. He said, "If you're out late at night and you have to ask your way home, you won't be able to understand anything, so stay at home!"*
>
> *My old-fashioned father thought that wherever a deaf person goes, they'll have trouble communicating. When I was older, I went to Tokyo. I wrote down the route on a piece of paper and wrote down all of the landmarks, so that if I got lost I would simply have to go through my memory to find my way.*

The Occupation forces instituted compulsory education for all Japanese citizens (including women and children with disabilities) in April 1948. Sano-san was eleven years old when the ruling went into effect, but compulsory education for deaf and blind students through middle school was not fully enforced across the country until 1953. The postwar conditions were turbulent and her family situation very dire. Her parents seemed to carry a lot of shame about their children's deafness. Compounding that, her stepmother was very cold toward Sano-san and her sister. All of both parents' energies and affections went toward the son produced in the second marriage.

1952–

At the age of fifteen, Sano-san was still mostly illiterate. However, she started to exchange letters with deaf friends and soon learned to read and write more smoothly. Her stepmother also became much more accepting of her stepdaughter's deafness. Whereas previously her stepmother would forbid both signing and pen-and-paper as means of communication, forcing Sano-san to speak and speechread, gradually her stepmother started to use these alternative methods to talk with her. Sano-san gained more friends in the deaf community, and even when she chatted with them in sign, her mother did not intervene but kept a polite distance. Sano-san talked about her eyes opening to the world through her deaf friends.

We see in the postwar period some of the changing attitudes toward deafness and signing. Whereas Nakano-san had very few friends in the deaf community in her early youth, Sano-san's circle of deaf friends started to expand more and more. She conversed with them in sign, improving her skill and knowledge of the language. Whereas Nakano-san had trouble communicating with her peers and the younger generation in sign because of her prolonged forced seclusion, Sano-san was able to converse easily with both older and younger deaf. This does not mean that she did not face discrimination within her own family:

1955–1960

My parents were both hearing. My younger sister and I are deaf. My younger brother can hear. But my sister and I are both daughters of my dad's first wife. My brother is my second mother's son. We're from different wombs (hara-chi-gai). My father only gave his affections to my brother. It was almost as if he wanted to hide my sister and me from society. When I became mature enough, I told my father exactly what I thought and my father was greatly surprised and let me go out more often.

After high school, Sano-san moved to Tokyo to work for a textile company.

When I went to Tokyo, I stayed in a company dormitory. Every month after I got my paycheck, I would go and buy my parents a present and on Saturday I would return home and give it to my parents. My mother was really surprised. "You really have been working hard," she said happily and stopped worrying about me.

One day, she went to a festival at the Ōtsuka School for the Deaf in Tokyo, where she met her future husband, who was also deaf. They started exchanging letters, continuing even after she returned to Ibaraki. She told her parents about her new male friend, and they encouraged the relationship. She eventually married him, and they settled in Ibaraki.

The first Welfare Law for Disabled Persons, passed in 1949, mainly addressed the issue of injured war veterans, and it took well into the 1950s for the Japanese government to become serious about other disability issues. The nascent Japanese Federation of the Deaf started to become more political by the late 1950s. In 1958, they began a grassroots campaign for the right to hold driver's licenses. It took fifteen years, but in 1973, the police bureau revised its categories of exclusion. Deaf persons were allowed to drive if they wore their hearing aids and were able to hear the sound of a car horn at a certain distance. Even before 1973, some deaf people especially in rural areas were able to obtain licenses because of sympathetic local administrators. However, Sano-san's parents forbade her to get a driver's license. She decided not to listen to them:

And so I secretly went to a driving school. After I passed my driving test, I went home with my shiny new driver's license and showed my father. He was very surprised.

*But my father told me that it's too dangerous for me to drive in a car and
strictly forbade me to drive. "What are you going to do if you get in an accident?" he asked me. But I said that all the other people are hearing, so there's no
problem. "No, no," he said and forbade me to drive.*

The ability to obtain driver's licenses was a pivotal moment for the
deaf community. It represented independence and freedom, and also the
power to enact social change. It is significant that the change was administrative and not legislative: the concept of deafness for driving purposes
was redefined so that most deaf (those who were able to hear the sound
of a car honking) were administratively reclassified as *not-deaf* even if
they could not hear well enough to communicate orally. Because the
government used an administrative loophole to redefine deafness for the
purpose of the driver's license, there were no additional requirements
(aside from wearing a hearing aid) placed on deaf drivers. In contrast,
some U.S. states require additional rearview mirrors or other assistive
technology.

In 1961, the Toho Pictures movie studio brought out *Namonaku
Mazushiku Utsukushiku* (lit: *We have no name and are poor, but are beautiful*,
released in the United States as *Happiness of us alone*), a major motion picture by director Matsuyama Zenzō, who had made his name with his
1959 epic *The human condition* (*Ningen no Jōken*). *Namonaku* was significant in being the first major film portrayal of deaf persons in Japan. The
love story unfolds between a man and a woman, both deaf. They suffer
through the death of their first child, caused because they could not hear
his crying for help, and other adversities. The movie closes with a typical
1960s three-handkerchief finale. Through the movie, the couple sign
with each other and are portrayed sympathetically. Like most other Japanese in the 1960s, they were simply trying to survive in a rapidly
changing Japan. Many informants have pointed to this film as representing the first turning point in general social acceptance of deaf issues.
Matsuyama went on to direct a number of other films around the topic
of disability.

What remains significant about the deaf who came of age after the war
is their ability to decide their own relationships, like the couple in *Namonaku*. Born in an earlier generation, Nakano-san was not only forbidden to choose her own life partner, but was denied one altogether. In
contrast, Sano-san's parents actively encouraged her to date a deaf man.
The birth of their child represented a turning point in Sano-san's life.

In Japan, becoming a parent is often considered the moment when one truly becomes an independent, self-supporting adult person (*ichinin mae*). Many companies will not promote someone who does not have children beyond the rank of section chief, on the assumption they do not know what it means to be responsible for other people. Thus, giving birth has special import in these accounts, as well as reflecting sadly on Nakano-san's life.

1965–

My husband is also deaf, so when I was pregnant, we wondered whether the baby inside my stomach would be deaf or not. We didn't think that there would be much connection between our deafness and whether the baby was hearing. But we wondered how the baby would do in a family environment where we both were deaf.

Our son was born and when I saw that he was hearing, I was relieved. I knew that both of us would take great care and raise him in a loving environment.[3] Our son grew up watching both of us sign so he learned some sign. When he was six, I told him, "You know your father's deaf, so you have to watch him carefully when you talk with him."

I remember when he was in first grade. You know my son was never teased, he never cried. He grew up strong. All the parents were invited to a school parent participation day. Everyone else was hearing. Someone asked my son, "Are your parents deaf?" He said, without any shame or hesitation, "Yes."

When he was in sixth grade, my son said out loud to a lot of people [in front of a class?], "My parents are deaf, but there's nothing wrong with that. There are lots of people who can't hear." Everyone was surprised but nodded their heads and agreed. He told everyone, "My parents are deaf, but there's nothing wrong with that." And he made a lot of friends.

My son would often invite his friends over to the house, saying "Come on, come on over!" I would bring them candy and snacks. He wasn't embarrassed at all that his mother was deaf. He told everyone who came to the house that I was deaf. I was very relieved that they understood. My son taught his friends a little bit of sign language, so they would use it to talk to me, I was so happy.

When he was in tenth and eleventh grade,[4] there was a PTA meeting. I was too embarrassed about being deaf to go to it. But my son said he would explain to everyone. But I said, "That's OK. Why don't you go and tell me later what happened when you come home." But he said, "Don't be so embarrassed by your deafness that you don't go!" I was so happy to hear him say this that I cried. My son interpreted everything that happened at the meeting so patiently for me.

My husband once told me, "It's a good thing that our son is hearing. You're deaf, so if you fell down and hurt yourself, broke your arm or something, he

3. For an exploration of hearing children of deaf parents in America, see Paul Preston's (1994) *Mother Father Deaf.*

4. The first and second years of high school are tenth and eleventh grade in the Japanese system of six elementary years, three middle school years, and three high school years (6–3–3).

*could take you to the hospital and interpret for you, so everything would go
smoothly."*

*My son told me that he wanted to major in a disability-related field in college.
He studied elder care [in college], graduated, and went to Tokyo. I asked him
what he wanted to do with his life and he said, "I want to build a nursing home."
We had been saving up some money for him, so we decided to give the money to
him so that he could build a nursing home [near here]. We told all our friends,
the people at the bank, as well as our business associates about how diligently
our son was working in the disability field. And finally, the nursing home was
built and our son married.*

*My husband and I are happily married. Our son is thirty-one years old and he
continues to work in the nursing home that he founded.*

When I asked if any issues arose because her son was hearing while
she and her husband were deaf, Sano-san replied:

*Yes, I think there is a difference when the child is hearing and the parents are
both deaf. I think our son is unusual in this regard. In many cases, the gulf between the parents and the child grows larger as the child grows up and often the
child ends up resenting the parents. But our son treats disabled people and elderly in the same way, he wants to help them. I'm very thankful that he grew up
to be a good person. Right now, we have a grandchild. Both my husband and I
help take care of our grandchild during the day.*

The birth of Sano-san's son had significant impact on her parents. Once
they saw that their grandchild was being properly brought up, they
were able to consider her a full-fledged adult. Their death later also
brought closure for Sano-san:

*When my parents saw me raising my son, they apparently calmed down a lot.
My father said, "Being deaf or hearing doesn't matter, everyone's normal." He finally understood. Sometime after that, my parents died. I feel very free right now.*

Horikawa Hiro: A *Dankai no Sedai* Deaf

Horikawa Hiro was born in 1945 or 1946, right after the defeat of Japan.
She falls just outside the strict definition of the baby-boomer *dankai no
sedai* (1947–1949), but her life story parallels that of many immediate
postwar generation deaf. The nine years that separate Horikawa-san
from Sano-san witnessed a tremendous amount of social and institutional change, mainly around the issue of education. Horikawa-san was
able to attend twelve years of primary and secondary school. She was

taught to read and write fluently in Japanese. Her signing still shows strong influences from Japanese grammar.

1945–1947

I don't have any memories of the war. I don't have any, but my mother has a lot. She remembers carrying me as a newborn baby, and hiding [in a bomb shelter]. One year later, when I was one year old, the war ended.[5] I don't remember anything from that time. My mother told me about that.

When I was born, I could hear. At the age of two, my mother carried me on her back and went for a walk in the mountains, something I enjoyed tremendously. But that day, the wind was very strong. The leaves of the trees blew around ferociously and a bug[6] flew into my eye and caused it to inflame seriously. She went to all of the neighboring hospitals but they all told her that it was too difficult to treat. Finally, she went to the Ashikaga Hospital in Tochigi and they finally agreed to treat me.

"If we inject her with the antibiotic, your child may not be able to hear again, is that OK?," the doctor asked my mother. My mother worried about this a lot. She had to decide. But she said, "Her eyes are [more] important, so please go ahead and her give her the injection." From that moment, I lost my hearing. I was two years old.

As mentioned in the preceding chapter, streptomycin-related deafness was common among young children in the immediate postwar period. By the time that Horikawa-san entered elementary school, four years had passed since the SCAP edict establishing compulsory education for all citizens, disabled and otherwise. Schools for the deaf had not yet been built in all the prefectures, however, so Horikawa-san was forced to go to a residential school in the neighboring Tochigi Prefecture.

1951–1952

My mother went to look for an elementary school for me. She went to the city hall and they told her to decide between deaf schools in either Gunma or Tochigi Prefectures. After worrying about this, my mother decided on Tochigi. I went to

5. Horikawa-san gave her age as fifty-two, which means she was must have been born in late 1945 or 1946. It is unclear if she gave her age a bit optimistically or if there is another reason for the small discrepancy. She may have been counting her age using the old Japanese system, which enumerates from the date of conception and not the date of birth, so that you are one year old at birth, not zero.

6. She signs *mushi* or "bug." As in English, there is slippage in the usage of "bug" to mean "insect" or "disease" (especially childhood disease, in the case of Japanese). While a literal bug could have flown into her eye (her signed description makes this seem likely), it is also possible that something infectious caused a disease of the eye. Horikawa-san was most likely too young to have remembered the details, and the "bug" could have been her mother's way of explaining to her what had happened.

the Tochigi School for the Deaf from the first grade of elementary school to my
third [and final] year of high school.[7]
*   I stayed in the dorms. There was a dorm for elementary children. My mother's*
house was far away, so I stayed in the dorms from first grade to the end of high
school. I came back home only during the winter and summer breaks.

The Tochigi School for the Deaf was one of the first postwar schools to experiment with signing in the classroom. However, various grade levels experienced different levels of sign acceptance, most probably due to changing school administrations. Both principals and teachers were rotated through the prefectural school system on a regular basis, usually without regard to special skills such as signing or deaf education. Teachers/principals were usually ill qualified at the beginning of their rotation, but by the end of their seven-year cycle the better teachers had learned some signing and could communicate with the pupils. Unfortunately, it was those veteran teachers who were then transferred out, often to regular schools.

The rotation system was designed to make sure that teachers and principals experience a broad range of educational systems. It ensured that schools had a constant supply of new blood and weakened the development of a strong teacher's union. Unfortunately, the rotation system has had an extremely negative effect on schools for the deaf and other special education schools because experienced teachers and principals are rotated out to regular schools and inexperienced, unqualified teachers rotate in.

1951–1963

By the time I entered elementary school, I already knew how to sign. The elementary school teachers also knew how to sign, although I know that in some other places signing was forbidden.
*   Communication was OK, but there were a lot of really smart people in my class. I was born in February and so I was younger than other people in my class.[8] I was slower than the other students. I was frustrated at being behind, so I studied really hard and was able somehow to catch up with the rest of the class. Everyone was so smart and I was stupid, so I had to study hard to catch up.*

7. That is, she received her whole education at the Tochigi School. During her education, the Tochigi School still used only the oral method of educating, i.e., they used no sign language in the classroom. The Tochigi Method of simultaneous communication was introduced in 1968.

8. In Japan, everyone who is born between April of one year to March of the next year attends the same grade level. Thus, students in the same class who were born in February are six months younger than those who were born the preceding August.

When I returned home, I used to exchange little notes with my mother and learned how to read and write. That's why I think everything turned out OK. Two grade levels below me, the students were forbidden to sign and were taught in a strict oral method. Everyone who graduated in my class knew how to sign.

There are some places where the teachers sign at the same time as they speak.[9] But even though our teachers used only signs, we understood them perfectly.

Starting with Horikawa-san's cohort, we see the introduction of speech technologies in the classroom. With the help of these technologies, Horikawa-san was able to learn speech and speechreading skills. She was aided by the fact that she had more residual hearing than many of the other children. If she had been born twenty years later, she probably would have been mainstreamed into a regular school system.

In my case, the teacher would put headphones on all of us. The teacher would turn around so her back was toward us. If we could hear her voice, we raised our hands. The ones who couldn't hear anything were determined to be profoundly deaf and didn't have to wear hearing aids.

The ones who could hear something were forced to wear these hearing aids that had this heavy central unit that you strapped to your chest and a plug that you put in your ear.

You had to wear these until the end of middle school [ninth grade]. After you graduated from middle school, you could take them off. At that time, my hearing was okay. After I got married, my hearing dropped. Around the age of forty-three, my hearing really started to drop. In the past, I could hear pretty well out of my right ear, but right now I can't hear a thing. I can only hear a little out of my left ear. When I was a student, I could hear the sound of planes overhead, or the noise of the television, or the sound of people talking; right now I can't hear things anymore. I can't hear planes anymore. But I can still hear the sound of cars honking, or the sound of the television, or my grandchild crying. But not anything else.

I can use the telephone to tell my son to come pick me up. After talking with each other, he comes by. The phone is okay. I can recognize the characteristics of my son's voice, so I can talk with him on the phone; but with other people, I can't understand a word.

Like Sano-san before her, Horikawa-san was able to choose her husband, also deaf, through her social networks on her own. The schools for the deaf were central areas for deaf interaction even after graduation. The alumni associations provided prime opportunities to meet potential spouses. Her parents were supportive of her decision. Horikawa-san also became active in the Women's Division of her local association of the

9. This is often referred to as sim-com or simultaneous-communication.

deaf, where she met Sano-san. She later went on to become a local leader in the Deaf Women's Division, which is how I came to meet her in that hot spring many years later.

> *After graduating from high school, I came straight back home and lived in my parents' house. I began working in a company and commuted to work. Three years later, I met with one of my old classmates who was now working in Tokyo. He graduated from the Tochigi School as well. I used to meet with all of my old classmates a lot. He invited me to a party. We started going out and later I married him.*
>
> *Later, my husband and I moved to Ibaraki. He had worked very hard in his business, commuting back and forth for about six years. He was asked if he could start up a branch in Ibaraki, sewing family crests for kimonos. He said yes.[10]*
>
> *I worked alongside him. We worked very hard each day. The economy was very bad in the beginning but it gradually got better.[11] We were able to put food on the table each day.*

The Horikawas gave birth to a son. Less than 10 percent of deaf couples give birth to deaf children. And in Horikawa-san's case, because the cause of her deafness was an ototoxic reaction to streptomycin, it was even more unlikely that their child would be born deaf. Their son was born hearing, but learned how to sign as he grew up. Surprisingly, he decided to stay in the family business of sewing family crests on kimonos. He married a (hearing) woman who decided to learn signing so that she could communicate with her mother-in-law. With the birth of their grandson, the Horikawas became a three-generation household living under one roof.

1980s

> *I wanted our son to go to college, but my husband said, "He doesn't need to go to college. He can work here with us." I thought about this a lot, but decided to send him off to college so that he could learn more things, become more cultured, and have a broader perspective on life.*
>
> *After graduating, my son worked at a bank company for three years manufacturing ATM cards. He learned a lot at that job and got more experience in the world. Then our son told my father, "I want to work here with you." My husband thought about it and agreed to let him work in the family business. My son studied [sewing] in Kanagawa for one year and came back. He got married and his wife lives here with us.*

10. It is a bit unclear who asked whom to set up the business in Ibaraki doing the family crests. My assumption is that her husband worked as an apprentice for a while before being allowed to become independent.

11. When Horikawa-san was in her late teens, Japan was celebrating the Tokyo Olympics in 1964, one of the chief examples of its rapid economic development.

> *Our grandson was born, so that makes us six people under one roof.[12] Our daughter-in-law is different from other people. She doesn't let things get to her or get into petty fights with other people; she's a very kind and gentle person. Her lifestyle is similarly relaxed; she gets along with everyone smoothly.*
>
> *Even when my daughter-in-law meets deaf people, she can communicate using sign, so everything's great. She says she enjoys using sign to talk to deaf people. She says that Sano-san is the easiest person to talk with. She says Sano-san's personality, habits, and other things really come out in her signing. Sano-san's grandchild and my grandson are the same age, so they're often playing at each other's houses. My son says he likes to invite Sano-san over and have a good time. All the time, all the time.*

By the 1990s, there was a *shuwa būmu* (signing boom) in Japan. Many popular TV shows had deaf protagonists and informal signing circles were becoming extremely popular. Horikawa-san's daughter-in-law was able to ride this boom of popular interest and attended a local signing circle.

Horikawa-san also faced parental opposition when she wanted to get a driver's license, despite being an adult woman with a teenage son. As with Sano-san, the ability to drive meant freedom from her parents.[13]

> *When Sano-san got her driver's license, I also thought that I would like one as well. My mother shook her head and said I couldn't. But I thought about it some more. My son was in middle school at the time and he was on the baseball team. Whenever he went to overnight training camps [gasshuku], he needed someone to come pick him up. He always had to ask his friend's parents [who were hearing], to pick him up as well. I thought that was an awful burden to place on them and decided to get the license by myself.*
>
> *And so, without asking permission from my parents, I went to driver's school and passed the exam. When I showed my driver's license to my mom, she was very surprised. I bought my car with my own money, but whenever I drove it, my mother would insist on sitting in the rear seat. I wasn't allowed to drive by myself. Even when I took my mom home to her house and said bye-bye to her, she would get worried and insist on driving back with me to my house. And then I would drop her off at her house, and we'd go around and around between my house and her house so many times. It was all very troublesome. When I finally let her off at her house and told her that I was going back alone, she started crying. She used to be worried that I got in a car accident and would always be calling.*

12. I am not sure who the sixth person is, but I believe it is Mrs. Horikawa's sister.

13. On December 27, 2000, the Metropolitan Police Department announced that they were revising section 88 of the Traffic Law to remove "inability to hear" as a disqualification for drivers licenses (*JDN* February 1, 2001:1), effective June 2001. Technically, the change would allow profoundly deaf persons who were previously disqualified like Horikawa-san's husband to finally obtain driver's licenses. This is the result of more than forty years of lobbying by the JFD. Unfortunately, the revised law allows for discretion on the part of the test examiners to deny licenses to "those who may potentially be unable to drive safely due to disability or illness."

I thought it was a nuisance and asked my older sister to talk to my mother. She told her, "Don't worry, she won't get in an accident. Even though she can't hear, her eyes can see normally. It's the same as a hearing person. When you close the windows of the car, you can't hear the outside sounds anyway. It's the same thing. So don't worry." After that, my mother finally calmed down.

I asked my mother once, "How come you insist on riding with me?" She said that if her daughter got in a car accident while she was lounging around at home, it would be troublesome [embarrassing?]. If she rode with me, at least if I got in an accident, we'd die together.

Mother would come to my house from time to time and I would take care of her. After a while, she passed away. Even though she's passed away, I still pay a lot of attention when I'm driving. I'm happy to have made this choice when I think about driving my son to school. It was better than having to ask one of his friends' parents to take him.

Right now, I take my grandchild to the hospital when he's sick. It's all right. I also drive to the local deaf association's events and activities. It's a lot of fun.

When I go teach how to sign at local seminars, I drive there as well. My husband also wants to get a driver's license, but he has absolutely no hearing. So he can't hear a car horn beep. Even if he uses one of my hearing aids turned up all the way, his ears hurt but he can't hear a thing. So it would be difficult for him to pass the exam, so he's given up hope of getting a driver's license. He says that he enjoys riding his bicycle up the mountains. He likes it, just like a mouse scampering around. So he doesn't mind.

But after we're done with sewing on a family crest on a kimono, I have to take it to the client by car with my husband. I don't like that at all. Do you know why? It's a long way to the clients' houses and the roads are wide. I like driving around the narrow roads nearer to my house. So I leave all the responsibility for deliveries to my husband. Even if it is raining, I make him take them by bicycle. She laughs. *I won't help him at all.* Laughs.

Funata-san: Late *Dankai no Sedai* Deaf

The youngest woman in the Ibaraki group was Funata Hatsuko, who was born in 1951 in the Yamagata area, which is about three hundred kilometers north of Tokyo. It is notable that although she was born well after the conclusion of hostilities, she still started her life story with the Pacific War. Perhaps coming after two interviewees who talked about the war, she felt compelled to include it in her own story as well.

1930s–1940s

My father went to Russia for the war effort. After the war was lost, he was sent to Siberia as a prisoner of war and lived there for many years. Every day, he was forced to work on a farm and dig in the fields. The only food was bread and milk. He was always terribly hungry and very cold.

The war ended around Showa 20 [1945] and Father came back to Japan in Showa 24 [1949]. He finally came back in one piece and healthy.

He married Mother in Showa 25 [1950]. Soon after, I was born.

I could hear when I was born. But when I was two years old, I caught a cold during the winter. I had a very high fever and the doctors gave me Su-to-mai [streptomycin], the same thing as before [in Horikawa-san's case], and the same injection made me lose my hearing. My mother was worried. She carried me on her back to many different hospitals. A doctor told her, "She won't get any better, she's permanently lost her hearing." My mother was devastated and gave up hope [of finding a cure for me]. Instead, she started worrying about how to best communicate with me.

She apparently worried a lot how I would manage to grow up.

The same theme of miscommunication also appears several times in Funata-san's narrative. Unlike Horikawa-san, who had encountered signing even before entering elementary school, Funata-san found learning to sign an eye-opening experience. She was a reticent child. It seems that she did not have enough residual hearing to be assisted by hearing aids. She struggled with her schoolwork.

1958–

When I was small, I didn't understand anything, I didn't think about anything. I didn't know anything about reading or writing or about words.

I entered a school for the deaf. Even when I was seven years old, I didn't know anything about reading or writing.

I was slow to learn sign, I think. When I entered elementary school, I was surprised to see everyone signing. I thought I had entered another world. It was the first time I realized that they were deaf, like me. But I was very resistant [to signing] at first. I wasn't one who talked a lot anyway, I just kept quiet and my mouth closed.

It took me a while to learn how to sign. When I was in first grade, I didn't know how to sign, even in second grade I didn't know. By third grade I knew a little and it was in the fourth grade that I gradually learned enough to be able to converse with signs. But all of the schoolteachers didn't know how to sign very well. They taught their classes only speaking. I would stare at their mouths and not understand a thing. So I fell behind in my studies.

It goes without saying, but like everyone else I didn't know how to read or write. That goes without saying. I was about three years behind in my studies. For example, even though I was in the third or fourth grade, I was only studying at the first grade level.

During class, no one could understand what the teacher was saying and everyone got very sleepy. We were forbidden to sign during class. Occasionally the teacher would throw blackboard chalk at someone; it would hit you on the forehead and hurt a lot. So when the teacher had his back to the classroom [to write something on the blackboard], we'd all sneak a conversation with our friends using signs. If we were caught signing, the teacher would hit us over the head with a stick. It hurt a lot. The school really reinforced the message, "Signing is bad! Signing is bad!" [this can also be translated No Signing! Signing is Forbidden!] The oral method was really emphasized.

That was the same up until high school.

So it goes without saying that I wasn't very good in my studies. I think everyone else was the same way.

When she was in the third grade, an incident occurred that made her aware of her deafness and her separation from hearing society.

1960–

When I was nine years old, I know it was rather late but I noticed something. There was a summer festival near my house. My two younger brothers were involved in some sort of game, song, or play that was happening on the event stage. They were having a lot of fun. I wondered why I wasn't participating. I wondered why I had never participated. Why? Why? I wondered as I watched the other people participating. Why? I didn't understand. At that moment, I understood that [it was because] I was deaf. I became overwhelmed with sadness (kuyashi-katta) and returned home and started bawling.

My mother asked me, "What's wrong? What's wrong?" Even if I wanted to tell her, I couldn't [because of the communication barrier]. Not being able to express myself, I cried for a long time. I cried for a whole day. My mother asked me, "What's wrong?" She must have realized, "Oh, everyone was participating in all of the events at the festival and having a good time. Only my daughter couldn't join in the fun." She started crying along with me. She held my crying body and comforted me.

That was the catalyst for me to start learning how to read and write. I studied seriously and changed.

After reorienting her life toward her studies, Funata-san had hopes of entering college. Unfortunately they were dashed. In 1969, colleges in Japan did not normally accept applications from deaf students. There were exceptions—the leaders of the JFD who graduated from Kyoto University in the 1960s—but the majority of these deaf college students were post-lingually deafened, had taken classes at regular high schools, were fluent in spoken and written Japanese, and were male.

One vice-principal of a school for the deaf chuckled when I asked him how many of his students went to college (this was in the late nineties), and told me perhaps one every once in a while. The expectation level in schools for the deaf in Japan remains extremely low. The disability job quotas enacted by the government actually exacerbate the situation since even high school graduates are pretty much assured a job, even if it is a dead-end "window-seat" job (*madogiwazoku*), so called because you sit by the window all day and look at the scenery.

1969

I really enjoyed studying until high school. I had this dream of going to college, but because I was deaf, my application was refused. It was the old days, so they refused to accept me.

So I began thinking about a job, my job counselor told me that a beautician might be a good job for me. But I'm short and I didn't like the idea of straining my neck looking upwards while I chop hair all day.

In Japan in the postwar period, many deaf persons found jobs as beauticians and barbers, and hair dressing is one of the occupational job categories for deaf persons—just as hot-type printing was for deaf persons in the United States. Frustrated by not being able to attend college and not liking the idea of straining her neck as a beautician, Funata-san started to think about the textile industry. She worked at what can only be described as a sweatshop.

1970s–

So that's why I began to think about kimonos. I thought a job sewing kimonos wouldn't be bad. I thought it could be something I could continue in the future.

So I left Yamagata for Tokyo and for five years I stayed at a [company] dorm there. It was very difficult. From early in the morning until late at night, we sewed all day long. For five years. All of the people [at the company] were hearing. There were only . . . two deaf people, including myself. No one knew how to sign so the only way we could communicate was through pen and paper. I learned how to sew the patterns by looking over the shoulder of my co-workers. For five years, I learned how to sew kimonos.

Many deaf women ended up working in factories, often in all-deaf cohorts. In her 1986 ethnography of Japanese factory women in conservative Nagoya, anthropologist Jeannie Lo mentions a group of deaf women who lived in the company dorm with her:

[There was] a community of six deaf women in their late twenties [who] lived on the seventh floor, isolated from the rest of the women. The deaf women worked in the factories since the noisy machines did not bother them. They communicated with each other in sign language, and with the other women with gestures and facial expressions. The deaf women will probably remain in Aoi dormitory until they are twenty-nine, when they must move into apartments of their own. They will probably stay in the factory, as it is difficult for them to find another job or to find a husband. With their handicap, they are considered "imperfect" by Nagoya standards and therefore unlikely to marry. (Lo 1990:60–61)

Returning to Funata-san, we find that she ends her life narrative rather abruptly with marriage to another deaf man (sometime in the late 1970s or early 1980s), childbirth, and the death of her husband:

1970s–1980s

After that, I met this fellow who had come from Aomori to Tokyo. We bought a house in Ibaraki and moved here. For sixteen years, we lived together.
But my husband passed away, he died. He died about ten years ago.
Right now, I live together with my only son.

Funata-san's life narrative was much shorter than either Sano-san's or Horikawa-san's. A considerable part of the reason for that may have been her unease at being perceived as taking interview time away from her older cohort. Although the three women are active in the same social events, it is clear that Sano-san and Horikawa-san are much closer to each other than to Funata-san. The two elder women also have connections through their grandchildren that Funata-san does not share.

Conclusion: Deaf Identity in Context

I was primarily interested in shifts in deaf identity through the postwar period in these interviews. However, I was stymied because there is no clear translation for *identity* in either spoken Japanese or Japanese Sign. The English word "identity" has two meanings. The first is our internal identity that gives us our essential being, that which makes us the same person when we wake up each morning (similar to the Greek concept of *eidos*), or sense of consciousness or self-consciousness. This is what makes us Bill or Keiko or Ichiro. The second meaning is an external identity, that which we share with others ("African-Americans" or "British," for example). The two meanings are often blurred in English as well as ASL, but it is primarily the second meaning of group identity that is the most interesting to me. For further discussion on the social theory of identity, see Alcoff (1988) or Calhoun (1994).

The Japanese term *jikaku* is the closest native term to the first notion, that of self-identity, and it has connotations of self-awareness or self-knowledge (the Kanji characters are written as "to see yourself," as from a third-person perspective). The JFD's (1997) Japanese Sign dictionary gives the sign for *jikaku* as "to become aware" (= *mezameru*, the sign for opening one's eyes or reaching a higher level of consciousness).

A loan word, *aidentiti*, has been brought into both spoken Japanese and Japanese sign (usually fingerspelled, occasionally using the ASL sign for *identity*)[14] to refer to the identity that is shared by people with a common feeling, often minorities. However, in both spoken Japanese and Japanese Sign, *aidentiti* is a cumbersome term. Furthermore, it is not in common use, and many of my informants did not know the meaning of the word. Delving into identity without having a term for it (or worse, constructing one by borrowing from English) seemed fraught with danger. For this reason, I asked the various informants for their life narratives. I assumed that if they saw themselves as deaf or had particular moments of deaf-awareness, these would reveal themselves in the natural course of telling their life stories.

The women in this chapter shared particular thematic elements which seemed to be core to their experience of being deaf in postwar Japan: crowded schools for the deaf, parents who did not understand their condition, educational and occupational barriers, deaf husbands, raising hearing children, the importance of getting a driver's license, and the importance of the school and alumni networks for close friendships.

The sign for *signing* is also the sign for *communicating*. In their narratives, we can also see how their construction of the difficulties they faced with the hearing world centered largely around the issue of communication. Only rarely, as in the story about not being able to hear the air-raid sirens, does the concept of disability or impairment as such figure in the women's stories. Rather, the women center on the problem of communication with parents, teachers, the outside world, and occasionally their own children.

This is the last coherent generation of the deaf in Japan. They share a commonality of experience and a group identity as deaf (*rōa*) even though their individual life courses have been quite different. In later chapters, we will see that after the 1960s, mainstreaming has meant that the next generation no longer primarily identifies with deafness and with other deaf.

14. Lately, some of the younger deaf have been using the ASL sign for *identity*, a fingerspelled "I" handshape placed like a badge over the heart.

CHAPTER SEVEN

The Postwar Generation of Deaf Activists

The tumultuous postwar period allowed a new generation of deaf activists to emerge in Japan. Compared to the prewar generation, they were considerably better educated, and this was significant in the new meritocratic Japan. Many of these young leaders were late-deafened, and because they had strong verbal skills they were able to go to the top colleges in Japan decades before the rest of the community. The new leadership was far removed from the lives of Sano-san and her friends in terms of both education and opportunity, but they shared the fruits of the new deaf political movement that emerged under the JFD in the 1960s and 1970s. In that sense, they can be considered part of the same generation in the deaf community.

Matsumoto Masayuki: Japan's First Deaf Lawyer

Matsumoto Masayuki was born with perfect hearing in Osaka during the Pacific War. When he was in third grade (1948; age nine), he contracted meningitis and became deaf. He was not allowed to resume schooling in his neighborhood elementary school and was transferred to the Osaka City School for the Deaf, where he did extremely well. He recalls in his memoirs that, in those days, a lot of signing was still used within the Osaka School for the Deaf and that he picked up signing rather naturally (Matsumoto 1997a:1).

Because of his strong Japanese language skills, after elementary school

93

Matsumoto ended up taking most of his junior high and high school classes at the neighboring regular (hearing) schools. Most of his deaf friends, however, remained at the school for the deaf. After high school, he entered the prestigious Kyoto University and graduated with a bachelor's in law in 1963, passing the extremely difficult national bar exam the same year. He spent two years (1964–1965) at the Legal Research and Training Institute, finally registering with the Osaka Bar Association in 1966.

The 1960s and 1970s were politically tumultuous in Japan. The San Francisco Peace Treaty signed on September 8, 1951, marked the official end of the American Occupation, and Japan returned to sovereign nation status on April 28, 1952. The first Treaty of Mutual Cooperation and Security between Japan and the United States of America (abbreviated *Ampo* in Japan) was signed in 1951. It occasioned considerable debate among politicians as well as in the general populace. Many leftists were proud of Japan's new pacifist constitution and felt that the United States might use the treaty to drag Japan into a war in Korea against its will. Things came to a head when the Security Treaty came up for renewal in 1960. There were massive public demonstrations and strikes involving literally millions of people all across Japan.

Tokyo University was at the center of these protests. The All-Japanese Federation of Japanese Students' Self-Governing Associations, often referred to by the abbreviation *Zengakuren*, was very influential at the former imperial university. If there was something ironic about the sway of Communism among the most elite students in Japan, it was lost on them at the time. Much more radical than the Japanese Communist Party, which they saw as part of the "old left," *Zengakuren* led a number of violent street demonstrations, including a particularly bloody conflict in 1960 with the police at the National Diet Building, the center of Japanese politics. Although it broke apart in the early 1960s, various factions and offshoots of *Zengakuren* continued its legacy of violent protest through the early 1970s.

Ironically, both the Korean (1950–1953) and Vietnam Wars (1961–1973) helped Japan's economy considerably even though it was not militarily involved in either conflict. Instead, it served as a major logistics hub for the American forces. The "Special Procurements" of military supplies by the American government during the Korean War served to jump-start war-torn Japanese industries and this effect was sustained through the conflict in Vietnam. In addition to the economy, both wars helped keep radical student activism strong through the end of the 1960s, a fervent mix of anti-American, anti-military, anti-emperor, anti-establishment, and other beliefs.

It was during this tumultuous period that Matsumoto attended Kyoto University (1959–1963) and became politically active within the Kyoto association of the deaf. At college, he became friends with some of the deaf youth group leaders who would later stage the silent coup (pun intended) that would change the direction of the national Japanese Federation of the Deaf in the late 1960s. These Kyoto leaders had backgrounds very similar to Matsumoto's in that they were also late-deafened and were also fluent in spoken and written Japanese. They also had strong leanings toward leftist ideals, a political dimension that they largely kept hidden from public view.

Deaf Ears at the Police Station: The Criminal Law System

Because deaf people were seen as beggars or worse, the criminal justice system had been an area of anxiety for the deaf community in Japan since the late 1800s, but concern peaked in the postwar period as confrontation with the courts was reconfigured into a human rights issue. As the first deaf lawyer, Matsumoto figures prominently in this narrative.

Much of the early struggle involved petitioning the courts to provide interpreters for the deaf in civil and criminal hearings. In the postwar period, the only hearing people that deaf people were likely to associate with on a daily basis were a closed community of family members, teachers at the schools for the deaf, and maybe some co-workers. If deaf people were arrested, they were forced to interact with a broader population of non-signing, non-sympathetic hearing people. There were no certified interpreters until the 1990s. Before then, co-workers, family, or schoolteachers would be asked to interpret for deaf defendants, if they were asked at all. The Meiji Civil Proceedings Act of 1891, which was based on European law codes, mentions the right to have an interpreter for the deaf present, but then immediately disclaims the requirement:

> When those pleading before the court do not understand the Japanese language or are deaf or otherwise mute, an interpreter (*tsūji*) shall be present. However, questions may be posed through writing and written

statements may be obtained from those who are deaf or mute. (Article 134 of the Civil Proceedings Act of 1890 cited in AJSIRC 1994:12)[1]

The wording in the legal code is weak, and in reality, interpreters were often not provided. Instead, deaf people were often forced to communicate via pen and pencil with the police. Their situation was complicated by the fact that many deaf at the time were illiterate and would not have known what the documents they were being forced to sign might mean. One of the founders of the Japanese Sign Language Interpreters Association, Itō Shunsuke, recalls the first time he was called to interpret:

> In 1949, I became a teacher at the Kyoto Prefectural School for the Deaf. I started to learn how to sign and how to be an interpreter. The first time I used my sign interpreting skills in public was when I was called to the Kyoto City "N" Police Station one day. A young man had been arrested for theft. He was uneducated and couldn't read or write. Even his signing was difficult to understand. I'm not sure if I was really acting in the role of sign language interpreter at the time. I put my signature [on the statement] and listed my role as the "sign interpreter" (*shuwa tsūji*). (AJSIRC 1994:12–13)

The *Japanese Deaf News* (*JDN*), the monthly newspaper of the Japanese Federation of the Deaf, reported with increasing frequency criminal cases involving the deaf in the postwar period. For example, in the February 1952 issue, the *Deaf News* noted the outcome of a trial of four deaf men accused of an armed burglary. In this incident, the victim reported to the police that burglars said to him, "Be quiet!" "Where's the money?" "Open the [bureau] drawers from the bottom!" "Shut up!" and similar remarks.

As the four suspects were all reported to be both deaf and mute, there was some question about whether the right people had been apprehended. Nonetheless, two of the deaf defendants were found guilty, while the other two were found innocent (*JDN* February 21, 1952:3).[2] There was no mention of any special legal aid rendered in this case relating to their deafness or use of sign or sign interpreters in the court.

In the same month, the *Deaf News* also reported the murder of a mother and daughter by a deaf family of four in Gunma Prefecture (*JDN*

1. The language is not very different in the 1996 revision of the Civil Proceedings Code (Article 154).
2. As the burglary had been committed in 1948 (it took four years for the decision to be rendered), there was considerable confusion over the actual turn of events in the newspaper account.

February 1, 1952:2). Three schoolteachers from the Gunma Prefectural School for the Deaf served as interpreters during the trial (*JDN* March 1, 1952:3).[3] These two cases are typical of criminal suits in the 1950s and early 1960s. While the *Deaf News* questioned whether the police and prosecutors understood the special circumstances of the deaf, larger issues of human rights had not yet been foregrounded. This changed with the next generation of deaf activists.

Kyoto School for the Deaf Protests (1965)

In November 1965, the year before Matsumoto graduated from the Legal Research and Training Institute, high school students at the Kyoto Prefectural School for the Deaf started to organize around the issue of high school education. Ironically, the protests occurred because the students were angry about the favoritism shown to the late-deafened and hard-of-hearing students by the faculty at the Kyoto School. They decided to demand more egalitarian education at the school, calling it the "3.3 Declaration of the School Boycott."[4] In the words of one of the protest leaders, Ōya Susumu (who much later became the head of the Ikoinomura nursing facility mentioned in chapter 4):

> We students talked with each other [about what we wanted]: we didn't want classes where there was favoritism toward the students with proper enunciation skills, we wanted classes where everyone could understand, we wanted a school environment that everyone could enjoy. We looked closely at the reality of our situation: the idea of entering college was considered a silly fantasy; we weren't even given the option of looking for employment at large corporations; we were expected to work like machines without hope until the end of our lives. (AJSIRC 1994:14)

Although the 3.3 Declaration resulted in some minor changes at the Kyoto School, the situation in schools for the deaf did not improve appreciably. The most significant impact of the 3.3 Declaration was in its

3. The *Deaf News* does not report what the final result of this case was. Since criminal trials can last more than a decade in extreme cases, it could have simply fallen off the radar by the time a decision was rendered.

4. 3.3 refers to the date of the protest strike (March 3, 1966). The use of the 3.3 number format and the language of the protest itself draw strongly from the cultural milieu of 1960s Japan. Protests against the Security Treaty (*Ampo*) and the Communist, Labor, and Burakumin protests were still very much in everyone's minds. Also, March 3 is "Ear Day" (*mimi no hi*) in Japan, promoting hearing health.

broader appeal to Japanese society. The story was picked up by the major newspapers as well as the federation's *Deaf News*. As in the Gallaudet Deaf President protests in the United States three decades later, deaf organizations around Japan were galvanized by the idea of these students protesting to improve their situation. This led to a new political sentiment among the generation emerging out of the postwar context.

Deaf activist Itabashi Masakuni contextualizes the 3.3 student movement in the milieu of Japan during the post-1960, post–Japan-U.S. Security Treaty period. Japan was going through a period of volatile social unrest with violent protests by the left encountering equally violent resistance from the right. Itabashi recalls turning on the TV or opening the newspaper and having the following questions continuously raised by various social activists and protesters:

- What is democracy? (*minshushugi to wa nandarō*)
- What are basic human rights? (*kihonteki jinken to wa dōiu koto nanoka*)
- What does it mean to protect our dignity as equal human beings? (*ningen toshite hitoshii songen ga mamorareru koto to wa*) (Itabashi 1991:360)

Using the same political language as the leftists, Itabashi explains that the framing of the deaf youth movement was clearly anti-discriminatory from the very beginning. Under the heading "Why did these problems occur," the Kyoto Forum on Deaf Education (1996) found that:

The social environment surrounding the school for the deaf at the time was one in which the problems caused by the nation's rapid economic growth and environmental pollution were increasingly challenged by local movements (*chiiki undō*) and other movements fighting for the protection of various rights (*shokenri*). . . .
The Kyoto Prefectural School Board published its *Dōwa* [Burakumin Anti-Discrimination] Education Guidelines in 1963. In the year that the "Student Strikes" occurred, the School Board was making its first steps in the civilized advancement (*bunmeika*) of [equal] education based on the national Constitution and the Fundamentals of Education Act. The Kyoto School for the Deaf established its first committee for *Dōwa* [burakumin] education in 1965. . . . Meanwhile, the attitude toward signing was becoming stricter and one week before the strikes the Principal announced at the Morning Assembly that, "I would like you to stop that gesturing with your hands and speak [with your lips]." (ii–iii)

In an environment where the rights of Burakumin students were being espoused at the same time as their own linguistic rights were being denied, the students at the Kyoto School felt they had no choice other than to strike. This and the Janome Murder Incident which occurred in the same year were later bundled under the rallying cry of the "Deaf Human Rights Proclamation" (*Rōasha no Jinken Sengen*) by deaf activists (Itabashi 1991:360).

Postwar Social Activism: The Burakumin Anti-Discrimination Movement

There are many plausible explanations as to why deaf political activism increased dramatically after the Pacific War. One could use a repression hypothesis, arguing that these groups were politically suppressed in the prewar and wartime periods and were simply bouncing back after the change in government. Complicating this view, deaf groups were not particularly politically active before the war and as with most other civil society groups in Japan, there is some evidence of willing government co-optation into the war movement (see the picture of the deaf students dancing for the soldiers in chapter 3).[5] There is no indication that they were repressed any more than the general population.

Then did the situation facing the deaf get worse after the war and during reconstruction, forcing more political mobilization because of a relative disparity? My interviews with informants born well before the war, such as Nakano-san, almost unilaterally show that the situation improved after the war: more social rights, more employment opportunities, better education, better social mobility, and so forth. Repression clearly does not play a role in activism in this case.

The context of postwar Japan is critical for understanding the ability of social protest groups to articulate a new form of activist politics. After the end of the American Occupation in 1952, there was a resurgence of the left in the face of strong government repression as well as violent internal political struggles among leftist groups such as factions of the Communist and Socialist parties.

In the introduction, I noted that the deaf movement appears to be one of the few successful minority social movements in Japan. The Burakumin movement, which has been mentioned several times, has been successful in achieving certain political and economic gains. However, unlike the deaf movement, it has had difficulty achieving positive social "spin" and acceptance. Because the Burakumin liberation movement be-

---

5. For examples of co-optation of other groups, see Sheldon Garon's provocative (1997) analysis in *Molding Japanese minds.*

came vocal right around the time the Japanese deaf movement was being born, and formed the backdrop to deaf politics of the time, a short history of it is necessary. Political leaders within the JFD claim no heritage with the Burakumin movement (despite the comments above regarding a feeling of unfairness in the Kyoto School Strikes), but it is still clear that the JFD's success has been predicated on the actions and political/social frames created by the Burakumin movement.[6]

The groups labeled as the former *burakumin* (literally: people of the village) are the descendants of a former caste status codified during the Tokugawa period. Nothing biological or cultural separates former burakumin from non-burakumin Japanese except for family lineage, an indicator on public records. During the Tokugawa period (1600–1867), the groups that made up what were later called the burakumin were considered outcastes—they had marriage and residence restrictions and their occupations were also restricted by law to categories involving physical or spiritual defilement: butchering, leather tanning, serving as executioners, and some others.

Although the burakumin and the caste system (samurai, peasant, merchant, artist) were formally abolished in 1871 with legal changes following the Meiji Revolution, even today the descendants of burakumin find themselves locked out of educational, occupational, and marital opportunities because of their purportedly tainted family status. To use an American example, it would be like being Black (encountering social, educational, and economic discrimination at all stages of life) but with no visible skin color difference. Indeed, many of the current and recurring scandals surrounding the burakumin problem involve underground blacklists that contain the names and addresses of former burakumin families, or the leaking of government or old temple records which also contain such private information. Major companies have been known to buy these blacklists so that they can (illegally) screen job applicants for potential "trouble."

The contemporary Burakumin anti-discrimination movement can trace itself to the prewar activities of a group called the Suiheisha ("The Levellers"), who drew heavily from Marxist and socialist theory. The 1922 Suiheisha call-to-arms, *Yokihinotameni* ("Toward a better day") by Miura Sangendō invoked Romain Rolland (French socialist writer), William Morris (British socialist architect and poet), and Maksim Gorkii (Russian novelist). The Suiheisha was active right through the middle of

6. For those not familiar with the Burakumin movement, there is a long list of excellent academic work in this area (cf. Donoghue 1957, 1978; DeVos and Wagatsuma 1967; Hingwan 1996; Tsurushima 1984; Mihashi 1987; Pharr 1990; Fowler 2000).

the war years, succumbing to government pressure to shut down only in 1942. After the war, they re-formed in 1946 as the National Committee for Buraku Liberation before settling on the name Buraku Liberation League (BLL) in 1955. From that period to the present, the BLL has been extremely politically active in pushing measures to eradicate discrimination and disparity.

The early BLL had the support of the Japanese Communist Party (JCP) through the end of the 1950s, mostly due to the efforts of the BLL president Matsumoto Jiichirō to bring together the Japanese Socialist Party (JSP) and JCP fronts of his organization. Matsumoto (no relation to the deaf lawyer) was a strong JCP supporter, but with his death in 1960, a schism emerged in the BLL over the issue of the nature of systematic discrimination. The Communist supporters in the BLL saw discrimination as a form of class distinction because of the employment restrictions and poverty. In order to overthrow the capitalist bourgeoisie, former burakumin and other lower-class workers had to unite, and any type of special measures to help only the residents of former buraku areas would in their eyes serve to divide the working class.

The Communists were a minority in the BLL. The rest of the BLL were content to work with the government on attaining special benefits for Buraku residents. In 1969, the Liberal Democratic Party (LDP, the conservative majority party in Japan) helped the BLL push through the Special Measures Law which gave buraku communities extra funds to improve schools, sewers, and other basic social services in their districts. The same year, the Communists in the BLL split off, creating the *Zenkoku Buraku Kaihō Ren'aikai* (abbreviated as *Zenkairen*).

One of the gains that the BLL had secured through the Special Measures Law was the *madoguchi-ippō* ("One Window") policy, whereby the organization was put in control of the funds that were to be disbursed. People who wished to apply for buraku scholarships, for example, had to go through the BLL prefectural associations. The BLL had had almost total hegemony over the *madoguchi*, except in the few areas where the *Zenkairen* support was strong enough for the Communist organization to be in control of the funds.

Burakumin were not the only active social protesters in Japan during the period. The conflict surrounding the U.S.-Japan Mutual Security Treaty in 1959–1960 heightened the general sense of political crisis on the left, especially among student groups such as *Zengakuren*, the national student organization, which also split into JCP- and non-JCP-affiliated (New Left) factions just before the Ampo crisis. This student activism continued well into the early 1970s, creating a broader frame for leftist political activism during this period.

That the 1950s and 1960s were politically tumultuous alone does not fully explain how a new generation of deaf political activists was able to take advantage of the new framings made possible by the New Left. One also needs to look at the demographics of the emerging deaf leadership cohort. As noted in chapter 5, during the late 1940s, there was a mass movement of the population toward urban areas at a time when the physical, medical, and social infrastructures were still rebuilding. The skyrocketing birth rate, number of epidemics, and introduction of powerful new antibiotics such as streptomycin caused the number of deaf children to increase dramatically in the turbulent postwar period.

In that environment, those who were post-lingually late-deafened had a significant advantage over those who were prenatally or pre-lingually deafened. The late-deafened were able to speak Japanese and speech-read with greater ease than their counterparts. This led to better educational opportunities and leadership roles in the newly reorganizing prefectural and national associations of the deaf.

The Tokyo Office of the JFD

The head office of the JFD moved from Kyoto to Tokyo in 1958. This was in part a recognition that while deaf activism was stronger in the Kyoto area, the center of politics in Japan was in the capital of Tokyo. If the JFD wanted to change national politics, it would have to be near the ministries and state politicians. Its first office was a cramped cubicle. The organization initially only had two employees. Takeshima-san, a deaf activist, was named the Director of the Tokyo Office. He was aided by Iizuka-san, a hearing woman who was the Office Manager, a lofty title during the long period when she and Takeshima-san were the only employees.

Iizuka-san learned how to sign when she moved into her husband's household after marriage. Her new in-laws were both deaf, and they taught her to sign. She recalls that their sign language was very "*rōsha-teki*" or "very deaf-like" (akin to Nakano-san's), so even now Iizuka-san has trouble signing at the same time as she speaks. This differentiates her from people who grew up in the middle generation. She suffers from terrible repetitive stress disorder from all the years of interpreting. When Iizuka-san even looks at people interpreting or at the sign news on television, she tenses up and her body starts to hurt incredibly.

Iizuka-san's husband's parents still remembered the old prewar fingerspelling and fingernumbering systems. In an interview, Iizuka-san recalled with a sigh that it would have been easier for her now, in her old age, if they had kept the old system because it was so much easier to sign numbers with it. The modern fingernumbering is quite painful for people with limited dexterity, especially the number 8, which involves the palm and all of the fingers except the pinky straight out.

The JFD as a whole began to become more political during this period. One of the best records of the change in direction is the *Japanese Deaf News*.[7] Until the mid 1950s, the mainstay of the articles in the *Deaf News* were mostly reports about what various people were doing, medical causes of deafness, and a series on the genetics of deafness. The only articles of political note were comments on changes to the social welfare law. For example, in 1950, the *News* reported that the Ministry of Health and Social Welfare officially recognized the JFD as a registered social welfare organization. In the 1960s, the JFD became more radical as new blood infused it.

The Bell Center

Around 1955, the *Japanese Deaf News* started reporting on the consolidation of the JFD into a much more structured organization as well as on the emerging push for a National Welfare Center for the Deaf (*Kokuritsu Rōa Kōsei Sentā*). It took nearly a decade of continuous lobbying and fundraising to secure enough funds for the project from both private contributions from deaf members of the JFD and the government. The groundbreaking ceremony for the building, named the Bell Center, was held in 1963.[8] In early 1964, halfway into construction, the project came to a halt because of cost overruns and delays. The *News* fretfully reported

7. This newspaper has undergone numerous changes. It first appeared in 1931 as *Rōa-Geppō* (Monthly Deaf News), then after the war, in 1948, it renamed itself the *Nihon Rōa Shinbun* (Japanese Deaf Newspaper). One year later, it became the *Nihon Rōa Nyuusu* for three years until changing its name in 1952 to *Nihon Chōryoku Shōgai Shinbun* (literally, Japanese Hearing Impairment Newspaper), which it has kept until the present day. As mentioned earlier, the JFD is conscious of the American bias against the terms "deaf-mute" and "hearing-impaired." With this and other JFD related material, I use the official JFD translation into English: *Japanese Deaf News*.

8. The name of the Bell Center is ironic since Alexander Graham Bell (inventor of the telephone) hated deafness. One of his goals in life was the eradication of all forms of deafness, in furtherance of which he proposed demolishing all schools for the deaf and preventing deaf people from marrying one another. Cf. Bell 1883.

a ¥125 million budget deficit (*JDN* May 1,1964:1), about $347,000 in US dollars at the time.

The JFD scrambled to secure ¥100 million within the year, saving the project. The center finally opened its doors in March 1965. Unfortunately, the project was doomed from the start. Cost overruns meant the Bell Center was heavily mortgaged. Furthermore, the project was hamstrung by government officials who, trying to turn it into a for-profit venture, designed the building so that the third floor and above were condominium flats. The management board of the building was heavily stacked with *amakudari* bureaucrats with no experience in either deafness or building management. The deaf community did not feel it had proper oversight over either the construction process or day-to-day management; its dream had been taken away.

Amakudari, literally "descent from heaven," is the practice in which retiring government bureaucrats take management, consulting, or board positions with companies in the areas where they previously had oversight responsibilities. Thus an ex-finance ministry chief might *amakudaru* (verb form) onto the board of directors of a bank. This is called the "revolving door" in American politics. Ex-bureaucrats carry with them their connections and knowledge of the system and are often very useful to their new employers. But there is a negative aspect. While they are still in the government, bureaucrats often pander to the companies where they may end up working after retirement or back laws that benefit the corporations more than the general good of the people.

The *amakudari* bureaucrats on the Bell Center board were not financially competent. Within a few years, without the ability to properly manage the building and suffering under the terms of its loans, the Bell Center went bankrupt. This was a sharp lesson for the young JFD in the hazards of cooperation with the government. In exchange for the resources to build the center, they paid heavily by giving up their independence in accepting *amakudari*, which ultimately led to the project's ruin. It was particularly painful, as a good part of the funds for the center had come from the pockets of deaf people all across Japan. For over ten years, it had stood as the dream of the community, and there was a strong perception that hearing people had maliciously ruined it.

The Janome Murder Incident

The same year (1965) that the Bell Center opened its door and the Kyoto School for the Deaf students went on strike, a deaf man was accused of

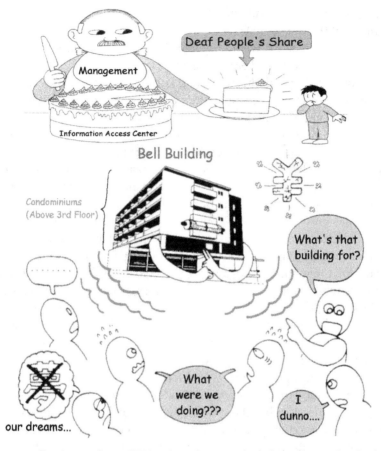

Figure 7.1. Two images from a JFD brochure depicting the feeling of betrayal in the deaf community after the Bell Center fiasco. Source: JFD (1997:18). Used with permission.

murder in what was called the Janome Restaurant Incident. Witnesses said the two defendants Satō Yoshikazu (age twenty-nine) and Kido Takashi (age thirty-two) had been provoked into a brawl at the Janome Sushi Restaurant in Tokyo by three hearing men who had been making fun of their deafness and use of signs. Trying to stop the potential fist-fight, the owner of the restaurant tried to reason with one of the deaf men, but unfortunately the men could not read the owner's lips, and further miscommunication ensued. Frustrated, the owner raised his thick wooden *geta* sandal and struck one of the young men in the face; he fought back and knocked the owner to the ground. On his way down, the owner hit the back of his head and subsequently died. The two deaf men were arrested on charges of assault and bodily injury resulting in death; no mention is made of what happened to the hearing instigators of the fight (Kawai 1991:380).

No sign interpreters were provided during the police interrogations. The defendants Kido and Satō were not provided with any effective way of communicating with their (hearing) lawyers. Although under the constitution defendants in Japan are guaranteed the right to consult in private with their lawyers, the police held that the sign interpreters were not legal counsel (*bengonin*, officers of the court) and insisted on monitoring any meeting with lawyers where interpreters were present, thus hampering the legal defense. In addition, it was questionable because of their lack of education whether the defendants fully understood their legal rights or were fully aware of the court proceedings.

This has proven to be a problem in the United States as well. Criminal defendants in America have constitutional rights that the police must inform them using a Miranda Warning: "You have the right to remain silent. Anything you say can and will be used against you. . . ." Deaf defendants with minimal schooling and poor English skills may not always understand the basic concept of these rights as used within the American court system. This is further obfuscated by neophyte court interpreters who may interpret the "right to remain silent" as "the right to *silence*" (as in a peaceful night's sleep) and not as "the right to not say anything self-incriminating using sign or any other form of communication." In a murder case in Maryland in 1975, the defendant signed a Miranda waiver as well as a confession, but there were suggestions that he understood the sign interpretation of "you have the right to have an attorney present" as meaning "it is all right to have an attorney present" (Lane, Hoffmeister, and Bahan 1996:354–355). The charges were later dropped.

In the Japanese case, the deaf community hastened to the support of the two defendants. The *Deaf News* reported that a fund-raising campaign by deaf persons, teachers at schools for the deaf, relatives, other civic organizations, ordinary citizens, school students, and others raised ¥120,000 toward their defense costs (*JDN* August 15, 1966:6). Unfortunately, they quickly came across an unforeseen roadblock. The support group went to all the law firms in the Tokyo metropolitan area trying to hire a private defense team. Most of the lawyers declined after learning that the case involved deaf defendants. There were similar problems in finding qualified interpreters familiar with legal language. The support group realized that their problems involved not only injustices within the court system but larger social and institutional prejudices against the deaf as well (Kawai 1991:381).

The Tokyo District Court ruled that Satō was guilty and sentenced him to ten months imprisonment with hard labor, suspended for three years. Kido, on the other hand, was sentenced to five years imprisonment with hard labor without a stay (*JDN* August 15, 1966:6). The JFD decided at its annual national meeting to lend its full support to the appeal (Itabashi 1991:360). Having just graduated from the Legal Research and Training Institute, the deaf lawyer Matsumoto Masayuki rallied to the cause of the defendants and filed an appeal in late 1966. This was Matsumoto's first appearance as a lawyer for the deaf. The appeal questioned the qualifications of the interpreters, especially in regard to whether they properly informed the defendants of the right not to have to provide self-incriminating testimony (*JDN* December 15, 1966:4).

There were also doubts as to whether the defendants had been able to follow the proceedings properly given that no interpreters were present for most of the questioning and trial. Apparently, when the mother of one of the defendants visited him in jail, she had to ask a classmate of his to come along in order to translate what was being said in sign. In those days, parents were often told by the teachers at the schools for the deaf to not allow their deaf children to use sign or to learn it themselves, although obviously some teachers were more sympathetic and learned sign themselves. Because of poor educational practices, many deaf adults had weak communication skills in written or spoken Japanese. One of the two defendants had graduated from a deaf middle school while the other had only finished third grade in Taiwan and was functionally illiterate (Kawai 1991:381–382).

According to Kawai Yohsuke, who was part of the legal support team, when the case went to the Appeals Court, Kido submitted numerous personal statements on his own behalf, but the justices were not able to understand their rather incoherent contents because of his illiteracy in written Japanese. The appeal justices affirmed the decision of the lower court but found Kido to have diminished mental capacity; in other words they considered him to be mentally retarded. They ruled the sentence be reduced to four years hard labor (ibid.: 382). The lawyers were greatly disappointed at the shallow level of disability awareness shown by the justices. They thought that if the judges were able to directly understand signing they would have seen that Kido's mental and linguistic abilities were normal and would have ruled on the basis of the actual appeal claims of discrimination and thus established precedents for the handling of deaf defendants.

As Kawai points out, furthermore, the justices did not realize that if

Kido were indeed functionally illiterate, there is no way that he could have understood and signed the written police statement/confession that condemned him. Kawai notes that when Kido signed with Matsumoto, his deaf lawyer, he showed intelligence and full comprehension (1991:384). The reduced sentence on appeal, while appearing lenient, only further emphasized the prejudice that deaf people were mentally incompetent. Resigning themselves to the situation, the team did not file further appeal.

The Janome Restaurant Incident, together with the Kyoto School Strike, served to awaken the political awareness of young deaf activists across the nation. The following year (1966), at the First National Debate Meeting of the Deaf Youth, there was a panel debate on discrimination and from the discussions that followed, the Youth Section of the JFD was formed. Matsumoto and some other deaf activists who had attended Kyoto University with him as undergraduates joined together. The Youth Section took the initiative in turning the JFD onto a new course. Soon after, the *News* blared the headline, "Protecting the Human Rights of the Deaf."

The courtroom experiences of the 1960s were important as means toward the end for the deaf organizations. In cases such as employment discrimination, an area that first came to the fore in the 1970s and has continued to be a problem to the current day, the ability of deaf organizations to quickly form working groups to bring legal and social pressure on behalf of plaintiffs has meant that cases have been resolved even before the actual trials began. Even given a limited voice within the courtroom, the newly reconfigured JFD underwent an extremely important growing and learning period in the 1960s.

Conclusion: New Strategies

A new generation of leaders emerged in the 1960s and 1970s with a different set of values and a vocabulary of "human rights" and "discrimination." While they fought their first battles in the courts, they quickly realized that the public relations value of the courtroom drama was just as important as the actual cases. Political alliances and mass mobilization were key strategies. Not only would they have to awaken the deaf community to their struggle, but they would also have to alert other (hearing) Japan to the injustices that deaf members of society were facing.

But just as changing contextual frames and demographics caused the rise in legal activism in the postwar period in the first place, changing social circumstances led to a shift from the courts to political and administrative realms. The number of incidences of abuse within the police/judicial system dropped at the same time that people realized that true power (and resolution of discrimination) would be found in changing the legal and administrative framework itself. They came to this realization while fighting for the right to have driver's licenses:

> The courtroom trial is a weapon in our fight to get a driver's license; but however important that weapon is, *you cannot change the law through the courts*. The [only] way to change the law is through the Diet. (*JDN* January 1, 1969:9; emphasis added)

The JFD steamed ahead with a human rights agenda. In 1975, its new president (one of the Kyoto University cohort) addressed the National Diet. In 1979, the JFD challenged the national Incompetence Law that declared all deaf and mute to be financially incompetent (meaning they had the legal status of minors). Whereas a 1958 *JDN* article was titled "*tsumbo* (deafies) can hear" (detailing a primitive way of electrically stimulating the auditory nerve), by the late 1960s the term *tsumbo* was labeled derogatory and a push was made to remove it from the vocabulary.[9]

The 1980s resulted in a new era of "cooperative welfare (*sanka fukushi*)" with administrative bureaucrats in the Ministry of Welfare. In this struggle, deaf associations were forced to balance the fruits of close cooperation with the government against the co-optation of the movement.

9. This follows the Burakumin movement's similar push to cleanse the Japanese language of derogatory terms. It is unclear, however, whether *tsumbo* was ever considered derogatory, although it is clearly now seen as *shigo* or a dead, old-fashioned word.

CHAPTER EIGHT

The Japanese Federation of the Deaf and
the Welfare State

As we saw in the previous chapter, the Japanese Federation of the Deaf emerged in the postwar period as the predominant social and political organization for the deaf in Japan and as a successful advocate for the rights of the deaf and hearing impaired. The JFD's first interaction with the state was through the courts, but it quickly found that the legal system was just as prejudiced as society as a whole, and shifted gears toward working with the government in improving the social welfare system. Here, the JFD's structure as a national federation with 47 prefectural member associations gave it a strong local and national presence as well as other political and social benefits.

The material benefits were also attractive. Programs that the government funded through the JFD included interpreter training, the distribution of inexpensive fax machines, captioned movies, speaker series, and social get-togethers at the local and regional level. These helped build and sustain community. But in order to receive the government contracts that would allow these things to happen, the JFD had to work closely with the government. This chapter details how the JFD managed to cooperate with the Japanese government at national and prefectural levels, without becoming co-opted in the process.

Cooperation and Co-optation in Japan

In his now classic 1985 book, *Weapons of the weak,* the political scientist James C. Scott talks about the everyday forms of subversion that members of minority, subaltern groups use to resist oppression. This text appeared at a moment in American academics when postmodernist thought regarding power had, in a sense, become hegemonic. Knowledge was power and resistance to power and ideology, to borrow a phrase, was futile. In the two decades since Scott's book was published, we have come to see the questions of power and resistance or structure and agency in much more complex terms, intertwined at their very roots.

In the narrative presented here, the balance between *cooperation with* and *co-optation by* the Japanese state plays a dominant role in determining how deaf organizations structure their political activities. A modern bureaucratic state attempts to keep acts of resistance within the confines of social norms and dictates, for example by opening the possibilities of lawsuits and lobbying activities.[1] The political scientist Frank Upham and others have written about the Japanese government's particular efficacy in engineering bureaucratic "solutions" to social unrest while grinding more obdurate citizens into the mercilessly lethargic court system. As noted in the previous chapter, court cases and appeals can easily drag on for over a decade.

One of the most effective techniques that the Japanese state has used to slow social change is a balance between cooperation and co-optation that negates the ability of protest organizations to move independently. They do this through the *itaku/amakudari* connection detailed in the previous chapter in connection with the Bell Center. Through the use of grants and contracts (*itaku*), groups with social problems are transferred "in-house" into a bureaucratic structure with both positive and negative incentives applied to work within the system. If you protest too much, you risk losing your funding. If you play along and accept *amakudari* bureaucrats into your organization, you will get more contracts from the government but are under much more surveillance, and the bureaucrats who revolve in through *amakudari* are not always competent administrators and may have vested interests.

In contrast with other nonprofits in Japan, starting in the 1980s and 1990s the JFD was able to reap the financial benefits of cooperation/co-optation with the government with few negative side-effects. The strategy adopted by the JFD to retain control was multileveled. At the top level, the Japanese Federation of the Deaf operated as an independently financed incorporated association (or *zaidan hōjin*) under the Ministry of

---

1. Riots and acts of terrorism being the most unstructured and thus most threatening to the state.

Health and Social Welfare. This meant that the majority of its basic operating expenses came from member dues funneled up through the prefectural associations supplemented by book and newsletter sales. The JFD
insisted that it was self-sufficient in this regard.

There are also no *amakudari* bureaucrats on the JFD board of directors.
There is a strict policy that only members of the JFD can be part of the
board of directors and only people who are deaf can be members of the
JFD (and of course no high-ranking government bureaucrats are deaf due
to educational and administrative discrimination). This lack of *amakudari*
means that the JFD is poorer than one might expect for a national organization of its size. The offices in Tokyo and Kyoto are cramped and dirty.
The staff are overworked and underpaid. One staff member admits that
they were *binbō-kusai* ("smelled of the poor") because they derive no direct operating expenses from government contracts.[2]

Normally, this would be the kiss of death for a large organization like
the JFD, which has a membership of over 25,000. They would not have
enough funds to provide adequate services in return for their membership fees. This is where as a federation of independent prefectural associations of the deaf, the JFD has proved to be flexible in manipulating the
system. The prefectural associations are a mixture of non-incorporated
and incorporated organizations, but the important thing is that their
legal status is independent of the national organization. This allows the
prefectural associations to receive money from the prefectural governments without tying the hands of the national federation politically.

The Prefectural Base of the JFD

The prewar Japanese Association of the Deaf had been a small organization with only 816 members in 1939. Most of those members lived in
Tokyo or the Osaka/Kyoto metropolitan areas. Membership was limited
to those in direct geographic contact with the organization. The postwar
Japanese Federation of the Deaf, by incorporating all of the prefectural as-

---

2. The JFD does have a few *itaku* projects at the national level. The largest is the Sign
Standardization and Promulgation contract under the Ministry of Health and Social Welfare. This mandates the JFD to work to create new signs, standardize current signs, produce textbooks, and do teacher/interpreter training. The second large contract is the International Deaf Leader Training Program, under JICA, which trains deaf leaders from
developing countries in Asia. But in both these cases, the *itaku* contract funds pay only
for expenses directly related to the projects, not toward the general operating budget of
the JFD.

sociations of the deaf under its umbrella, was much larger. In 1948 it had 3,387 members, and that had nearly tripled by 1970, to 9,514 members.[3]

Rather than a single national membership, the JFD operates on a federal system whereby members are affiliated with one of the 47 prefectural associations. Since most people tended to stay close to the schools of the deaf where they graduated (and where all their friends were), this system has worked well, especially on a social level. Through their local associations, deaf adults can continue to get together with their old school friends, meet potential spouses, travel in groups to resort towns, and so forth.

The origins of the federal system lie in the turmoil of the postwar period. Local deaf associations based around schools for the deaf or major metropolitan areas remained strong during and after the war. However, regional and national communication and transportations systems were barely adequate even for hearing people. Informants told me that if a deaf person at the time wanted to relay a message to a friend in a neighboring town, he would have to bicycle over to the friend's house because there were no fax machines and telegrams were inordinately expensive. Even the annual meetings of the JFD were a major effort in the 1950s because conference participants from southern Kyushu or northern Hokkaido would have to take a combination of boats and steam trains over a period of several days to get to central Japan. A decentralized federal system in that period made more sense than a centralized national organization.

The prefectural associations were a major source of social support for deaf people in the postwar period. Up until the late 1980s, mainstream Japanese society was largely inaccessible to the deaf. Japan had no TTY (real-time teletype machines for the deaf) or TTY relay operators that could bridge a call between a deaf TTY caller and a hearing telephone user. Fax machines were introduced in the 1970s, but only became affordable in the mid-1980s. Even then, they were not real-time. There was no television closed captioning in Japan until the late 1990s, and even now not all programs are closed-captioned. If you wanted a captioned movie, you would have to go to the lending library at the local deaf center. You did not commonly see people signing publicly until the late 1980s.

Up until the same period, it was virtually impossible for a deaf person to get a white-collar job, so most deaf were in the manual trades—factory workers, beauticians, tailors, seamstresses, shoe shines, and so forth. We can see this clearly in the occupational choices made by the three deaf women discussed in chapter 6.

3. Source: JFD Annual Board Meeting Reference Materials (2004).

With their welfare supplements from the government, all three women and their deaf husbands lived comfortable middle-class lives despite their blue- and pink-collar jobs. Nonetheless, deaf people remained marginalized in Japanese society. The prefectural and local associations of the deaf worked to counteract this by providing access to all of the cultural events that helped their membership feel that they were part of the Japanese nation. They hosted summer picnics, fall sports events, end-of-year parties, new year's parties, *mochi* rice cake–making parties, spring cherry blossom viewing, and many other activities. You could travel with your association to a hot spring resort or hike through the Japan Alps. Through your association, you were assured friendship (often with people you had known since you were school kids) and ease of communication. The organizations built a parallel Japanese society complete with all the fittings. This helped their membership feel *Japanese* (for a similar example in New Zealand, see Monaghan 2003b).

The local associations also provided a wide array of social services. Many were registered as social welfare organizations under the prefectural departments of social welfare. This close relationship with the government on the local level allowed them to get funding and access to prefectural facilities. Many prefectural deaf associations moved their offices into the prefectural social welfare buildings, saving on rent. When the signing boom of the late 1980s and 1990s occurred, this close working relationship with the government also permitted the prefectural associations access to funds to set up interpreter-training workshops (hiring local deaf persons to teach the classes); a few maintained the interpreter dispatch services, and others created video lending libraries with open-captioned movies and dramas. All of this ensured that their clientele would come back to the local associations for friendship and succor.

The Role of the National Japanese Federation of the Deaf

Since the local prefectural associations handled almost all of the member services, this freed the national JFD head office to focus on two things: politics and publications. Under its bylaws, the national federation was nominally separate from the prefectural member associations. While the latter could not organize or protest for social change without disrupting their collegial relationships with prefectural administrations, the national JFD as a separate organization which received very few government funds could lobby on the behalf of all the deaf in Japan without risking financial repercussions from the government. The two-tiered federal system allowed the national JFD and prefectural associations of the deaf to have access to funds as well as the ability to mobilize for social change at the same time. And it would not be an exaggeration to say that this structure enabled the JFD to become one of the most powerful disability organizations in the postwar period.

The national office was also responsible for publication of the JFD newsletter, quarterly magazine, Japanese sign dictionaries, and research reports. The monthly JFD newsletter in particular served as a mechanism for raising the consciousness of deaf community about the injustices they suffered. The number of subscriptions each prefectural association could raise was seen as a vital indicator of how strong that community was regarding the deaf political movement (*rōasha undō*). The sign language dictionaries served as a linguistic unifying mechanism—the series was called *Watashi-tachi no Shuwa* (*Our signs*), with an emphasis on the shared nature of the language.

Because of the wide array of benefits offered at the local level as well as the power of the national office, membership in the JFD swelled in the postwar period and reached its peak in the mid-1990s. Yet despite its strength, the JFD will only shrink in the future because of four main factors: (1) fewer deaf children being born, due to the falling birth rate in general as well as maternal disease prevention measures; (2) lower enrollment in schools for the deaf owing to medical advances in hearing technologies and mainstreaming; (3) the aging of the bulk of the membership, with the Elderly Section of the JFD the only division experiencing growth; and (4) less interest on the part of younger deaf people in joining the JFD and being involved in their form of deaf political activism.

Money and Power at the Local and National Levels

Only a very small portion (3.7 percent in 2004) of the national JFD operating budget is derived from private or corporate donations. Funds apart from membership dues and newspaper subscriptions are rarely solicited from individuals, and if they are, they are usually project-specific—such as fundraising for development projects in Southeast Asia, or donations to help the lobbying effort for changing laws that forbid deaf persons from certain jobs (for example, doctors and police).

The JFD is adamant that its entire operating budget comes from its

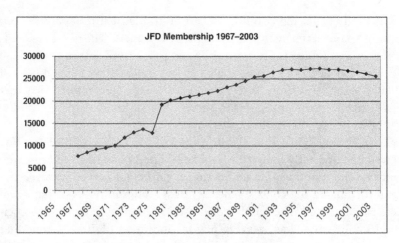

Figure 8.1. JFD membership, 1967–2003. Source: JFD (2004 et al.).

membership and other private sources and not the government. In 2004, the annual prefectural membership varied between ¥5,500 and ¥10,000 (US$50–90), depending on location. Of this, a considerable amount was tithed up to the JFD, constituting 37 percent of its operating budget (over 50 percent if you exclude the ¥50 million balancing loan on the books). In addition, the JFD received revenue from subscriptions to the *Japanese Deaf News* and the quarterly magazine *Mimi*, and sales of its instructional sign and deaf history textbooks. Finally, the JFD received some money for acting as consultant for soap operas ("dramas") and movies with characters who are deaf or who sign.

The estimated budget of the JFD was roughly ¥173 million in 2004, or about US$1.6 million. This is small for a nonprofit organization of its size. The line item that reads ¥0 for "*itaku* project income" is notable. The JFD maintains that it is not reliant on government funds for operations and the official budget does not recognize any such funds. *Itaku* is a term that frequently comes up in connection with government-involved Japanese nonprofit organizations (NPOs); basically they are government contracts to do projects.[4] In the United States nonprofit organizations generally come up with their own project proposals, apply for government

4. Sheldon Garon (1997:160) discusses the mechanisms by which the government pierced the state/public-subsidies barrier in 1959. Garon presents a good argument for *itaku* as "social management," but he underestimates the degree to which organizations on the ground (like the JFD) can actively manipulate and benefit from *itaku* projects if handled correctly.

Table 8.1. Japanese Federation of the Deaf Budget for Fiscal Year 2004

Item	Yen	Percentage
Membership fees	63,750,000	37
Business income	22,995,000	13
Donations	6,500,000	3.7
Miscellaneous income	5,020,000	2.9
Itaku project income	0	0
Funds transferred in	18,800,000	11
Loans	50,000,000	29
Balanced transferred forward	6,147,837	3.5
Total income	**173,212,837**	
Business expenses	32,377,000	18
Administrative expenses	90,069,000	52
Funds transferred out	500,000	0.29
Reserve fund	266,837	0.15
Loan payments	50,000,000	29
Total expenditures	**173,212,837**	

Source: http://www.jfd.or.jp/info/gaiyo/yosan.html (accessed December 6, 2004)

funding, and after receiving the grants, tend to utilize the funds as they see fit, within reporting and administrative guidelines. In Japan, *itaku* contract projects are rigorously determined and controlled by the government.[5] As one JFD staff member put it in an interview, "*itaku* projects are things that the government should be doing, but aren't. So they contract us to do them."

For example, in the 1990s the Ministry of Social Welfare was nominally responsible for writing guidelines and implementing a proper institutional structure for sign interpreters (since interpreters of the deaf in Japanese are almost all volunteers or semi-volunteers under the coordination of the local welfare offices).[6] Since the ministry did not want to spend the time creating such a program, it allocated money and *itaku*-contracted it to the JFD. The same types of *itaku* projects also occur at the prefectural and local levels. The *itaku* themselves are not necessarily neg-

5. This is similar to the Dutch case as pointed out by Pekkanen (2004b).

6. In the United States, the guidelines for interpreter-training programs and interpreters' tests are created by the Registry of Interpreters for the Deaf (RID), a nonprofit organization.

The quasi-governmental aspect of the *itaku* projects can be compared to the role of professional organizations in the United States such as the bar associations for lawyers. That is, the bar is not a part of the state apparatus, but the state has authorized certain powers for it to act on behalf of the government.

ative; it is the loss of financial and political control often associated with receiving an *itaku* that makes them such a contentious part of social welfare politics.

That being said, having member-based organizations such as the JFD run the *itaku* programs themselves is infinitely better than having the government run them—or worse, having them managed by a for-profit or nonprofit organization run by non-disabled persons. The JFD and other disability organizations have tried to fight the move by the government to a payer-based model of social welfare, which would turn them into mere *consumers* with no control over services provided. While that move seems inevitable given government finances, the blow is lessened by running the *itaku* contracts through their own organizations. The JFD is more successful here than some other disability groups who are not seen as self-reliant by the government. That is, while the JFD can directly or indirectly control the majority of the interpreter dispatch services, paratransit systems for people in wheelchairs and group homes for people with psychiatric disabilities are for the most part run by able-bodied persons.

At the national level, the JFD's major *itaku* projects are the "Research on Standardizing Signing" (*hyōjun shuwa kenkyū jigyō*) and "Popularizing and Increasing the Use of Sign" (*shuwa fukyū teichaku jigyō*) projects, both under contract from the Ministry of Health and Social Welfare. Under the first project, the JFD worked to standardize and develop new sign words as well as edit and publish dictionaries and textbooks. Under the second project, the JFD taught its member groups how to organize sign circles as well as more formal sign classes, introduced new signs, and did public relations work to encourage the use of sign in different areas.

Generally speaking, government *itaku* projects are tied to the presence of *amakudari* board members. A ministry bureaucrat will retire, find his way onto a board at a nonprofit, and soon after that the organization will receive a large *itaku* project from the same division of the ministry that he retired from.[7] This has not been restricted to the Ministry of Social Welfare—similar activities were uncovered at the Ministry of Finance in relationship to the Yamaichi Securities company. Red flags were finally raised when the stock trading company went spectacularly bankrupt in 1997, although such practices had been going on for quite a long time. It would be difficult to find a government ministry in Japan that does not engage in *amakudari* of one form or another. At the prefectural level, ex-

---

7. The male pronoun is used deliberately.

bureaucrats often retire to head local nonprofit association boards. In a recent scandal, Osaka City was found to have given ¥100 billion (approximately $960 million) in contracts during fiscal year 2003 to sixty-six "nonprofits" that were made up of "old boy" retirees (*Asahi Shimbun* March 17, 2005:1).

Instead of allowing the main organization to be co-opted by *amakudari* retirees, one tactic that the JFD has adopted is allowing its affiliated organizations to split off and become nominally separate legal entities. Only the subsidiary group that is directly receiving the *itaku* funding has seeded *amakudari* bureaucrats on its board. Thus, the main organization can still maintain 100 percent deaf control on its own board. For example the Culture and Information Center for Hearing Impaired Persons (*Chōryōku Shōgaisha Jōhō Bunka Sentā*) in Tokyo operates a video captioning program and lending library. It sends its captioned videos (of popular dramas, informational videos, movies, and the like) to Deaf Information Centers all across Japan.[8] The board of directors of the Culture Center in the late nineties was heavily seeded with *amakudari* members, and the director was an ex-ministry official generally considered to be clueless about deafness and signing.

Nonetheless, according to the Culture Center and JFD staff with whom I talked, there was no way around this. The center was an extremely expensive venture and needed the *amakudari* members on its board to ensure that the money would keep flowing. Since the center was independent of the JFD, the *amakudari* bureaucrats on its board could not interfere with the internal affairs of the JFD anyway. In this case the center staff was competent and included people who were deaf, so the important activities of the center were able to go on despite the lack of qualifications in its board of directors.

In the past, the JFD was directly involved in lobbying efforts, for example, lobbying for legal change so that deaf people could drive automobiles or for full financial independence and legal majority status. More recently, the JFD appears to have changed tactics and is now using the branching tactic for political mobilization as well. For example, the movement to change laws that forbid deaf people from certain occupational positions is being run by a nominally independent group, rather than the JFD itself. Although the group is stacked with people from the JFD leadership, its independent status makes it easier to solicit support

8. Source: Culture and Information Center for Hearing Impaired Persons (*Chōryōku Shōgaisha Jōhō Bunka Sentā* 1995). Information on the internal structure and critique was obtained from informant interviews.

from other disability groups and gives it greater freedom in lobbying efforts since it is not representing the JFD in its activities. (This is a common tactic in the United States as well, with 501c(3) groups that are not allowed to be overtly partisan splitting off a political lobbying wing: Pekkanen 2004b).

To a remarkable degree, these splinter groups have remained closely allied with the JFD. One might expect, for example, that the smaller organizations might begin to develop different ideas from those of the national organization about what is best for the deaf community. One factor in maintaining unity has been the general cohesion of the middle generation under the mantra of the social welfare-based *rōa undō* (deaf movement)—a unifying discourse that has so far yielded results. As the middle generation becomes too old to retain control and a new generation of deaf begins to take leadership positions within the JFD, new political strategies will become important as more dissension and conflict among the subgroups and the national organization appear.

Itaku Contracts at the Prefectural Level

The forty-seven prefectural associations of the deaf that are nominally separate from the JFD are in reality part of the same umbrella network, and the JFD claims all of their members as its own. The prefectural associations receive a significant portion of their operating expenses from *itaku* funds. Most of the prefectural association offices are located in social welfare buildings owned by the prefectural government, and in many cases, their support staff are prefectural civil servants as well.

Prefectural associations can take one of three legal structures. The three corporate forms available are the "incorporated social welfare organization" (*shakai-fukushi-hōjin*), "incorporated association" (*shadan-hōjin*), and "incorporated foundation" (*zaidan-hōjin*), all under the auspices of the prefectural division of social welfare.

As of 2005, sixteen of the forty-seven prefectural associations in the JFD remain unincorporated (in Japanese, *nin'i dantai*). Being unincorporated causes considerable problems. For example, the Yamanashi Association of the Deaf (founded in 1935) had long resisted incorporating. According to one of the local board members, the membership feared that the group would lose its independence and that their membership fees would rise if they incorporated. This meant that renting its small office space, office equipment, and so forth had to all be done in the name of one of its board members. In addition, it meant that the Yamanashi Association was ineligible for most *itaku* funds from the prefectural government.

This became an issue in 1994 when the Yamanashi prefectural government decided to build a new welfare building and include a Deaf Information Center (the Ministry of Social Welfare has decided that one goal is to have a Deaf Information Center in each prefecture).[9] Unfortunately, the prefectural government would award the *itaku* project to run the facility only to an incorporated body, so the contract went to a *shakai-fukushi-hōjin* incorporated entity created by the government to run the center and staffed by hearing personnel. The community lost control over the center's operations. It is clearly not in the best interests of prefectural associations to remain unincorporated as they are left out of many of the *itaku* projects that directly affect their members. In 1999, the Yamanashi group was incorporated as a *shadan hōjin*.[10]

Shakai Fukushi Hōjin

The first category of incorporated organizations, *shakai-fukushi-hōjin*, consists of groups that are closely involved with the state in social welfare activities. Of all of the organizational structures, this has the least financial and political independence from the state and is the most minor form allowed. However, because *shakai-fukushi-hōjin* receive most if not all of their operating funds from their *itaku* projects (for example, a sign interpreter dispatch program project or sign interpreter-training course project), the state implication works both ways—the state cannot easily cut off funding to a *shakai-fukushi-hōjin*, once it has been started. Only six prefectural associations were at this level as of 2005. On the plus side, this structure allows the associations to move into the prefectural welfare services building, saving a considerable amount of rent, as well as having prefectural employees as the support staff. On the significant minus side, a *shakai-fukushi-hōjin's* activities are mainly limited to the scope of its *itaku* projects.

9. In 1991, the Diet passed a revision of the Welfare Law for Disabled Persons. Section 33 of the bill required Deaf Information Centers to be erected in each prefecture. These usually have multiple functions. The first is a walk-in video lending library (the larger ones also have their own video production facilities and captioning equipment). They also provide job and personal counseling services and interpreter training and dispatch (in some cases). The goal of having a Deaf Information Center in each prefecture was a priority for the JFD.

10. The specific details of the Yamanashi incident are extremely complex; readers are referred to Ogura (1997).

Shadan Hōjin

The large majority of prefectural associations (24 of 47) are *shadan-hōjin*. This type of incorporated body is in between *shakai-fukushi-hōjin* and *zaidan-hōjin*. They have enough resources to be able to rent their own office space and staff workers. They are able to engage in their own activities without having to justify them as being directly "social-welfare" related or part of their *itaku* projects. In contrast with the Yamanashi Association mentioned above, the Ibaraki Deaf Association had incorporated as a *shadan hōjin* by the early 1990s and were awarded the operating contract (*un'ei itaku*) for the prefectural Deaf Information and Welfare Center. The center is a separate building and facility from the prefecture's other operations and it houses the Ibaraki Deaf Association as well as the two interpreter dispatch centers (sign interpreters and real-time transcribers) (cf. IPWCHIY 1992).

Zaidan Hōjin

Only one prefectural association in late 2005 was at the top level of *zaidan-hōjin*, the Kumamoto Association of the Deaf, on the southern island of Kyushu. This has been a traditional powerhouse of activism and is unique among the associations in having enough financial resources to own its own building and more or less dictate its own politics in the region.

Positives and Negatives of Incorporating

One downside to achieving *shadan-hōjin* or *zaidan-hōjin* status is that an organization becomes ineligible for many of the more lucrative *itaku* projects. The government wants to maintain close control of the projects, so it prefers to give them to *shakai-fukushi-hōjin* organizations. The way the more financially independent associations usually work around this is to split off a smaller, focused group that only works on that *itaku* project.

For example, the Fukuoka Association of the Deaf is a *shadan-hōjin*, but the prefectural government wanted to give the Deaf Information Center grant to a *shakai-fukushi-hōjin* in order to retain more control, so the Fukuoka Association created a new *shakai-fukushi-hōjin* entity solely for the purpose of running the center. In that way, the association was able to keep closer control of the center than if the state had decided to run it itself. The ability to act in this amoeba-like fashion greatly depends on the political strength of the organization. The Yamanashi Association, for example, just was not organized or strong enough to create its own branch entity; thus it lost the contract and the ability to provide direct input in the operation of the center.

In summary, of the forty-seven prefectural associations (in 2005), sixteen are unincorporated, six are *shakai-fukushi-hōjin*, twenty-four are *shadan-hōjin*, and only one (Kumamoto, as noted above) is *zaidan-hōjin*.[11] There is a gradual escalation as the remaining unincorporated organizations move up to *shakai-fukushi-hōjin* status and the *shakai-fukushi-hōjin* graduate to *shadan-hōjin* once they organize more and build stronger financial resources. It is unlikely that any of these groups will become powerful enough to become *zaidan-hōjin* in the near future.[12]

When an association incorporates, aside from the usual legal strictures of incorporation (the necessity to organize a board of directors, bylaws, and the like), one other significant change occurs: a legal name change. Although most of the prefectural associations were named the XYZ Prefectural Association of the Deaf (*rōasha kyōkai*) before incorporation, the government welfare office usually places pressure on them to include in their corporate bylaws a statement to the effect that the hard of hearing are part of their population group. This is in part to help attract younger deaf or hard-of-hearing people who might not always identify as deaf.

Most of the associations in the JFD (35 of 47) are named some variation of the XYZ Prefectural Federation of Hearing-Impaired Persons (*chōkaku shōgaisha renmei*). In many prefectures, deaf and hard-of-hearing groups have traditionally had bad blood between them. The two groups are forced together under the auspices of a single prefectural organization by the government, which wants to reduce its administrative overhead despite the fact that the groups may have little in common other than a hearing problem.

To give some examples of differing needs, the deaf groups want sign interpreters and sign training workshops, while the hard-of-hearing groups (which consist of individuals who do not sign but speechread /speak) want text captioning of public events using overhead projectors or computer video captioning. Deaf groups want to maintain schools for

---

11. As of September 21, 2005. Verified through the organizational contact list internally published by the Japanese Federation of the Deaf.

12. And there is the distinct possibility that as local groups become weaker because of decreasing membership in the JFD, it might be possible for an incorporated group to "fall" to a lower category.

the deaf and use signing in the classroom while the hard of hearing want to improve the situation for students who are mainstreamed into local school systems. Although there are indeed points on which they agree, the larger *itaku* projects have mostly been sign related, which the hard of hearing resent.

One prefectural association head gave an example of the bad blood in his community. The association received some *itaku* money to increase the use of signing among doctors and nurses. Part of this campaign was the distribution of buttons that read, "I can sign!" with a little cartoon of someone signing, that doctors and nurses could pin on their jackets. The hard-of-hearing association, learning of this project at the last moment, managed to veto it, claiming it did not help the hard of hearing who could not sign.

Organizationally, the joining of the two groups can create quite a mess. For example, the Tochigi Prefectural Federation of Hearing-Impaired Persons has under it the Tochigi Association of the Deaf and the Tochigi Association of Hard of Hearing and Late Deafened. Because the deaf members numerically outnumber the hard of hearing at least 10:1, the head of the deaf association is also the head of the prefectural federation (since these are elected positions with the same people voting for both their own group and the umbrella group). In this chapter, I usually referred to the prefectural federations of hearing-impaired persons as if they are synonymous with the prefectural associations of the deaf, largely ignoring the hard-of-hearing associations within the federations. This reductionary gesture is in fact what the JFD does itself (leading to no end of complaints from the hard of hearing) since in most cases it does not make sense to try to differentiate between the incorporated national federation and the deaf associations it encompasses.

The Importance of the *Itaku* Projects

The state allows the associations to incorporate as social welfare organizations in order to become eligible for their grants. The *itaku* projects at the prefectural level usually fall within several categories: sign promulgation and teaching grants; interpreter dispatch service grants; overhead projector dispatch service grants; job counseling grants; and Deaf Information Center grants. By running the projects, the deaf associations center themselves within the deaf community by becoming the provider of essential services. So both the government and the deaf organizations benefit from this system.

In many prefectures, the association has control over the interpreter dispatch service (contracted from the prefectural association welfare services department). This means that all deaf people who want to have an interpreter present at their school PTA meeting, job interview, doctor's appointment, or similar occasion must contact their local association. The dispatch services looks at their roster of registered interpreters and dispatches one, if available. The interpreters, who are generally housewives who are freelancing, are paid a nominal fee (around ¥800–1,000 an hour, or $8–10) and travel expenses. These funds come from the prefectural government. The association runs the interpreter-training program and also administers the interpreter licensing exam for the prefecture.[13]

Another important service is sign training programs. The prefectural government wants to encourage hearing citizens to learn basic signing and also increase the number of registered sign interpreters. The *itaku* contract to the prefectural associations usually has them set up both informal signing circles and more formal sign interpreter–training courses. The signing circles, which usually meet once a week in a welfare building or cultural center, are now common in most towns in Japan. One or two deaf people run the circle (they are paid a nominal fee, although some are volunteers) and teach basic sign, but the main purpose is social. Most of the students are housewives who take the course and never return. But a good number do go on to take the sign interpreter–training courses, which are run by deaf teachers who have more training in teaching skills. A savvy prefectural association head will make strategic choices in choosing the teachers for the signing courses, since teaching these can be both lucrative and socially prestigious.

13. In contrast, in the United States, interpreter services are the responsibility of the public facility that the deaf client is visiting. If a deaf person goes to a hospital or school, for example, the Americans with Disability Act stipulates that the hospital or school must make a reasonable effort to provide appropriate services ("reasonable effort" does not necessarily mean an interpreter, which causes no end of grief and threats of ADA lawsuits) to accommodate that individual. Any public facility (including private enterprises such as movie theaters, airplanes, and hotels) must meet the ADA requirements. However, the government is not involved in the dispatching of interpreters. Many states do have an interpreter licensing program, but others delegate that responsibility to a nonprofit, the Registry of Interpreters for the Deaf. Professional sign language interpreters in the United States charge between $40 and $80 an hour, depending on their skill level. Most are full-time professionals.

Finally, if a prefectural association can swing itself control over a Deaf Information Center, this can be quite a boon to its own organizational efforts. It often means that the organization will gain its own office space, classrooms, theater hall where it can show captioned videos and movies, video lending library, and so forth. The center, and the *itaku* money it brings to hire staff, can provide a secure and bounded physical space for deaf people to come and benefit from the association's work.

The JFD at the national level is outside of the system, whereas its prefectural associations are within the system, the best of both worlds. The nominal independence of the JFD from its prefectural associations as well as from any major *itaku* contracts gives it more leeway to interact with the government on an adversarial (by Japanese standards) basis, something that a mere *shakai fukushi hōjin* could not. However, there are times when even the JFD is too closely associated with the government to act independently.

One of these was in 1999 when the JFD decided to protest laws that prevent deaf persons from following a number of professions (medical doctors, pharmacists, police officers, and some others). In this case, what was interesting was that the JFD created a new group solely for the purpose of challenging the laws. Even though the coordinating committee and staff members of the group were all drawn from the JFD, on paper it was a separate entity with JFD "support." Members of this group held a demonstration, marched to the Ministry of Social Welfare, and lodged a formal protest.

The name of this ephemeral group was the "Headquarters for Focused Planning to Revise Laws That Discriminate against Hearing Impaired" (*Chōkaku Shōgaisha wo Sabetsu-suru Hōrei wo Kaisei suru Chūō Taisaku Honbu*). It was composed of nine organizations: the JFD, the Japanese Federation of Hard of Hearing and Late Deafened Persons, the National Federation of Schoolteachers of the Deaf, the Schools for the Deaf Alumni Association, the Research Group for Sign Interpreter Issues, the Research Group for Real Time Transcriber Issues, the National Organization of Parents of Hard-of-Hearing Children, the National Federation of Parents of Children with Hearing Impairments, and the National Federation of PTA Groups at Schools for the Deaf. Of these, only the first two are officially recognized *hōjin* associations, both under the Ministry of Health and Social Welfare. The seven unincorporated groups would in the United States be considered subcommittees, working groups, or sections within the two parent organizations. They share office space and staff with the larger organizations and receive direction from them. But as both the JFD and the Federation of Hard of Hearing have strict rules that only deaf/hard of hearing may be members (this is in part related to their *itaku* funding), the parents and teachers of deaf children are nominally separate. Normally it would be hard for these unincorporated groups to meet with the ministry, and normally it would be difficult for the JFD to make such a forceful protest statement. But by creating a separate, temporary group, they manage to squeeze through a loophole in the system.

Participatory Welfare

This amoeba-like ability to spin off subgroups that engage the government at different levels is what one JFD leader termed "participatory welfare" (*sanka fukushi*). That is, instead of viewing welfare as manna from heaven, the suckling teat depicted in the ASL sign for welfare, he felt that the Japanese deaf community must engage directly in welfare and participate in its creation and execution.[14]

I would like to be able to say that the JFD has been making the best of both worlds and that its strategy of multilevel flexibility is a resounding success. In many ways, it is. But the system's failures are also interesting to note. The acceptance of *itaku* contracts at the ground level has forced complications on the prefectural associations. Specifically, the Ministry of Social Welfare would like to solve all of its deaf and hearing-impaired problems in one fell swoop, but historically the organizations of the deaf and the hard of hearing have had different agendas. In some cases, such as the Tochigi Association of Hearing Impaired, the government has more or less forced the two to form under a single organization's banner in order to get *itaku* funding, over which the two have promptly squabbled like neglected siblings.

There has also been pressure to make the deaf organizations more representative, that is, to include not only the deaf but all persons with hearing impairments. This has led a number of organizations to change their titles from "deaf" (*rō*) to "hearing impaired" (*chōkaku shōgaisha*). Unlike the move in the United States away from biological terms to cultural ones (homosexual to gay; negro to Black), the trend has been the opposite in Japan due to this need for what could be called *marugakae* or total

14. In their (1996) book *Islam and Democracy*, John Esposito and John Voll talk about the mainstreaming of Islam, the process by which Islamists are no longer marginalized in Indonesian politics. Although the term *mainstreaming* has particular connotations in deaf discourse which render it unusable in the political context, the process is very similar.

inclusivity.[15] Another way to say this would be "represent-ability"—the ability to represent the entire spectrum of a disability group (everyone from the hard of hearing to totally deaf), a different concept from those prevalent in the United States—"inclusion" or "diversity"—although the end result is similar.

One of the arguments that the government raised in denying the contract in 1994 to the Yamanashi Deaf Association was that it had only 270 members, out of a possible 3,000 registered hearing impaired in the prefecture (Ogura 1997:6). The association tried to argue that the remaining 90 percent un-enrolled were late-deafened or elderly individuals who lost their hearing naturally (and were thus uninterested in the services that a Deaf Information Center would provide). But the prefectural government did not find that the Yamanashi Association was sufficiently inclusive.

Unfortunately, this forced focus on inclusion has had an ironic impact on deaf youth. As we will see in later chapters, the youngest generation of deaf, many of whom have grown up mainstreamed in hearing schools, do not identify as deaf or hard of hearing at all. They do not find themselves attracted to either the welfare or the discrimination aspects of the JFD's political mobilization. Although often pressured to join the prefectural association by their local city office, they do not find much appealing in the JFD. On the opposite side of the spectrum, the ennui felt by some deaf youth has also led to a cultural backlash with the emergence of a radical Deaf Culture organization that strongly advocates a U.S.-style identity politics. The JFD has found it extremely difficult to recruit youth since the young are usually on either extreme of the political ground on which the JFD has so carefully staked its central-leftist position.

Welfare Backlash

There is little of the U.S. type of stigmatization of "welfare," *fukushi*, in contemporary Japan. As Japan becomes a rapidly aging society, the question of social welfare services for the elderly and handicapped has

15. Professor Takeshi Ishida of Tokyo University provided me with the insight on the *marugakae* or inclusion model of postwar disability groups (personal communication November 16, 2004). Other postwar disability groups in Japan have operated on this same type of single-disability, total inclusion model: the Japanese Federation of the Blind (est. 1948) and the Japanese Ostomy Association (1959) are two examples. In contrast, the disability groups emerging in the past two decades (with the exception of D-Pro and other cultural Deaf groups) have generally been multi-disability organizations.

dominated politics for the past half-decade. Although there are shifts away from total governmental control toward a consumer-payer system (driven mostly by the fact that with Japan's dropping birth rate, its previous system was becoming rapidly unaffordable), as well as grave concerns about the long-term viability of the social welfare system, there is almost no debate about *whether* such a system should exist. No tropes of "welfare mothers" giving birth to inner-city children merely to live off government money have yet sullied the sociopolitical imaginations of the Japanese.

Ironically, the backlash against welfare has come from within the deaf community. In his 1991 book, *The requirements for independence: an introduction to the social welfare of/for those who cannot hear (Jiritsu he no Jōken: Mimi-no fujiyū na Hito no Fukushi Nyūmon)*, deaf activist Iwabuchi Norio criticizes the attitude of Japanese deaf citizens who he says always clamor for handouts, ranging from half-price train tickets to free rolls of fax paper. This is what has prevented Japanese deaf people from gaining true independence, in his view. For his inspiration of what is needed for true independence, he looks toward the Americans with Disabilities Act of 1990, which seeks to outlaw discrimination based on disability and to equalize access, but does not itself provide any proactive welfare benefits.

Comparison with the United States

Although it is not within the scope of this chapter to engage a full comparison between civil society NPOs in Japan and the United States, a few paragraphs about some of the obvious differences are in order. First, American organizations such as the National Association of the Deaf (NAD) tend to be largely national in scale, whereas Japanese nonprofits tend to be more locally based. U.S. organizations tend to use direct mail, engage in direct lobbying activity with the government, and eschew the organization as social meeting ground.

First, let us look at the different membership structures. The NAD has 27,000 members, approximately half of whom are hearing. The JFD has approximately 25,000 members, all of whom are deaf (JFD 2004:113). Given that the United States has more than double the population of Japan (267 million vs. 126 million), the JFD has almost twice the membership per capita. But it should be remembered that not only are the members held closely within the prefectural association structure, organizing their social and political activities around the local groups, but also that the prefectural state governments actively "persuade" deaf persons in their area to join the local associations in order to become eligible for welfare benefits.[16]

Demographics certainly play a major role in this difference. The high population density of Japan combined with an efficient public transportation system (that is either half-priced or totally free for people who carry a government issued Disability ID Card, like most deaf persons) allows deaf persons to mingle easily with one another. In addition, Japan still does not have widespread TV captioning, nor are real-time TTY telecommunications devices widespread, which means that deaf persons must physically meet in order to communicate efficiently.[17]

Furthermore, NPOs in Japan are not eligible for discount postage. Whereas the NAD or any other registered U.S. nonprofit can mail out 150+ standard, pre-sorted, envelopes for less than a penny apiece through the U.S. Postal Service, the JFD and other Japanese nonprofits must pay the standard rate of ¥80 per piece (as of 2004). A mailing list of 1,000 members means an outlay of ¥80,000 (approx. US$760), prohibitively expensive for most small groups. Some NPOs in Japan have found it cheaper to print up all the envelopes, stuff them into a large suitcase, fly to South Korea, and mail them from there (Pekkanen 2002)! In the United States, the large discount given to NPOs makes it more cost-efficient to have a large mailing list of contributors, especially given the Christian tradition of tithing to charity.[18]

In the United States, many nonprofit organizations hire professional lobbyists to target key politicians or lawyers seeking landmark cases. In Japan, the parliamentary system makes courting individual politicians difficult, and the court systems have proved to be a long and very uncertain method of enacting social or legislative change. Instead, NPOs in Japan have focused on lobbying at the bureaucratic level; thus the importance of building strong relationships with ministries through the *itaku* system and avoidance of direct confrontational tactics.

16. In the JFD's case, there is no organization of equal power to compete for these state resources since D-Pro, the only other major Deaf organization, eschews state welfare benefits. So by default there is only one window.

17. TV captioning and the spread of TTY text telephones been mentioned as reason American deaf clubs are no longer as powerful as they used to be. You no longer have to be at the club to meet your deaf friends have a good time. You can stay at home, watch a closed-captioned movie on television, and then chat with your deaf classmate in the next town using your TTY text telephone or Internet.

18. Another irony of the American NPO situation is that in order for donations to 501(c) entities to be classified as charitable giving, contributors may not receive anything of value in return. This means that most members of such organizations receive at most a newsletter and constant junk mail pleas to donate more.

Though I never heard the use of the term *madoguchi-ippō* in reference to the deaf situation, the *madoguchi ippō* system that the Buraku liberation organizations were forced into is the same system that functions in the deaf community with the use of the *itaku* funds. One difference, however, is that Buraku Liberation League prefectural units appear to have much more discretion in the use of their funds, leading often to accusations of impropriety (that is, non-BLL members not receiving funds due them; Reber [1999]). The government has reined in the deaf prefectural associations much more closely through the use of the *shakai-fukushi-hōjin* system.

The JFD has benefited from elements of the BLL's rhetorical strategy as well. Along with the *fukushi* welfare avenue the JFD has also been using the *jinken* human rights frame and discourse. Although it would be hard to argue for an extant minority rights frame in Japan, it is clear that the BLL has managed to create a strong human rights frame in its stead (cf. Tsurushima 1984; Goodman and Neary 1996; Reber 1999).

One of the ironies is that although the JFD is similar in hegemonic strength (both politically and numerically) to the BLL (only a small minority of deaf belong to D-Pro, just as a small minority of former Burakumin belong to *Zenkairen*), they are on different sides of the political spectrum. The BLL has had strong Japanese Socialist Party and Liberal Democratic Party support and an antagonistic relationship with the Japanese Communist Party.[19] The JFD, on the other hand, is politically very much on the left, and many of the leaders are sympathetic to the Japanese Communist Party.

Conclusion: Cooperative Rewards

This chapter has described the basic structure and functioning of the Japanese Federation of the Deaf. One of my major goals was to illustrate

---

19. For an explication of the 1950s animosity between the JCP and JSP, see Kohno (1997). The JCP competed with the JSP for the support of the labor unions. Furthermore, the JSP was strong enough to create a coalition government with the other big parties (notably the LDP) and had no political need for the JCP, despite their ideological similarities. The schism culminated in the JSP stating that it was not connected in any way with the JCP in order to deflect growing anti-Communist sentiment in the Diet.

Related to the JCP's antagonism toward the BLL, it is often said that the reason the JCP is so strong in the Kyoto area is to counterbalance the BLL, not for any love of the JCP in and of itself by the Kyoto residents. Many point to this as evidence of lingering anti-Burakumin sentiment in Kyoto.

how the JFD and its affiliate prefectural associations used the *itaku* contract system and nonprofit corporate structures (the various *hōjin* entities) to their benefit. Most prior research on nonprofits in Japan has approached the issue from a top-down legal perspective which more or less assumes that the laws create the categorical boundaries and discourse in which the nonprofits exist. What I have tried to show in small part here is that far from being limiting, these laws can yield a bounty of opportunities for the deaf associations able to take a savvy approach to them. The deaf associations have shown an amazing ability to split amoeba-like into smaller, more regulated entities in order to reap the benefits of the *itaku* projects, thus having their cake (project funding) and eating it too (avoiding strict government control of their funds). This helped the JFD maintain its strong membership through the mid-nineties.

Unfortunately, a new generation of deaf youth emerged who were largely indifferent to the social and political benefits of joining the JFD. In the next two chapters, we will explore the social and educational changes in the 1970s that created this new cohort as well as how their new identity politics are changing notions of social activism within the community.

CHAPTER NINE

Deaf Students in the Post-Mainstreaming Era

Early during my fieldwork I visited Sapporo, the capital of Hokkaido, the northernmost island of Japan. Hokkaido is remote and peripheral, both geographically and emotionally, from the center of Japan. I stayed at the home of the Nakanes, a married couple who were both deaf. The Nakanes owned a small business that catered to the needs of deaf individuals in the Sapporo area, selling fax machines, door bell and phone flashers, and, most recently, digital cell phones that allowed for short e-mail messages to be passed between cell phone users. These were very popular among younger deaf people.

The husband took me to visit the Sapporo School for the Deaf, from which he had graduated over thirty years ago. Like most other schools for the deaf, the Sapporo School is K–12 and government-run. He had stayed in the dorms during his years there, as his family lived too far away for him to commute. The Sapporo School still had residential facilities, but only a few of its high school students still lived in them. The majority of students now commuted from home by train. Like most schools for the deaf in the late nineties, the Sapporo School was facing greatly lowered enrollments due to the falling birthrate and increase in mainstreamed students.

The Sapporo School for the Deaf was famous for being very strongly oral, which meant it emphasized speech and speechreading skills and disavowed signing in the classroom. Nakane-san and I were shown the kindergarten, where the small children were taught how to vocalize by holding balloons in front of their mouths, which let them feel the vibrations of speech. In the elementary school, all the children wore large hearing aids. The teachers held microphones hooked to a FM loop amplifier system, wired into the floor of the building. The students could hear the teacher's voice, but they could not hear each other, obviating both distractions and peer bonding. The high school had a PC with speech analysis and feedback software. From a speech audiologist's perspective, it was cutting-edge technology and the school was very proud of it.

Nakane-san and I chatted in sign throughout the school tour. He told me how although the technology had changed, the severe oralism of the school and its rejection of signing had not. None of the teachers (who were all hearing) knew how to sign, so our continuing subversive critique of the school fell upon blind eyes, so to speak.

At the end of the tour, we were ushered into the school principal's office. Like almost all principals of schools for the deaf, he had previously no training in deaf issues or sign language. He was simply in rotation. In several years, he'd be transferred out to another school in the prefecture, most likely a hearing one, and a new principal would be rotated in. Sitting in his office, Nakane-san and I again chatted in sign while the principal organized some of his papers.

I gave the principal my Yale University business card, indicating that I was a doctoral candidate in the cultural anthropology program. He seemed very honored that I was visiting his school. He talked with Nakane-san and asked him what changes he noticed in the school. Although the principal didn't know sign, he did know enough to speak slowly, enunciating carefully. We engaged in some more polite chatter. I interpreted for Nakane-san when he missed some words that the principal spoke, speechreading being an inexact art form even for the most advanced practitioners.

At the end of the day, the principal walked with us to the front door of the school to see us off. As we said our farewells, he leaned over to me and said in a clear, slow voice:

"You have wonderful enunciation."

He had thought I was deaf. The idea of a hearing person who could sign without voicing, who wasn't an interpreter, and who was interested in the deaf community, had escaped him.

Whither Deaf Children?

By the 1970s, Japan had fully recovered from the war and the economy was booming. Memories of that terrible period of time were quickly fading. Except for the rather cramped housing and air pollution in the cities, the quality of life had improved considerably, and the general populace was settling into comfortable middle-class lives with all the creature comforts that modern science and industry could offer. In the 1970s, two changes significantly impacted the deaf community. The first was the combination of the rapidly plummeting birthrate and advances in medical technologies that resulted in many fewer children being born deaf. The second was the growing popularity of mainstreaming deaf children into regular school systems (also called academic inclusion or integration). The conjunction of these two forces meant that enrollment in schools for the deaf dramatically fell during this period. Deaf children in the post-mainstreaming era have a very different sense of self-identity from those of previous generations.

The decreased birthrate was caused by multiple factors. After the war, there was a baby boom as a result of men returning home after a protracted leave of absence coupled with the knowledge that children could finally be raised in a secure social and economic environment. In 1947, the year after Horikawa-san was born, the total fertility rate was at its peak of 4.54 children per woman. This soon began to fall. By 1960, it was down to 2.00, where it stabilized for about a decade. Part of the drop was a natural recovery from that temporarily elevated condition. Smaller apartments in the cities, nuclear families, the lack of availability of grandparents to serve as caregivers, and the postwar meritocratic educational system meant that greater investment in fewer children was the smarter choice for parents.[1] In 1975, the birthrate began a downward curve, dropping to 1.54 children per woman in 1990. By 2000, it was 1.36, the lowest in Japanese history. This is well below the natural sustainable rate of 2.08 children per woman and means that Japan will face a rapidly shrinking and aging population (National Institute for Population and Social Security Research 2002). The introduction of a vaccine for rubella in 1969 meant that there would be no more large cohorts of deaf children born. There would never again be a deaf high school baseball team trying to make it to the national championships.

The impact of fewer children was multiplied by the increase in mainstreaming deaf children starting in the 1970s, a movement that in many ways represented success for the deaf community. More and more deaf children were now living with their parents and going to local schools. Previously, deaf people had been thought to be lower in intellect and less capable than hearing people. Mainstreaming meant that deaf children were recognized as being just as intelligent as their hearing peers.

---

1. For an analysis of the factors behind the dropping birth rate, see Muriel Jolivet's (1997) *Japan: The Childless Society.*

Impact on the Schools for the Deaf

The drop in the birthrate and mainstreaming had a disastrous effect on schools for the deaf. In 1975 the total enrollment at all the schools for the deaf in Japan was 13,897 students. By 2001, enrollment had dropped by half to 6,719 students. The number of "hearing-impaired" children as classified by the government was 26,000 in 1965; just over thirty-five years later, it had dropped 41 percent to 15,200. During the same time span between 1965 and 2001, the general population of Japan had increased 30 percent. While the category of people with disabilities as a whole has been increasing by about 2 percent each year because of the aging society, from 1991 to 2001 the total number of hearing-impaired adults in Japan dropped for the first time in postwar history, from 358,000 to 346,000 (Prime Minister's Office 2003:123, 126). With further advances in medical technology, deafness as we know it now could cease to exist.

The influence of the precipitous drop in the number of deaf children over the past three decades cannot be overestimated. Many of the schools for the deaf that I visited in the late nineties had significantly lower enrollments than any other time in their history. Classrooms that used to hold forty or more students now held the entire grade year of three or four students. Entire grade years were missing at some schools,

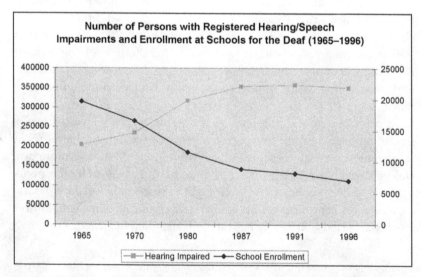

Figure 9.1. Number of persons with government-registered hearing or speech impairments vs. Enrollment at schools for the deaf.

Figure 9.2. Plummeting enrollments at schools for the deaf has meant small class sizes of three to four students per grade. Author photo.

even metropolitan ones. The overall atmosphere was quite similar to that of ghost towns.

For example, in 1998 at the Kyoto School for the Deaf, the largest school for the deaf in the prefecture, there were only: 2 first graders, no second graders, 4 third graders, 2 fourth graders, 3 fifth graders, 6 sixth graders, 2 seventh graders, 4 eighth graders, and 2 ninth graders. At the high school level there was a larger cohort of what are called U-turn deaf (more on this later in the chapter): 15 tenth graders, 10 eleventh graders, and 24 twelfth graders. Of the senior high school students, 19 were in the "regular" academic track and 30 were in the vocational skills track (Kyoto Prefectural School for the Deaf 1998).

Mainstreaming as Success or Failure

Starting in the 1970s, partly due to the dramatic success of the previous generation of deaf adults such as the deaf lawyer we met in chapter 7, parents began to have higher hopes for their deaf children. Rather than allowing them to be removed from the family and placed in residential schools for the deaf, parents began demanding that the local school systems accept their children at neighborhood schools. As luck would have it, the process of mainstreaming was aided by the falling birthrate. Local school systems could afford to put more resources into a smaller number of children and welcomed these children back.

Assistance for the mainstream students came in the form of the *nanchō-gakkyū* (hard-of-hearing grade levels), where deaf students were provided with speech and speechreading instruction, and other instructional aids. At larger school systems, the *nanchō-gakkyū* were self-contained classrooms (schools within schools), but in many smaller schools they were provided as resource rooms that students could go to during the week for additional tutoring, speech training, and coaching. I know of no regular schools that provided sign language instruction or interpretation as part of their special education curriculum. The main emphasis of the *nanchō-gakkyū* was integration using oral methods of speech and speechreading.

Before mainstreaming, at the Kyoto Prefectural School for the Deaf, the number of elementary school children enrolled reached a peak in 1952. We can follow as these children entered middle school, where enrollments peaked in 1955; and high school, where they peaked in 1966 and 1970.[2] Since then, the number of children in elementary and middle school has declined every year. This is what you would expect demographically especially if you assumed that there were fewer and fewer deaf children being born, as the statistics seem to indicate.

There is, however, an anomaly in the pre-school numbers at the Kyoto School that challenges this assumption. After a peak in 1939 there was a steady drop in enrollment in the kindergarten program. There was a short spike in the immediate postwar period, but enrollment dropped again in 1948. Now what is notable is that despite decreases in all other grade level enrollments, there was an *increase* in the number of pre-school children starting in the 1970s and peaking in 1973. This increase in pre-school did not lead to a corresponding increase in the number of elementary school children three years later, because most of those pre-schoolers ended up mainstreaming.

In 1967, from a low of 17 percent transferring to regular schools there was a rapid increase in mainstreaming to a peak of 100 percent just three

2. Source: The Editorial Board for the 100th Anniversary of Deaf and Blind Education (1978) and Kyoto Prefectural School for the Deaf (1998).

years later in 1970. From there, the trend starts back down, but remains above 50 percent through the end of the 1970s. Although the mainstreaming rate stabilizes at about 50–70 percent, one thing has become clear: the path for deaf students had opened into hearing schools and this had the effect of drawing students away from the schools for the deaf.[3]

The children with the most academic potential (or the most persevering parents) were chosen for mainstreaming. As the term *nanchō-gakkyū* or "hard-of-hearing" grade levels implies, these were often the students who had some residual hearing or were post-lingually deaf and already had a base of spoken/written Japanese on which they could build. In the postwar generation, these were the very students who would become class presidents and later leaders in the Japanese Federation of the Deaf.

The culling of the top layer of students for mainstreaming reinforced the prejudice among parents and students that schools for the deaf were academically weaker than regular schools, creating a self-fulfilling prophecy. As the weaker students stayed behind, the curriculum shifted to meet their needs. Schools for the deaf became sites for an increasing number of children with multiple disabilities (deafness and mental retardation, for example).

Identity Formation in the Post-Boomers

The post-mainstreaming generation began graduating from high school in the 1980s and 1990s and are currently in their twenties, thirties, and early forties.[4] Those who mainstreamed out of kindergarten or elementary schools often identify themselves as hearing (*kenchō*), hard of hearing (*nanchō*), or hearing impaired (*chōkaku-shōgai*), and not as deaf (*rōa*). Many of these young deaf adults cannot sign or learned how to only after graduating from high school. Many see themselves as simply not hearing very well, and they avoid deaf groups and associating with

---

3. Other factors behind this are that after kindergarten children have picked up some degree of speech skills, they (or their parents) want to attend an elementary school that is closer to their own homes where their neighborhood friends are. Also, many children do not have a positive impression of schools for the deaf (especially if speech skills are forcibly taught at a young age), and want to leave as soon as they can. The Nara School (see below), which does not teach speech skills until the elementary school level, does not have this attrition problem.

4. Those that graduated from kindergarten in 1970, the first wave of mainstreaming, would be around 34 years old at the time of my fieldwork, 1997–2000.

other deaf persons because of the communication barrier. Often, even if they qualify, they do not carry the disability ID card despite its numerous social welfare benefits.

In one family that I interviewed in Tokyo with two girls who were hearing impaired, only the older sister identified herself as deaf. She went to a school for the deaf and signs fluently. The younger sister identifies herself as "not-deaf," goes to a hearing school, and does not sign, even though she has roughly the same amount of residual hearing as her *"defu"* sister. One teacher of the deaf in Osaka, deaf himself, told me, "in the past, our entire class would join the local deaf association when we graduated from [a high] school [for the deaf]; but now, kids go to mainstream schools and might never meet another deaf person."

Deaf leaders in the JFD are concerned about this new generation who do not identify as deaf since this will have disastrous results for the community in future years. In addition, they are concerned about people who are audiologically deaf, but who have no sense of themselves as deaf individuals, cutting themselves off from the community support and information resources made available through the traditional deaf organizations.

The teachers are caught in a conundrum. It is clear that it would be extremely difficult for a student from a deaf high school to matriculate into a good four-year college. The high schools for the deaf are often two to three years academically behind the hearing schools, and they do not do college exam preparation. If we look at the post-graduation track record of the Shakujii School for the Deaf in Tokyo (1980–1995), for example, we see that only one or two graduating seniors a year continue their studies. The schools they enter are almost always trade schools. Looking year by year, we find that in the span 1980–1995, only *one* student from that high school has ever entered a four-year college (in 1985 at the Japan Sports College) and *none* have entered a general education four–year program (Tokyo Shakujii School for the Deaf 1995). The majority of the graduating deaf seniors in Japan are going into manual labor, office work, or trades.

Mainstreaming in the United States

In the United States, less than a quarter of deaf or hard-of-hearing students are now attending traditional schools for the deaf. The rest are going to local schools supplemented by resource rooms or self-contained classrooms (Gallaudet Research Institution 2000–2001 cited in Karchmer and Mitchell [2003:23]). This is the result of the Education for All Handicapped Children Act of 1975 (PL94–142; later renamed the Individuals with Disabilities Education Act or IDEA), which mandated the "least restrictive environment" for children with disabilities. Most school boards interpreted this as meaning integration in local regular schools rather than seclusion in special schools. Reviewing the literature on whether integration has produced better academic results for deaf students compared to schools for the deaf, Karchmer and Mitchell find that, to the contrary, "there is little independent explanation of achievement differences attributable to student placement (2003:33)." In other words, students in schools for the deaf improve academically at the same rate as their deaf peers in integrated school settings.[5]

The situation regarding integration changes when American students decide to go college. Enabled by full-time interpretation provided by the Americans with Disabilities Act, the education deaf students receive at higher-tier regular colleges is considered to be superior to that at Gallaudet University, the nation's only four-year college for the deaf. Sociologists Barnartt and Scotch write that the "unhappiness with the ADA can be seen in the attitude expressed around Gallaudet University that the ADA has been a disaster for the university, since it permits deaf students to seek college education anywhere" (2001:172)." This leaves the university with a growing problem of academically weaker students. One can argue that this has also been the case at many women's colleges and historically Black colleges as well. Whether regular colleges in fact serve deaf students better than Gallaudet University has not yet been studied.

Japanese Colleges

For Japanese deaf students, the problem is that getting into college has traditionally been based on performance in written and oral entrance exams. Schools have not proactively recruited minorities or disabled stu-

---

5. That being said, Karchmer and Mitchell's data also show that deaf and hard-of-hearing students consistently lag behind their hearing peers in standard achievement tests regardless of educational setting. The highest performing 10 percent of deaf students test only at roughly the median or average level of their hearing age peers. The median deaf/hard-of-hearing student tests below the bottom 10 percent of his or her hearing age peers (2003:32).

dents.[6] In fact, colleges have been known to forbid the use of sign interpreters during the oral interviews for the entrance examinations, citing the policy against external assistance. Furthermore, even if a deaf student is able to get in, Japanese schools and colleges are not currently required by law to provide interpreters, and the local sign interpreters provided free by the city government are rarely qualified to interpret at the college level.

Through the 1990s, college was only a dream for most deaf students in Japan. The situation gradually improved as lower-tier colleges began to implement open admissions in order to boost flagging enrollments due to the falling birthrate. Second- and third-tier colleges and technical schools are now actively recruiting students with disabilities. In 2003, four graduates at the Shakujii School for the Deaf mentioned earlier went on to noncompetitive four-year colleges. However, the competitive first- and second-tier colleges still remain largely inaccessible to students who have not gone through the regular school system supplemented with rigorous after-school *juku* cramming. The majority of students are still going on to non-career track white- or blue-collar jobs immediately after high school.[7]

It was my impression that the students who remained in the schools for the deaf in the 1990s were aware that they were considered slow compared to their mainstreamed or hearing peers. Since they could not enter good schools, the great majority of the graduates of schools for the deaf entered the job market directly, aided by the Employment Promotion Law for Disabled Persons which stipulates that at least 1.8 percent of the employees of large companies have registered disabilities. This quota system ensures that most who want a job can find one, although not necessarily in a field they want to enter.[8]

6. This ignores the issue of parents who use bribes or family connections to get their students in through the back door. To be fair, American colleges have also had a special place for "legacy" children.

7. Source: http://www.shakujii-sd.metro.tokyo.jp/sinro/frsinro2003.html (accessed October 31, 2004).

8. Source: http://www.roudoukyoku.go.jp/seido/shoukai/shougai-houkaisei.htm (accessed December 6, 2004). People with very serious disabilities count as more than one person, those with minor disabilities as less than one person. The law does not stipulate what positions these employees must be in or their working conditions. Many companies bypass the quotas by hiring many disabled part-timers or staffing only low-level clerical jobs. The fines for not meeting the quota are so low that many companies simply opt to pay them rather than deal with hiring disabled employees. Japan has no equivalent of the Americans with Disabilities Act, which mandates an equalization of job opportunities regardless of disability status, although it should be mentioned that the ADA has

Cochlear Implants: Powerful Hearing Aids
or Genocide?

When I first went to Japan in the mid-1990s to start the research that led to this book, I was surprised that the Japanese deaf community was not up in arms about cochlear implants like their American brethren. Before we get into that question let me first explain what a cochlear implant is and why American deaf activists believe they are "genocidal." The first single-channel cochlear implants were developed in the 1970s by research laboratories in the United States and Europe. Most forms of hearing loss are caused by damage to the very small hair cells that line the inner ear. If an electrode is implanted in the inner ear canal or cochlea, auditory nerve cells can be directly stimulated. While the first "single-channel" implants could only transmit a single frequency, by the 1980s multichannel implants were developed that allowed for multiple frequencies.

Cochlear implantation is a surgical procedure conducted under general anesthesia that requires drilling into the cranium in order to place the electrode and signal receiver. For the most part the surgery is destructive. The process of threading the electrode into the inner ear damages the remaining hair cells, and the electrode cannot be easily removed or replaced. The area where the receiver is embedded in the skull remains vulnerable to shock, and recipients are at a greater risk of meningitis. After the implantation, patients cannot be examined using Magnetic Resonance Imaging (MRIs), as the powerful magnets would pull the device literally out of the cranium.

Cochlear implants became controversial in the United States in the mid-1980s after the Food and Drug Administration approved their use in infants with profound hearing loss. At first the minimum age for implantation was two years; now it has dropped down to twelve months for certain devices. The implantation teams, which consisted of surgeons and audiologists, usually recommend that implanted children be taught using strictly oral methods of speechreading and speech. Bertram discusses "techniques applied to encourage parental cooperation" (1996:57) in preventing the children from signing, which was seen as lessening the likelihood of their successfully learning how to speak and speechread.

---

been relatively useless in improving the employment condition for those with severe disabilities in the United States.

Parents were told that, with due diligence, their deaf child could become just like a normal child after the implants. The name of one company, Advanced Bionics, reflects the optimism implicit in these devices.

Some radical Deaf activists in the United States in the 1990s seized on the cochlear implant as a central issue in articulating their position as a linguistic and quasi-ethnic minority. They argued that cochlear implants were a form of genocide, that Deaf children were literally being killed and reborn as hearing children (Lane 1993).[9] The ASL sign for cochlear implant is the index and middle finger digging into the back of the neck, like vampire fangs. These members of the Deaf community were successful in affecting social debate on this issue in the broader hearing community. For example, in 1995, an article in the *Wisconsin Law Review* was titled, "Making decisions for deaf children regarding cochlear implants: the legal ramifications of recognizing deafness as a culture rather than a disability" (Brusky 1995). A documentary titled *Sound and Fury* directed by Josh Aronson (2000) about the cochlear implant controversy received an Academy Award nomination in 2001, and has since been screened many times on public television.

In Japan, on the other hand, there has been relatively little public debate on cochlear implantation. Part of this is owing to the late introduction of the device. According to the Association of Cochlear Implant Transmitted Audition (ACITA), the first adult implant was in 1985, but children were not implanted until 1991. National health care did not cover the devices until 1994, at which point the acceptance rate accelerated. As of December 2002, only 2,500 people had them implanted. While in other countries, pediatric implantation represents about 50 percent of total implants, in Japan it has been only 30 percent, with the large majority going into adults (Association of Cochlear Implant Transmitted Audition [ACITA] 2002).

In Japan, doctors, parents, and the deaf community have framed cochlear implants as powerful hearing aids rather than as genocidal devices. They believe that a profoundly deaf child with a cochlear implant is still a deaf child and will still need special educational and medical services. Implanted individuals are still eligible for the disability ID card and all the social welfare benefits of a person with disabilities. The

9. More recently, the issue has become much less volatile. On October 6, 2000, the National Association of the Deaf, the leading national organization for the deaf in the United States, issued an official position statement recognizing and respecting the decision of deaf individuals and parents with deaf children to choose to have a cochlear implant.

cochlear implant does not change the person's fundamental state of being—that of being deaf. In addition, many Japanese parents have been reluctant to have surgery performed on their children who from the outside appear to be normal. If the implant was just a powerful hearing aid, then perhaps the child could get by with regular hearing aids. The tendency has been to wait and see how the child would develop.

Furthermore, Japanese signing has not been framed as a different language from spoken Japanese. Audiologists and educators have not dissuaded use of signing in Japan as vehemently as their counterparts in the United States, where the issue of signing or speech has occasionally taken on the tenor of a religious war. The JFD has focused on deaf social welfare and not deaf culture, so cochlear implants represent a new assistive medical technology and not a threatening new cultural force. During my fieldwork, D-Pro tried to raise the issue of cochlear implants as genocide, but there was relatively little interest in the topic even within the deaf community.

U-Turn and L-Turn Deaf

There are some emerging trends in contemporary deaf education. The first is the "U-Turn Deaf." The term refers to students with disabilities who were originally in early intervention programs at the kindergarten level, mainstreamed into regular elementary schools, and then "U-turned" or returned back to schools for the deaf at the middle or high school level. From an oralist educational perspective, these children failed out of mainstream schools. Indeed, some students did return to the schools for the deaf because of educational difficulties, but during my school visits I also met some children who returned out of choice.

The U-turn figures are quite startling. Kyoto School for the Deaf had its peak enrollment in 1956 when it had 11 kindergartners, 164 elementary, 107 middle, and 35 high school students. The students filtered through the school, causing the number of high school students to peak at 87 in both 1966 and 1970. Since then, the drop has been precipitous. By 1977, there were 47 kindergartners, 39 elementary, 26 middle, and 37 high school students. Fewer elementary school students than kindergartners (even not adjusting for 3 years of kindergarten vs. 6 years of elementary school) indicate the influence of mainstreaming practices (Kyoto Prefectural School for the Deaf 1998).

There is a also a similar phenomenon called "L-turning" which refers to children who were mainstreamed from kindergarten, but L-turned (that is, made a sideways step or lateral transition) into special education programs in middle school or high school. The reasons for L-turning are similar to those for U-turning: difficulty with the schoolwork, problems integrating socially into the classroom, not feeling prepared for high school exams. The U-turn and L-turn terminology is common among educators and academics working in all fields of special education in Japan, including those with other physical or intellectual disabilities.[10]

By 1998, we see the influence of U-turn and L-turn students in the Kyoto School for Deaf statistics. For example, that year there were 29 kindergartners, 17 elementary, 8 middle school, and 49 high school students (Kyoto School for the Deaf 1998). The large number of high school students compared to the middle schoolers indicates that students were transferring to the Kyoto School to complete their education. The U-turn children were entering kindergarten at the school for the deaf; mainstreaming at the first grade level and remaining in the regular school system for their compulsory education (elementary and middle school); and then returning to the schools for the deaf for high school (grade ten).

There are several reasons why students return to the schools for the deaf. School becomes much more difficult at the middle school level as students prepare for high school exams. In Japan, elementary and middle school students are socially promoted into the next grade level even if they do not finish a previous year. This means that students who are having problems are left ever further behind. Private high schools have entrance exams, and most of high school at these rigorous programs is preparation for college "entrance exam hell," so U-turning or L-turning at the tenth grade makes sense. As the story of the young woman in the next chapter indicates, she started to experience more problems fitting in at her local school as she grew older. She ended up going to a college for the deaf as a result.

However, despite the educational system's negative opinion of these students, I also saw reflections of pride in the choice to come back. Deciding to return to a school for the deaf may not be psychologically easy, but social integration is facilitated by the small class sizes. Many of the U-turn and L-turn deaf who were mainstreamed out of kindergarten do

---

10. These terms are also used in other social settings. A young man who was born and grew up on a farm, moved to the big city for college and a job, and then returns to the farm to take care of his aging parents is said to "U-turn" to rural life. If he brings his wife who was born and grew up in the city, she is said to be an "L-turn" migrant to life in the boonies.

not know how to sign. Others only know how to sign using a Rochester method–like system of meticulously fingerspelling each letter of each word. Reentering schools for the deaf, they need to learn or re-learn how to sign and re-assimilate into a deaf environment. But for many it is a welcome change from the demanding and often lonesome situation of being the only mainstreamed deaf student in a hearing school system.

Nara Prefectural School for the Deaf

Perhaps the most promising aspect of deaf education in Japan is the appearance of schools for the deaf that are adopting a much more lenient approach to signing and deaf education. The Nara Prefectural School for the Deaf is a good example. Instead of forcing speechreading and oral speech training on their kindergartners (which is the emphasis at most other schools), the Nara School emphasizes the fun nature of learning and group skill-building exercises. The Nara School is also unique in having the first deaf kindergarten teacher in Japan. Formerly, deaf adults could not become kindergarten teachers because the certification examination included tests of piano playing and singing skills with no accommodation made for people with disabilities.

The Nara School's emphasis on enjoying learning and de-emphasis on speech training has had significant impact on its retention rates. The Nara School does not experience the massive flight of students into mainstream elementary schools from the kindergarten level. The kindergartners there think that learning is fun and that the school for the deaf is an exciting place to be, and they enjoy being with their deaf peers.[11] Speech training comes later, academic quality is better than the other schools, and the school positively bustles with kids. Other schools are slowly looking to the Nara School for inspiration, but it is still seen as a radical, experimental approach, and the long-term effects on the deaf community and deaf education are still to be seen.

There are other indications that the Ministry of Education is becoming more flexible regarding deaf education. In May 2004, the *Japanese Deaf*

11. A significant difference is that children are not hooked up to loop amplifiers to hear their teacher's voices. The loop-microphone system is designed to eliminate peer-peer conversation so that children are not distracted by the other children in the room. Only the teacher can talk to the students. The Nara School, on the other hand, greatly encourages peer-peer communication (both manual and oral) as a primary means of social and linguistic development in their students.

News reported that twelve deaf teachers had been hired at the elementary through high school levels as well as around thirty staff members at schools for the deaf across Japan (*JDN* May 1, 2004:2). The mainstreamed generation is coming back to schools for the deaf—in an even bigger U-turn arc than before—this time to teach.

Another major change in the last five years has been the growing flexibility and willingness of Japanese universities to accept students with disabilities. Japanese colleges and universities have been suffering from plummeting enrollments due to the greatly decreased birth rate at the same time that their government subsidies have also fallen because of budget cuts. This has caused many schools, especially rural colleges, to be more creative in their recruiting. Some have eliminated entrance exams altogether and embraced open enrollments. In 2004, Gunma University announced that it had just hired two trained staff members to provide interpreting services for two incoming deaf students (*JDN* May 1, 2004:11). With no mandate from the Ministry of Education or disability law requiring it, this was the first time that a Japanese college had decided to provide full-time support for its students.

Conclusion: Mainstream Opportunities

Mainstreaming opened up educational and linguistic opportunities for deaf students. Children could choose a variety of options: to go to the special schools for the deaf; attend "hard-of-hearing classes" built into their local schools; or participate in a regular classroom on a full-time basis. Linguistically, they could choose more traditional forms of Japanese signing used by the elderly or the more linear style used by middle-generation deaf. Or they could forgo signing all together and speak and speechread in spoken Japanese.

The middle generation wanted to become part of greater Japan, but because they could not, they created their own parallel version of Japan inside the local associations of the deaf. There, they gained a sense of themselves both as Japanese and as JFD members. By the time the youngest generation emerged in the late 1970s, they were given the opportunity to actually become part of the larger Japanese nation-state by attending local schools rather than schools for the deaf, and their parents decided to move their children in that direction.

Americans tend to view choice as a positive—an opportunity to discover who you truly are. But from a social perspective, you can view

choice as fracturing. Identity is not so much a result of a personal decision as something that emerges from the context we are in, the people
that we are surrounded by. Identity in this sense is profoundly social.
With mainstreaming, the deaf community fractured several ways. First,
mainstreamed children no longer identified as deaf, isolating their peers
at the schools for the deaf. The younger generation as a whole became
detached from the postwar generation.

Many times, educators and parents decided what type of school the
children would go to, and thus what kind of language education they
would receive. But in other cases, the children themselves decided to
mainstream, to join their hearing peers. In either case, these decisions
had profound impact on their political and personal identities. In the
next chapter, we will explore the life of a young woman who chose herself to mainstream into a regular elementary school but later U-turned
into a college for the deaf.

CHAPTER TEN

Life History: Yamashita Mayumi

A Deaf Youth in Contemporary Japan

As noted in the previous chapter, the 1970s witnessed huge changes in deaf education because of the falling birthrate and the introduction of mainstreaming. Enrollment in schools for the deaf plummeted as children were pushed into the regular school system by their parents.[1] Improved technology can also be credited with part of this change. With integrated circuit (IC) chips, hearing aids could be made smaller and more portable. Children with residual hearing (like Horikawa-san, described in chapter 6) who might have still stayed in schools for the deaf were encouraged to integrate into the mainstream.

In this chapter, we look at the life course of the youngest of my interview subjects, "Yamashita Mayumi," born in 1980. At the time of the interview in 1999, she was a nineteen-year-old second-year student at the Tsukuba College of Technology.[2] Yamashita-san was considerably more nervous than the other subjects that I interviewed. She does not seem to have a fixed internal narrative of her life course yet. Part of this may be her youth; another part may be that she is still coming to grips with her self-identity. Because she stayed so close to the interview questions, I have retained that format when presenting her narrative. I have, how-

1. For an autobiography of a young woman born in 1969 who stayed at the school for the deaf until graduating from high school, see Tamura (1994). For the memoirs of a hard-of-hearing woman who was born in 1958, was mainstreamed, and then decided to go to America as an exchange student and discovered her "deaf identity" (and ASL), see Takamura (1993).

2. Because of her age at the time of her interview, I have used a pseudonym even though she consented to the use of her name.

ever, edited the questions and responses so that they follow a linear temporal sequence through her life.

1980

KN: Where were you born?
I was born in Hokkaido, near Sapporo.
KN:Do you know how you became deaf?
I don't know if the reason I lost my hearing was due to being born that way or if I lost my hearing due to a high fever when I was a baby. I don't know.

Yamashita-san attended kindergarten at the Sapporo School for the Deaf, the school that figures in the opening anecdote of the previous chapter. The Sapporo School, like many other schools for the deaf in Japan in the 1970s, was very aggressive in encouraging parents to send even three- or four-year-old children into their Early Intervention Programs. The Sapporo School is infamous within the deaf community for being very demanding in its oral (speech and speechreading) skills program.

1983–

When I was in kindergarten, I attended a school for the deaf. I learned kōwahō (oralism; speech-reading/speech skills) there.

The speechreading/speech classes [at the kindergarten] were very severe. At that time, I wasn't able to sign at all, but of course I would gesture or mime or things like that. I always felt that the teacher would become angry if he/she caught me, so I set as a personal goal that I would try to avoid all types of miming. The school had a bulletin board with the "Goal of the Month" and under it was always written "I Will Not Mime." At that time, I didn't understand the reasoning behind that. . . . I didn't really understand anything at all, all I knew was that I had to make more of an effort all the time toward making my lips move.

When I visited the Sapporo School in 1997 as part of my fieldwork, I was surprised at how demanding their oral education program was. Even the smallest of children were encouraged to vocalize, and signing was strictly forbidden. Unlike regular kindergartens in Japan where the primary emphasis is on learning social skills through playing, the Sapporo School was very authoritarian in emphasizing the importance of early linguistic speech competence. It was not surprising that after three years of very difficult speech training that many young children would want to leave the school and integrate into regular school systems. Yamashita-san was no exception, leaving for a regular school at her first opportunity.

1986–

From elementary school to high school, I attended regular[3] schools.
KN: Why did you go to a normal elementary school?
Well, I was only a kindergartner, so it wasn't possible for me to think too seriously about it, but all of my friends in the neighborhood were going to the same regular school, and I wanted to go there as well. I think my mother's rationale was that . . . well she never said this directly . . . but that if I went to the school for the deaf, I would fall behind in my studies. One of my schoolteachers told her that because I was able to orally communicate somewhat, I should do fine in the regular school system.
KN: Were you put in a special class for the deaf?
No, they had nothing of the kind. It was really a regular school. They didn't have a special program for the hearing impaired, so I was put in regular class. The teacher would use a microphone in class. That made the sound a little louder, so it was a little easier to understand. But at that time, I had absolutely no idea myself what the best method [of learning] would be. So I personally thought this was that best way [since I didn't know any better].

One of my classmates came from the school for the deaf, but most of my classmates from those kindergarten days went to schools for the deaf. Only I and one other boy transferred to regular school. But he went to a school that was far away; I have no idea what happened to him.

Despite mainstreaming, lack of smooth communication with her (hearing) classmates was a major problem. In addition, she did not have the opportunity to develop friendships with deaf peers. This is typical of many mainstreamed deaf children, whether in Japan or in the United States.

KN: Did you have any trouble communicating with your classmates?
When I was small, I would just play [with the other kids] normally. You don't need any form of verbal communication if you're just playing tag or other kids' games. But especially when I entered middle school and high school, the need for communication grew much more and I remember many difficult times. When I was small, I really didn't think of anything at all. I was deaf and all of my friends were deaf, I thought that was normal. It wasn't a burden at all.

I didn't experience any discrimination myself. I've heard [of cases] of teasing and discrimination, but I never experienced it myself. It might have been that the people around me were particularly understanding. It was nice.

There were some problems with my hearing friends because I couldn't hear. For example, if I was with a couple of my friends and I couldn't understand what was being said, I'd stay quiet. One of my friends would ask me, "Why aren't you listening to what I'm saying?" or "You don't even bother to try to listen to the conversation." I had particular problems with that friend because the size of her[4] lip/mouth movements made it difficult for me to understand her. I found that I

---

3. The sign she is using for "regular" is transliterated *futsū* or normal.
4. Gender is assumed for the purpose of English translation; the original signing does not indicate gender.

would intentionally keep my distance (keien) from my friends with small mouth movements, and talk more with my friends who had larger movements. And so my friend with the small mouth movements got angry with me and said, "Why do you avoid me and talk all the time with those [other] girls?!!" That was an example of one problem I had.

Social Discrimination and Contemporary Attitudes toward the Deaf

Yamashita-san was fortunate in experiencing little direct discrimination at school or in the home, although the prevailing assumption of both her teachers and her parents was that she should try as hard as possible to be "normal," meaning hearing. In chapter 3, we explored how the teachings of Buddhism, Shinto, and Confucianism affected the social environment of people with disabilities in Tokugawa and Meiji era Japan. In many ways, even at the turn of the twenty-first century, they continue to influence how mainstream Japanese think about people with disabilities.

For example, the Japanese social welfare system still establishes the social welfare of people with disabilities as the responsibility of the state, just as in the Nara period Confucian system. Disabled persons are required to register with the Ministry of Health and Social Welfare if they wish to receive disability benefits, which are quite substantial. As in the *tenkenron* laws of the Nara period, there are various grades of disability, ranked from Grade 1 or most severe to Grade 5 or the lightest.

Influenced by Buddhism, many people continue to believe that misfortune in this life was created by bad deeds in a former life. One of the largest Buddhist sects preaches that disability can be caused by past bad acts or karma that are affecting a household. They will help purge this karma through diligent religious practice and frequent monetary contributions. This sect is infamous for their frequent and aggressive proselytization of families with children who have disabilities.[5]

Even in contemporary Japan, some families will hide disabled siblings or children from peers, co-workers, and especially future in-laws. Conservative families are reluctant to marry a daughter or son to a house that has disability in the "blood." Private detectives are occasionally hired before the betrothal to make sure there are no unpleasant surprises hiding in the back room, so to speak. Those in favor of this practice argue

5. Discretion is the better part of valor when dealing with religious sects in Japan, especially those with powerful political connections and a history of filing libel suits against scholars. Those who wish to know the identity of this organization are welcome to ask me individually.

that it is pragmatism and not prejudice. If a daughter were to marry into a family with a mentally retarded son, for example, she might become responsible for caring for this brother-in-law after his parents died. What parent would want that for their daughter? Or so the argument goes.

A schoolteacher at a school in northern Japan that I visited in 1997 said that the mother of one of her students had considered joint suicide (mother and child) when she found out her child was deaf. As late as 1998, a NHK survey found that in response to the question, "Do you think abortion is absolutely unacceptable, somewhat unacceptable, somewhat acceptable, or absolutely acceptable if the baby is very likely to be born seriously handicapped?," only 10 percent found it absolutely unacceptable; 13 percent somewhat acceptable; 42 percent somewhat acceptable; and 20 percent absolutely acceptable (The Roper Center for Public Opinion Research; NHK Survey May 1, 1998).

The belief that disabled children will be a burden to the family and society and that suicide (or abortion) is a valid option still runs deep. This often has religious or moral overtones. Akiie Henry Ninomiya writes: "In May, 1986, a mother strangled her one-year-old child who was diagnosed as mentally retarded. Her mother-in-law blamed her for having a disabled baby by saying, 'Our family does not have such sinful dirty blood; because your family blood is contaminated and sinful, a disabled child was born'" (1986:205).

In a moving section of her 1995 autobiography, Murayama Miwa, a poet and disability activist who has cerebral palsy (CP), writes about one of her friends who was killed by her mother in a joint suicide-homicide (*muri shinjū*). Many mothers of severely disabled adults worry that after they die, there will be no one to care for their children. A few commit joint suicide-homicide so that their adult children will not suffer without them and won't be lonely by themselves in the other world (the afterlife). Murayama-san's friend was about the same age as she was, twenty-six at the time, and an activist and leading light in the disability community. But because she had severe CP, her friend could not stop her mother from killing her.[6] Deeply shocked by the news of her friend's death, Murayama-san went home and told her father, "If you want to die, please die by yourself. I will continue to live after that, so you don't have to worry about me" (1995:101). It was after that that Murayama-san decided

6. Disabled people being killed by their caregivers is a worldwide phenomenon. However, Japanese parents are among the few who kill themselves at the same time so that they can continue caring for their child in the afterlife. It is this persistence of paternalism even into the next world that frustrates disability activists such as Murayama-san.

that in order to live fully, she would have to live separately from her parents. When I met her about ten years later, she was running a local center for independent living for people with severe disabilities in Tokyo.

In the late 1990s, a young Japanese man born with no arms and no legs became a hit celebrity. Ototake Hirotada's (1998) *Imperfect limbs* (*Gotai Fumanzoku*), a very upbeat and positive chronicle of his life, became an instant best seller in recession-weary Japan. According to his narrative, when Otatake-kun (as he is known) was born, his mother rather than rejecting him, thought he was the cutest thing she had ever seen. His book talks about how he, with the support of his family and friends, made it to Waseda University, one of the top private universities in Japan. With his book, Ototake-kun also gained an instant fan-club of Japanese women who (like his mother) declared him "*kawaiiii*" (so cute).

Signing in the Schools

Returning to Yamashita-san's narrative, one of the notable aspects about schools for the deaf in Japan is that there is considerably more signing by teachers at the higher grade levels than the lower ones.[7] While orally educated kindergarteners are easily prevented from signing by their teachers and parents, elementary school children will begin to sign with each other, and go on to do it even more in middle school and an overwhelming amount at the high school level. One teacher explained that "You can't help it (*shikata ga nai*)." From the teacher's perspective, easy topics at early grade levels can be explained using oral methods or pictures. However, upper-level students have a lot of difficulty with complex or abstract topics unless they are explained in sign. Yamashita-san, however, was mainstreamed from elementary school through high school, so she encountered very little signing before entering the Tsukuba College of Technology.

1990s

KN: Did you know how to sign when you were in school?
No, I didn't understand anything; I didn't know any signing at all back then. I might have known about signing when I was in elementary school or middle school, but I think back then that I thought signing wasn't something that some-

---

7. The proponents of the bilingual-bicultural educational method (Israelite, Ewoldt, and Hoffmeister 1992) would argue that it would be better for the children to attain a strong first-language (L1) in a sign language before attempting to learn an oral language (L2). This pedagogical philosophy obviously has its roots in bilingual education (Spanish, etc.) in North America and is not without its critics.

one like me used, but rather something that elderly people (ojīsan to obāsan; lit-erally: grandpas and grandmas) used. I thought that the way that deaf (rō) people communicate had changed. And that's why I thought I and other people in my generation didn't sign. I thought that was normal.

I think I first experienced the limits of speechreading in high school. When I was in elementary school or middle school, I thought I could simply ask the teachers to open their mouths a little wider. When I entered high school, I couldn't understand a single thing that the teachers said. I thought I had reached the limit of speechreading then.

I asked Yamashita-san whether she ever though of U-turning back to the school for the deaf. As the figures from the Kyoto School given in the previous chapter indicate, many mainstreamed deaf students return at the high school level because they cannot keep up with the "exam-hell" in regular high schools.

1990s

KN: Did you ever think of going back to the school for the deaf?
Never. I never thought once of going back to the school for the deaf. I think the reason for that was that I had many bad (kurushii) experiences when I was there in kindergarten. I didn't want to repeat those types of bad experiences again my-self, and my mother had heard that students at the school for the deaf were be-hind in their studies. I had accomplished everything up to now by myself, so I never thought of going back to the school for the deaf simply because I was falling behind in school. But I do remember thinking several times about going back to the school for the deaf when my relationships with my friends became difficult. But I thought the education I was getting at the regular school was the best.

After graduating from high school, Yamashita-san enrolled in the Tsukuba College of Technology (TCT). The school was founded in 1987 by the national government and accepted its first cohort of students in 1990. It is technically part of Tsukuba University, the preeminent national university sixty kilometers northeast of Tokyo. However, the only re-sources shared with the university are the physical education facilities. TCT is a three-year technical college for the blind and the deaf. Most of its deaf programs are vocational: Design, Mechanical Engineering, Architec-tural Engineering, Information Sciences, Electronic Engineering, and a General Education division.[8] In 1998, the year that I visited Yamashita-san, there were 168 students enrolled, 46 of whom were women.

8. The division for the visually impaired teaches: Acupuncture/Moxibustion (a tradi-tionally blind vocation); Physical Therapy; Computer Science; and General Education. In 1998, there were 128 blind students enrolled.

The General Education majors in both hearing and visually impaired divisions exist just on paper. In 1998, there were no students enrolled in either division in that major.

KN: Why did you decide to come here [to a deaf college]?
*Well, I was undecided for a long time, but I remember thinking at that time that
I was about to enter society as an adult. It would be nice if rather than entering
a regular college where I would have the same types of [communication] problems with my [hearing] friends, it would be nice if I came here and had an easier
time while discovering new interests in my life.*

*The reason I entered the Tsukuba Technical College was to meet other deaf
people and to expand my own horizons. Up to now, I had gone to regular schools,
and there were many times that I had always exhibited reticence toward hearing
people. I had never reflected much upon my own situation [as a deaf person]. By
entering this school, I though that I would not have to be so self-conscious about
other people and that I would be able to do the things that I enjoy doing. So I entered here and am in my studies.*

It was at Tsukuba College of Technology that Yamashita-san learned
how to sign for the first time. She is on the verge of coming to terms with
her identity as deaf; it is likely she will experience her own "deaf-shock"
soon.

KN: What did you think about learning how to sign?
*I had the impression that signing was old-fashioned (dasai), but it's become a bit
attractive to me now. I want to learn how to sign, but at this school, many of the
students in my same grade level don't sign.*
KN: Your classmates don't sign?
*Most of them went directly into regular schools. Three of them graduated from
schools from the deaf and were Recommended Students[9] here. But just because
you go to a school for the deaf doesn't mean that you use sign language.*
KN: Were your parents against you learning how to sign?
*I think they thought that way when I was in kindergarten, but now that I'm here
[at this college], my mother's thinking has changed a little. I think her rationale
is that since I'm able to communicate orally and all that's needed is for me to pay
attention to my pronunciation, I think she's happy with that and so it doesn't
matter if I learn signing at this point.*
KN: What do you plan on doing when you graduate?
*When I graduate, I don't think I'll want to work at a regular company. I have some
interest in deaf education and using my own experience in schools for the deaf,
would like to go into this field. But I still can't decide. I can't make up my mind.*
KN: One last question, have you ever heard of this group, D-Pro?
No, I've never heard of them, who are they? [I explain.] *Oh is that the case . . .
Do they do that on a regular basis? Daily? . . . Oh really . . . and what type of
activities do they do? . . .*

9. Most colleges have at least a two-tier system where regular students go through the
famous "exam hell." But there is usually at least one back door for "Recommended Entrance" (*suisen nyūgaku*) students who are allowed into the college on the personal rec-
ommendation of their high school principals. Of course, there are usually rumors of
other ways of entering college through other types of "recommendations," usually monetary.

> *Even if someone told me not to vocalize, I don't think I could do that. I was ed-*
> *ucated all my life in the oral method, to vocalize. If I was told not to vocalize, I*
> *don't think I could [communicate] properly.*

D-Pro, Deaf-Shock, and the New D-Groups

I was interested to know whether Yamashita-san had heard of D-Pro or other cultural Deaf groups, but they do not appear to be active yet at TCT. In other parts of Japan, some mainstreamed students are discovering their cultural Deaf identities as they become adults—when they enter college or when they hit the internal glass ceilings in their companies. The typical pattern is that they are invited into or join signing circles on campus or in their neighborhood. There they meet other deaf, hard-of-hearing, or "hearing-impaired" persons and gradually start to form an idea of themselves as deaf. At the same time, knowledge of American Deaf culture and politics has been imported to Japan, and it is these younger deaf students and adults who are the most keen on learning about how deaf identity is organized in the United States.

"Deaf Shock" is the name of an organization of the culturally Deaf in the Osaka area formed in the nineties. One of the members told me that its name comes from the feeling of shock that one gets when one realizes that he or she is a member of a cultural/linguistic minority and not merely disabled. "Deaf Shock" (*Defu Shokku*) itself is a loan word from English. In general, Deaf Shock and the new groups are notable in their use of American loan words and ASL loan signs. In their writings, they often use the roman character D to denote cultural Deafness and a culturally Deaf person. They identify as *"defu"* and reject the Japanese terms *"rōa"* and *"chōkaku shōgaisha."*

One of the interesting aspects of these "D-groups" or "Defu-groups" as they are known, is that not only are their members much younger than the JFD members but also there is very little intergenerational and intergroup contact with the older groups. Very few members of D-Pro (the principal group in Tokyo) are active members of the JFD or Tokyo Association of the Deaf and vice-versa. The separation is most striking when one attends D-Pro–sponsored events, since most of the audience is below the age of forty, whereas the opposite is usually the case at JFD meetings.

D-Pro itself was created in 1993 at the Ikaho Onsen, a famous hot spring in Gunma Prefecture, several hours north of Tokyo by train. Ironically, or perhaps deliberately, the group chose the same resort where the newly born Japanese Federation of the Deaf had its first postwar meeting in 1947. But from the beginning, D-Pro set itself up as something *different* from the JFD, a total break from the past, a new form of separatist deaf movement with the wish to introduce American-style identity politics into Japan.

D-Pro has been active in inviting prominent Deaf activists from the United States to Japan. The Deaf cultural activist M. J. Bienvenu has been their guest in the past, and in 1998 they invited the Deaf poet, linguist, and activist Clayton Valli. The age gap and lack of intergenerational ties was most apparent in Valli's case since he (in his late forties at the time) was easily the oldest person there, with most of his audience a full generation younger.

D-Pro and the other D-groups have been able to attract a growing number of younger deaf in the metropolitan areas. In taking an overtly American perspective, they also erect the same definitional boundaries between deaf and hard of hearing that we find in the United States and the same conceptualization of the deaf-of-deaf (deaf children of deaf parents) at the core of the Deaf community.

There is a process of "imagined community" building within deaf communities in Japan. Within the D-groups, signing is done without voicing or mouthing. This was not the version of signing used by the D-Pro members when they were still in high school, and so there is a process of language learning or alteration when they join the D-group. I often heard laments from former teachers of deaf students: "She had such a beautiful voice before she joined D-Pro. . . ." The tone of such comments almost made it seem as if the teachers thought D-Pro was a cult, and at least that was how many of the (hearing) teachers viewed it. Older deaf people approach D-Pro warily as well.[10]

Studying D-Pro

It was my original intention to focus on D-Pro for the fieldwork that led to this book. I was attracted to D-Pro because it seemingly represented a

10. Although it may draw the ire of D-Pro, the resemblance between D-Pro and the New New Religions (cults) is more than skin deep. In both cases, we have charismatic women leaders and a target population of highly educated students suffering from ennui over their existence. D-Pro offers the closeness of a tightly woven organization that sees itself as the carrier of the true Deaf and pure JSL spirit, dividing the world into neatly organized categories of the Deaf, Hard of Hearing, and Hearing. For comparative data, see Maeda (1997), Miyai (1997), or Metraux (1998). Another useful comparison would be with the "panic sites" described by Napier (1996).

new social movement—a phrase I use here both in the literal sense of a new type of social movement and in the technical sense of a social movement based on individual identity rather than group membership. America has been the birthplace of many new social movements which share many similarities in identity construction: feminist, environmentalist, gay/lesbian, for example. As mentioned before, the "Deaf" culture movement in the United States has successfully built on the frame of identity politics and minority civil rights established by these other groups.

In Japan, however, minorities have had a very difficult time establishing a foothold in politics and society. Two of the larger minorities groups, the resident Koreans and the Ainu, have argued for political power based on their non-Japaneseness, finding considerable external leverage that way. Other minorities, such as former Burakumin and gays and lesbians, have struggled over the issue of self-definition. The former Burakumin may face discrimination based on their legacy, but who are they now and what does that mean? Gays have faced the most social opprobrium not for homosexual acts, which, like most private acts in Japan, are largely ignored by society, but for their lack of appropriate public heteronormative ones, such as marriage and child rearing. Any minority group in Japan suffers from this lack of a minority frame to build upon. This is why D-Pro was exciting to me.

But in an ironic twist, it was that which attracted me to it that ultimately made it impossible to study D-Pro to the same degree as the JFD. For while the JFD encourages and indeed depends on a close working relationship between hearing people and deaf, D-Pro is an organization whose fundamental aim is to develop a separate but equal Deaf culture. While my stumbling signing was overlooked within the JFD, for D-Pro it was a painful illustration of how hearing people mangle signing for their own purposes, twisting control of the language from deaf people. It was a sign (quite literally) of oppression. I was also more visible as a hearing person in the close-knit quarters of D-Pro than I was within the much larger JFD. Although I interviewed the key leaders, attended several meetings (business meetings as well as cultural events), and read all of their publications including their early newsletters, my access to D-Pro was limited compared to the JFD. Because I worked in the JFD Tokyo office, I had a good sense of the daily rhythm of life that I never managed to find with D-Pro. A thorough ethnography of D-Pro and the other D groups in Japan remains to be done by either an American or Japanese Deaf scholar, a reminder to "native" scholars such as myself that there are always multiple layers and intersectionalities within our home countries that we must negotiate.

Comparisons with Brazilian *Nikkeijin* and North Koreans in Japan

Other native scholars have been struggling with the issues of minority identity in Japan. Gaku Tsuda has written on the situation of Brazilian *Nikkeijin* (Japanese descendants) and the reconstruction of their ethnic and national identities as revealed through performance. In the late 1800s, Japanese emigrated to Brazil seeking better lives. A hundred years later, their descendants returned to Japan as migrant workers. Although their ancestors were Japanese, many of the Nikkeijin had totally assimilated to Brazilian society, and it was only changes in Japanese immigration law that made it easier for descendants of Japanese to return as temporary workers that brought them back to their "homeland":

> Not only are the Japanese-Brazilians ethnically excluded as foreigners in Japan, they become acutely aware of their Brazilian cultural differences, experience ethnic discrimination, and recognize many of the negative aspects of Japanese cultural behavior. In response to such negative ethnic experiences, many Japanese-Brazilians experience a resurgence of Brazilian national sentiment in Japan as they distance themselves from the Japanese, assert their cultural differences, and strengthen their Brazilian national identity. In this manner, the dislocations of migration can produce a form of deterritorialized nationalism where national loyalties are articulated outside of the territorial boundaries of the nation-state. However, ethnic or national identity as a form of self-consciousness is not simply a matter of internal experience, but is actively displayed, demonstrated, and enacted in practice. The signifying nature of practice culturally constitutes power relationships by either consolidating existing hegemonies or generating resistance. (Tsuda 2000:56)

Replacing "ethnic" with "deaf," we arrive at much the same scenario that causes the younger deaf to reach out to the United States for new forms of identity politics. Without the unifying trope of the *dankai no sedai* generation, they feel an ennui and dislocation from both the mainstream and the older deaf generations.

Generational difference plays a significant role in the twentieth-century changes for the deaf. We can draw parallels between second-generation and third-generation North Koreans in Japan described by

Sonia Ryang (1997) and the third-generation deaf described in this book in the effort to find their true ethnicity in their past or in other nations. Ryang's description of the facility by which third-generation North Koreans in Japan are able to play with their "Korean-ness" is perhaps indicative of what will happen with the next generation of deaf youth.

Conclusion: Identity in the Post-Mainstreaming Generation

The post-mainstreaming generation has had to contend with the lack of identity that many younger deaf feel as well as the competing new identities that are emerging from groups such as D-Pro. They are caught between the Scylla of apathy and the Charybdis of radicalism. Donald Grushkin writes about a very similar phenomena facing the hard of hearing in the United States (2003), a category that in many ways resonates with the youth generation in Japan. Ironically, much of this new activism centering around cultural deafness is a result of a greater acceptance of deaf people and a drop in economic and social discrimination against the deaf due to JFD activities over the past half-century. But others are likely to view D-Pro, like all new identity-based movements, as being too fervent at times, and there is a difficulty in building a history when one is building a new movement at the same time. D-Pro members struggle with constructing themselves both as Deaf and against the older generation.

The D-groups, especially D-Pro, have come in for some harsh criticism, mostly from deaf people in the older age groups and from hearing people related to the deaf community. Their thinking is too "American" and they simply "copy American Deaf ways," or they are "too radical" or "too exclusionary." One teacher at the leading school for the deaf said he felt the group was "leaning toward the right wing" (*uyoku-teki*). This statement at first did not make sense until one of my deaf informants decoded it for me. By "right wing," the teacher meant nationalistic. D-Pro advocates a proud ethnic Deaf identity that could be seen as ideologically not so far from the right-wing militarists with their sound trucks blaring in central Tokyo arguing for national pride, the expulsion of foreigners, and the return of the Northern Islands.

It is difficult to tell whether this movement will put down roots or not. Certainly the soil is fertile enough with the post-mainstreaming generation hungering for some sense of identity. And in the last five years since the turn of the millennium, D-Pro has changed its strategies by deemphasizing the overt use of American Deaf movement literature and has tried to become more natively Japanese. For example, they have moved away from the use of the loan word *defu* and have begun to use the term *rōsha* instead. They are active participants in the Japanese Deaf History Association (*Nihon Rōshi Gakkai*). The group has grown in size and become much more organizationally coherent.

However, as of 2005, D-Pro has not yet incorporated as a nonprofit organization. Because of its small membership, the national and prefectural governments do not recognize D-Pro as an organization representing the needs of people with hearing impairments, so it has yet to receive *itaku* contracts to run sign interpreter programs or provide deaf social welfare services (which would in any case be anathema to its political goal of being separate yet equal).

This lack of government recognition has limited D-Pro's appeal to those who are solely interested in its message of identity politics, unlike the JFD, which is also able to appeal to people because it provides social and information services. In the next chapter, we will see how the generational rift between the JFD and D-Pro has also developed along linguistic lines. Both groups, as well as the national public television network, are struggling for the power to be able to define what is called "Japanese Sign Language" (*Nihon shuwa*).

Postscript

In 2004, as I was preparing the final manuscript of this book, I learned that at age twenty-five, Yamashita-san had just been hired at the Suginami Middle School for the Deaf in Tokyo as a math teacher (*JDN* May 1, 2004:2). This is probably the ideal location for her to make use of her skills and talents, and to work toward making sure that other deaf children do not feel the self-consciousness and separation from her peers that she did as a mainstreamed child.

CHAPTER ELEVEN

Language Wars and Language Politics

*Or, How an Itinerant Anthropologist Introduced a
New Sign into the Japanese Sign Lexicon*

Location: Hotel Ikeda, Atami Hot Springs (100 km. south of Tokyo)

*Event: End-of-Year Central Committee Meeting of the JFD Research Group
for Defining and Promulgating Japanese Sign Language*

The conference room at the hotel was moderately large by Japanese standards. Four long tables were arranged in a square in the middle of the room. Sowa-san, the senior JFD staff member in charge of the meeting, deaf himself since an early age, started setting up the A/V equipment, an S-VHS video camera and television. The hotel staff members brought in a coffee pot and cups. Shigihara-san, a young hearing woman who was my supervisor at the JFD, and I arranged the chairs, six on each side of the table. Sowa-san asked for the blinds to be closed. It was a shame because the windows presented a stunning view of the deep azure ocean and Ōshima Island in the distance, but the sun shone so brightly off the surf that it would backlight the signers at the tables and hurt everyone's eyes. With a sigh, Shigihara-san and I closed the blinds.

This was the 1997 end-of-the-year meeting of the Central Committee of the JFD's Research Group for Defining and Promulgating Japanese Sign Language, an *itaku* project from the Ministry of Health and Social Welfare. The Research Group was responsible for coming up with new sign words, describing and defining them, and promulgating them, usually by publishing them in a series of books called *New signs*, but also by teaching them at JFD-led teacher-training seminars across the nation.

During the year, each regional block of the JFD was assigned to think up new sign words. For example, the Hokkaido Block was responsible for new "newspaper" words. They scanned the daily newspapers looking for vocabulary items that were not currently in the JFD's Japanese Sign dictionaries, wrote them down, and brainstormed new signs. The Central Committee's job was to look over these suggested new signs and decide whether to adopt them. Rarely were the signs adopted without much discussion and modification. It was a lexicographer's dream—creating a new language. We had lugged several boxes of reference books from the JFD's Tokyo office: thick Japanese language dictionaries, etymologies, Japanese Sign dictionaries, and even a copy of an ASL dictionary.

The committee came to order. As junior staff facilitators (and women), Shigihara-san and I sat in the corner strategically near the coffee pot so we could fill any empty cups around the table. Shigihara-san took some notes, but she also interpreted for me. While I had been in the field a few months, I had not picked up enough Japanese Sign at that point to understand some of the regional dialects and idiolects being used, so her help was appreciated.

Takada Eiichi, the then-president of the JFD and in his mid-sixties, opened the meeting with a few quick comments. As usual, Takada-san spoke while signing, so no interpreting was needed. He was one of the young leaders in the 1960s who, after graduating from Kyoto University, took over the JFD and infused it with its current political activism, vesting in it a language of civil rights for the deaf. He was famous, both nationally for speaking in front of the Diet on deaf issues, and internationally for his work with the World Federation of the Deaf.

Sadahiro-sensei, a hearing man in his late sixties or seventies, and the next ranking officer in the group, then got up and gave a quick speech as well. He signed without voicing, so Shigihara-san interpreted for me. Kawai-san, the then-leader of the Tokyo Block (deaf himself, and slightly paralyzed from polio[1]), got up and gave a few short words, again vocalizing while signing.[2] Kawai-san was also one of Takada-san's co-conspirators in the period of fervent political activism in the 1960s and 1970s.

Sowa-san gave a short introduction to the background of the group.

---

1. Indicative of the bluntly descriptive nature of sign-names as well as the closeness of the community, Kawai-san's sign-name depicts his weakened legs—it can best be translated using the non-PC term "crippled."

2. Yes, it is ironic that I needed interpreting for the hearing person and not for the deaf ones.

Since 1980, the JFD has been receiving an *itaku* contract from the Ministry of Health and Social Welfare that has been funding this research group. One of the major concerns of the *itaku* project was producing new words, and one requirement was to create at least a hundred new words for the ministry each year. This the group presented in a series of reports to the ministry as well as the aforementioned *New Signs* books that come out each year as a result. The research group had to show the ministry how it was accomplishing its three assigned tasks: creating new signs, popularizing their use, and establishing a solid lexicon of sign vocabulary.

We then did a round of introductions. Twenty-two people were at the meeting that day, including the three JFD staffers, Sowa-san, Shigihara-san, and myself, as anthropologist participant-observer. Five of us were hearing, including Shigihara-san, Sadahiro-sensei, and myself. The majority of people in the room were in their fifties, sixties, and seventies, and the number of famous names (for that generation) in the community was astonishing. This was a handpicked committee that included only the people the JFD felt had both the knowledge and the social status within the community to come up with new signs.

Sadahiro-sensei was a teacher at a Hiroshima school for the deaf. He was one of the first to really recognize the utility of signing in general education in the postwar period. He has served as an interpreter and ally of the JFD for over forty years. His story, narrated to me by Shigihara-san on the side, is that he was first assigned to the deaf school in Hiroshima out of the blue; he had previously had no background in deaf education. This was in the 1940s, right after the war. Apparently over a third of Sadahiro-sensei's co-workers at the old Hiroshima school have since died of radiation poisoning from the Bomb.

In any case, as a new teacher Sadahiro-sensei noticed that some of the teachers could communicate very well with the students, and others could not. He asked the students themselves, and they said that it took a while before they got used to speechreading a new teacher, and some people were more difficult than others. He wondered how they communicated out of school and saw that the students used signing with each other. The school policy was that signing was forbidden, but the students still used it inside the dorms, where few hearing teachers lurked. Sadahiro-sensei decided to learn it himself. There were of course no formal sign classes, so he asked the students to show him. It was not, in his terms, "proper signing," but he saw that it really worked to liven up the classroom. Sadahiro-sensei was instrumental in setting up the first sign interpreter program in Japan. He also was the one who helped them find the first JFD Tokyo office, a cramped twelve-by-twelve-foot cubicle.

Other people in the room included Takeshima-san (deaf; sixties) who used to be the director of the Tokyo office and Iizuka-san (hearing; sixties), who was the office manager under Takeshima-san. Both of these people were influential in the early JFD era, and we met them in chapter 7. Itō Masao (deaf; seventies) was a leading scholar within the deaf community and is cited many times in this book. The list goes on. The room was a veritable blue-ribbon collection of famous twentieth-century figures in JFD history.

The Hokkaido Block leader started his presentation. The group had been scanning the daily newspapers looking for new words in circulation. Japanese is a voracious and adaptive language. Not only has it swallowed the writing systems and lexicon of classical Chinese, but also English, Portuguese, German, and French. New words flood into the Japanese language at an incredible pace, fueled by widespread literacy, a high educational standard, a common myth of cultural homogeneity, and powerful media companies. Words are fads in Japan: *ryūkōgo* ("word in fashion") refers to these faddish words which, just like Chanel handbags and Eminem CDs, are enormously popular one year, seemingly coming out of nowhere, but by the next year are *shigo*, dead words. All of Japan, seemingly, is caught up in these new words. All except for the deaf, who are not subject to the same hegemonic media assault. But the first act of hegemony is to operate through desire. And in this case, it was the desire of the deaf community to want these new words, and the desire of the Ministry of Social Welfare not to have anyone left out of the social pack.

A New Sign for "Digital"

The first word chosen was a loan word from English: *dejitaru* or "digital." The late nineties was the beginning of the "digital boom" in Japan with digital cameras, digital video discs (DVD), digital video camcorders (DV), and so forth.

Digital. How to sign digital. The Hokkaido Block had previously brainstormed this and videotaped their suggestion: *The left hand is held at chest level with the index finger pointing up (as if signing "1") while the right-hand index finger makes a sine wavelike gesture next to it.* The presenter stopped the videotape and nervously sat down. We began discussion.

There was a bit of confusion. People did not understand the 1–sine-wave thing. The leader stood up and described analog and digital: how digital waveforms approximate analog ones, thus the "1" and a sine wave. We scurried to the reference books to look this up. The first criticism came up: "it looks too much like 'Amway.'" This was right before the 1998 Nagano Winter Olympics, of which Amway was a major sponsor. "What does Amway look like?" asked another committee member. "Amway is a 'd' finger held up with a sine wave next to it," was the reply.[3] Since one of the goals was distinct signs that cannot be confused with one another, the Hokkaido "1"–sine wave suggestion was struck down as being too close to an existing sign. People started to think about other ways to sign "digital."

Knowing that I am a techno-nerd, the committee member sitting next to me asked me what I thought "digital" looks like. I was surprised. I was there just as an observer, and I did not think anyone would be interested in an opinion from a hearing person, but I gave it my best shot: "Well, I would sign it '10101010'," fingerspelling the 1–0–1–0–1–0 on my right hand, right to left in the American style.

The member thinks this is a great suggestion and brings it to the board's notice. I'm a bit shocked. They end up modifying the sign, but the new sign for *digital* becomes: *on the left hand, the "1" sign is made, on the right hand, the "0" sign is made. Move the "0" back and forward in front of you as if to indicate motion in the sign.* I am finally published, but would my adviser approve? Had I just broken the Prime Directive of Anthropology?

Creating New Signs in Japanese Sign

In a 1997 editorial essay, then-JFD president Takada Eiichi noted that the federation was unique in actively and deliberately creating new signs to fill out the lexicon. In his discussions with American and European deaf leaders, he had learned that there were no equivalent language-building programs in these countries. He argued for the importance of the project in order to help bring deaf people in Japan into mainstream society.

In American Sign Language, a large portion of loan words (words borrowed from spoken/written English) are fingerspelled: you spell out

3. "1" and "d" look essentially the same in that the index finger points up, but with "1" the remaining fingers are in a tight fist, while for "d" they are held in a loose open fist.

61 | デジタル

● 丸めた右手を人差指を立てた左手の横を通って前の方に２回動かす

Source: New Signs. The Report of the 1997 Research Group for
Standardizing Sign Language. Tokyo: Japanese Federation of the Deaf. pp. 36.

平成 9 年度標準手話研究所事業報告書。
東京：全日本ろうあ連盟。pp 36。

Figure 11.1. A new sign for "Digital." Used with permission.

each letter using the manual alphabet, for example, P-H-D or B-A-N-K. Although faculty at Gallaudet University and the other American colleges with large numbers of deaf students invent and disseminate new signs as they teach consecutive generations of deaf students, there is not enough media or organizational hegemony in the United States to create a solid new lexicon of signs. Furthermore, ASL has optimized fingerspelling to the point where a fingerspelled word is just a blur on the hands, just as fast as a sign word. ASL signers can "read" fingerspelling at a tremendously fast pace.[4]

In addition to fingerspelling, ASL also has a tradition of *initialized* signs. ASL has very strong roots in deaf education (in France, then later in the United States). Over two hundred years ago, a French educator,

4. When I took speed-fingerspelling at Gallaudet University in 1995, we were taught to recognize sequences of fingerspelled handshapes: M-A-N, E-R, P-R-O, and so forth. Both when fingerspelling and reading fingerspelled words, you used these as building blocks to speed-reading and spelling. My ASL tutor told an anecdote about her deaf daughter knowing that the refrigerator was fingerspelled R-E-F but not being able to connect that to the actual spelling of "refrigerator." Other fingerspelled words like BANK or DOG have similarly turned into very rapid handshapes and lost much of their immediate association with fingerspelling. This is perhaps similar to the way certain loan words in Japanese have lost their foreignness, *tempura* being a prime example. Unit 4 of Valli and Lucas (1995) discusses this form of lexicalized fingerspelling and loan signs.

the Abbé de L'Epée, established the manual (signing) method of deaf pedagogy. L'Epée used initialized signs, signs that took the first letter of a spoken word and matched it with a sign morpheme to produce sign equivalents of spoken words. For example, from the basic sign that means "group" or "gathering of people" made by moving your two cupped hands in a semi-circle, you can develop: "F"-group = FAMILY, "C"-group = CLASS, "G"-group = GROUP, "I"-group = institution and so forth by fingerspelling the F, C, or G letters with your hands as you make the circle. This French system was carried over to the United States by Laurent Clerc, who helped Thomas Gallaudet establish the first school for the deaf in Hartford. Many ASL words are developed using this initialized sign system, and it has become a basic means for new words to be added to the lexicon (that is, most new signs in ASL use some form of initialized sign structure). So much is this so that if you see a new sign, you can do a morphemic breakdown of its "initialized" component (fingerspelling letter) and base morpheme to deduce what the sign means.[5]

Unfortunately, Japanese Sign has never had a similar base in the classroom since the Ministry of Education never officially permitted its use in the classroom. This would not be an issue if Japanese fingerspelling could be used to sign words that were not in the lexicon. Unfortunately, Japanese fingerspelling is a clumsy system. ASL fingerspelling tends to be linear across the chest. As you spell right to left, your hand makes very few up-and-down motions and there is limited wrist movement. This is a major cause of ASL's fingerspelling speed and efficiency. On the other hand (so to speak), Japanese fingerspelling is up and down, left and right, back and forth as it tries to compensate for the 46 characters in the kana syllabary and voicing markers. This makes for a fingerspelling that is tiresome to sign and even more tiresome to read.[6]

Furthermore, unlike spoken Japanese, which has intonational markers, or written Japanese, for which there are Kanji and two kana systems to differentiate between homonyms of native words and foreign loan

5. This system of a fingerspelling component that indicates the first letter of the English word and a base ASL morpheme that indicates the class of meaning seems remarkably similar to the way Kanji characters are put together: a root radical that indicates the class that the character belongs to (category of words related to plants, trees, humans, etc.) and another component that indicates the pronunciation of the character.

6. There are also many wrist motions in Japanese fingerspelling. This contributes to many repetitive stress disorders among interpreters (carpal tunnel syndrome; tennis elbow, etc.), who are the ones who fingerspell the most (fingerspelling is not nearly as common in Japanese sign as in ASL).

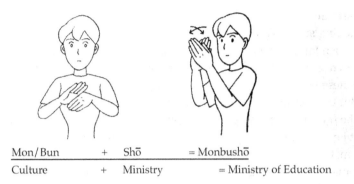

Mon/Bun	+	Shō	= Monbushō
Culture	+	Ministry	= Ministry of Education

Figure 11.2. Signing *Monbushō* (Ministry of Education). Source: Yonekawa (1997: 1968). Used with permission.

words, Japanese fingerspelling cannot differentiate between words with the same syllabic spelling: the fingerspelled word HANA can mean nose, flower, or beginning, for example. It remains a clumsy system and although attempts, such as the Tochigi fingerspelling method which speeds up fingerspelling, have been made to make it more efficient, these have not caught on.

Aside from fingerspelling unknown words, Japanese sign has some other methods for creating new words. One is the obvious use of compound signs. Both native signs and the constructed Kanji signs are often used for this purpose. One example would be the sign for Monbushō (the Ministry of Education), shown in Figure 11.2.

Unfortunately, Japanese signers do not like this type of compound sign (this is true of ASL signers as well). While compound signs are used for proper nouns, the preference is to have a single sign for all other noun forms. A key issue is the speed of signing and comprehension. There are few pauses between words when signing and a tendency to treat a single sign as a whole word or signifier, so it is hard to distinguish a compound sign from two separate signs functioning on their own.

Why the Need to Create New Signs?

Why does the JFD feel compelled to invent new signs and publish them? The Ministry of Welfare gave the organization an *itaku* contract in 1980 in order to increase the vocabulary of deaf signers, to make sure that they were able to keep up with contemporary Japanese (both the people and the language), and to standardize Japanese Sign, helping both interpreters and deaf alike in intercommunicating. Furthermore, creating a matching sign lexicon furthers the education ministry's desire to firmly establish Japanese as the national language as well as helping the JFD in its own goals of blurring the difference between Japanese Sign and the Japanese language, as discussed in chapter 2.

But there is another, more profound reason; one that is more unsettling to the JFD and one that it does not publicly talk about.[7] For despite stating that Japanese Sign is any sign communication used by any deaf person in Japan, the JFD is very protective of Japanese Sign. After all, the JFD's most popular series of sign textbooks is titled *Our signs (Watashi-tachi no Shuwa)*.[8] Within the last two decades, there have been two threats to the JFD's over Japanese Sign, one from the radical deaf and one from well-meaning hearing persons. With its centrist and nonexclusionary position, the JFD is caught between a rock and a hard place.

The Rock: D-Pro on the Right

As we have seen, D-Pro is a cultural deaf organization created in Japan in 1993 by a group of young deaf people strongly influenced by the bicultural/bilingual model of deaf society promulgated by cultural Deaf activists and scholars in the United States (cf. Padden 1980). Here is D-Pro's own description (from a undated handout in English) of "bilingualism/biculturalism":

> Deaf people have two languages, spoken and written Japanese and Japanese sign. We live in two cultures, the culture of hearing people and the culture of the Deaf. Even though Deaf people have two languages and two cultures, Japanese sign and the culture of the Deaf have always been regarded as inferior and worthless, ignored and not respected. Even Deaf people themselves have believed themselves to be worthless and inferior.
> Now, Deaf people have come to understand their own language, Japanese Sign Language, is as perfect a language as any other language in the world and is not inferior at all. They have realized that even if their own

7. One unstated private reason would be that bureaucracies exist to replicate themselves. That is, once the committee was assigned the goal of creating at least 100 new signs a year, that in itself became its raison d'être. Certainly, although no one will admit it, some of the new signs created by the working group are fluff signs, designed to meet the year-end quota. This is no different from any other nonprofit which has to hustle at the end of the year to meet state contract goals.

8. The first-person plural possessive pronoun comes across more strongly in Japanese than in English. *Ours* means *not-yours*. When the first volume of *Our Signs* was published in 1969, Japanese Sign was in a considerably more marginal position in society than it is now, and the JFD was much more politically radical.

way of communication, activity, behavior, value, belief and so on, is different from that of hearing people, who are the majority, they do not have to feel inferior and/or guilty. These differences are the result of "cultural difference." Of course, it is important for the Deaf people to acquire Japanese and the culture of hearing people. Bilingualism/biculturalism is the philosophy that those two languages and two cultures should be equally, but separately, respected. (D-Pro, n.d.)

One of the central beliefs of D-Pro is that there exists a pure Japanese Sign Language. It is signed without mouthing or vocalizing words and does not use the Japanese grammar system. It is a visual-spatial language and is the true language of Japanese deaf persons.

D-Pro has begun codifying this pure JSL grammar through various textbooks it has published, and its position makes one thing clear: the signing used by the JFD leadership, the style of speaking while signing, is not *Japanese Sign Language*.

This has been stated by D-Pro leaders on numerous occasions. While I was at the Tokyo office of the JFD, we would often have people who attended D-Pro lectures come in and tell us the latest atrocities. As noted in the introduction, the D-Pro leadership like to call the JFD "a Hard-of-Hearing people's group (*nanchōsha dantai*)." Certainly, from the outside, and looking only at the leaders (many of whom, admittedly, were late-deafened), the JFD is not "pure deaf." The JFD is proud that it accepts anyone with a hearing loss, regardless of their signing capabilities or deaf heritage. JFD leaders are shocked when a D-Pro member lectures that only people born of deaf parents know true JSL. They are also shocked when they are called "hard of hearing," when they all identify as deaf.

I noted in the introduction how at one of these horror-story sessions, the director of the Tokyo Office threw up her hands and exclaimed, "That's sign fascism! (*sore wa shuwa fashizumu yo!*)" She spoke out loud at the same time she signed this, so according to D-Pro, she was not signing JSL even in her moment of ultimate exasperation. To mix political metaphors slightly here, Pierre Bourdieu once described this type of imagined linguistic purity as an "illusion of linguistic communism" (1991:43).[9] Whether fascist or communist, it is clear that politics and political control over definitions are at the heart of these language claims. These are all forms of what Woolard and Schieffelin (1994) call "language ideologies."

9. In a similar vein, in a video by BBC TV (1997), a deaf Nicaraguan man states: "Our [sign] language is not something we got from other countries, *it is pure Nicaraguan*. It is ours" (emphasis added).

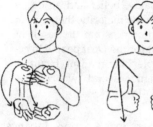

Figure 11.3. Signing "Rich" Source: Yonekawa (1997: 330, 845). Used with permission.

JFD "RICH"
(FAT-WITH-MONEY)

D-Pro "RICH"
(BUSINESS-SUIT)

D-Pro members have been challenging the JFD's control of Japanese Sign in other areas as well. At the research group meeting described above, one of the participants lamented that while he was demonstrating new signs at a teacher-training seminar, suddenly a D-Pro member challenged him on the sign for RICH-PERSON. The JFD lists RICH in its dictionary using a sign best described as "FAT-WITH-MONEY" while the D-Pro member insisted that the real sign was "BUSINESS-SUIT." The JFD member was clearly disturbed by this development.[10]

In one of the great ironies of the situation, Kimura Harumi, the prominent leader of D-Pro, is also the head teacher at the only national interpreter-training program in Japan. Funded by the Ministry of Health and Social Welfare, this program is run out of the National Rehabilitation Center for the Disabled (NRCD) in Saitama Prefecture, just north of Tokyo.[11] This is cause for no small chagrin at the JFD. Unlike the JFD-led

10. This is most probably just a regional difference in Japanese sign, although I have seen only the FAT-WITH-MONEY variation myself and never BUSINESS-SUIT used in the context of RICH. In private, many signers will compare how they sign various words, but a public challenge is very rare indeed. That the D-Pro member would challenge a JFD member (both deaf themselves) was unheard of. And that the JFD member would emphasize that the challenger was D-Pro, in and of itself, is also significant. Both D-Pro and JFD see themselves in opposition to each other.

One of the interesting things is that the JFD does not highlight the rich regional variation in Japanese Sign. For example, there are at least three different ways to sign "NAME" depending on where you live and went to school. Most people know the variations since you see them all the time. But even the largest sign dictionary published by the JFD has only one sign for "NAME," and the same goes for the other signs with large regional variation.

11. All of the prefectural interpreter-training programs are run by JFD affiliates. It is odd that the government chose to put Ms. Kimura, a very young woman by Japanese standards (late twenties), in charge of the national interpreter program. It's even odder, since the government likes to take centrist positions, and Ms. Kimura is famous for being radical. The story behind this placement is not one which I was able to elicit.

interpreter courses where the interpreters learn to interpret using a grammar that closely approximates the spoken sentences being interpreted and to mouth the words at the same time (to facilitate speechreading of unknown words); the NRCD course has the interpreters closed-mouthed and using a spatial grammatical system—what D-Pro calls pure JSL.

The victims in this case are the interpreters who go through the NRCD course. The program prefers hearing people who have relatively little sign knowledge (and so are not "infected" with the JFD's "hard-of-hearing" way of signing). They are taught through the bilingual/bicultural model (which emphasizes differences between Deaf culture and hearing culture) and learn to sign in the manner described above.

But once they graduate, they fall again in the domain of the JFD, since the JFD controls almost all of the interpreter dispatch centers and JFD members are the ones most likely to request interpreter services (because of sheer numerical majority). The negative response to the NRCD interpreters is quite strong. The older deaf have complained to me that they cannot understand the (new) signs, and that since the words are not mouthed, they cannot speechread them either. They are not able to understand the nonlinear grammar system the interpreters use. As a result, not many NRCD interpreters are able to get jobs at interpreter dispatch centers unless they are retrained to sign in the more mainstream style.

If the fundamental focus of the JFD is on equality, the fundamental focus of D-Pro is on difference. This has two facets, the focus on culture building (separatism) and the focus on oppression and discrimination. For D-Pro, interaction between different groups leads to fundamental inequalities. The language of communication itself becomes the basis of oppression:

> Kimura: If we [Deaf] try to interact with hard of hearing or late-deafened persons on an equal basis, sim-com is the method of communication that we [have to] use. That is the very definition of oppression (*masani yoku-atsu*). It is biased in one direction. Of course, I hope that someday we are able to interact on an equal basis, that's what should happen. . . . I understand Hasegawa-san's position to be an example of Assimilation-type Discrimination (*dōka-gata sabetsu*) (Uenō 1996:118).[12]

---

12. *Dōka* (assimilation), and more specifically, *dōwa* (social integration) are loaded terms that refer to the policy of social integration of former burakumin outcastes. Strictly speaking, *dōkagata-sabetsu* or the process of discrimination (*sabetsu*) through assimilation is an oxymoron. Etymologically, *sabetsu* refers to the creation of difference or disparity. Unless of course, D-Pro is arguing that deaf Japanese are essentially different from hearing Japanese and any attempt to make them the same would be an inherent violation of their civil rights, which seems to be the case.

The cultural and linguistic divide between the generations is quite severe. For while D-Pro insists that there is a separate Deaf culture that involves sign language and the embodiment of deafness, the JFD leadership for the most part dismisses the idea of a separate deaf culture. According to the JFD, signing is how its members communicate, but language itself does not constitute culture. The deaf Japanese of the JFD do not see themselves as culturally apart from other Japanese. They are deaf and they need to sign to communicate with other people, but otherwise they are the same as everyone else. In response, D-Pro labels this an assimilationist type of discrimination.

The JFD's goal in creating and disseminating new signs is to unify the deaf community—both internally with a shared lexicon and with the larger Japanese nation. The emphasis on having "current terms" so that deaf individuals do not feel outside of contemporary discourse is important for both the JFD and the Ministry of Health and Welfare. Both have a vested interested in the deaf community's being seen as part of the Japanese nation and speaking the national tongue. At one level, this is a fundamentally unifying strategy derived from general Marxist principles of not splitting the proletariat, although it has an ironically nationalistic aspect.

D-Pro's strategy has been to conduct a systematic analysis of grammar, differentiating between what is just "sim-com" (they use the English term referring to signing while simultaneously voicing using a spoken grammar system) and what they see as "pure JSL." This allows the to divide the community into those who sign using pure JSL and those who do not, an essentially divisive strategy that separates the new activist generation from the older assimilationist generation.

The Hard Place: NHK on the Left

Although defining the lexicon has been a key strategic goal, the JFD finds itself battling another entity that threatens its control of Japanese sign: the quasi-public broadcasting television network, NHK. Since 1983, NHK has been broadcasting two television shows using sign: *Everyone's Sign*[13] (a weekly hour-long sign language course) and *The Sign News* (a fifteen-minute daily news show).[14]

---

13. The JFD's textbook series is *Our Signs*, where "our" is clearly intended to indicate the deaf—whereas the title of NHK's show clearly redistributes ownership to all Japanese.

14. NHK also has a show that airs issues of importance to people with disabilities, including special segments on deafness.

Although it would seem that *Everyone's Sign* would be the most immediate source of threat, it is not. The level of sign taught is relatively basic, and it helps popularize signing, so there is no issue there. In fact, many JFD members often appear as guest instructors on *Everyone's Sign*.

The real threat is the *Sign News* program. This short program is eclectic. It takes video footage from the main news program, pulls the highlights, and has newscasters give the news in Japanese Sign. All of the signing is both open- captioned and overdubbed or simultaneously voiced.

This is where the danger is. *Sign News* takes the daily headlines and translates them into sign, but there are always new words popping up in the Japanese vocabulary that do not have signs assigned to them yet. *Sign News* has to work around this problem, which is especially severe for a news program (terms that have arisen just recently, for example, include SARS, Mad Cow, Islamist, Coalition Provisional Authority, Long Term Care Insurance, and Six Party Talks). Like most other signers, the *News* newscasters eschew fingerspelling; in any case no one can fingerspell at the same speed that the voiceover is reading the text, so there is no point. So the newscasters have to invent new signs and ways of expressing new ideas.

What intensifies the problem is that with the open captioning and overdubbing, the *Sign News* is an ideal way to learn Japanese sign. It is as if you were trying to learn a foreign language and always had a running transliteration into your own language. The ratings for the *News* are abysmally low, but a good number of the viewers are interpreters and teachers at schools for the deaf (while staying in many homes, I never saw a deaf family turn to the *News*; most said that it was too much of a bother to watch it).[15] However, any new sign that the *News* uses, the interpreters and teachers pick up, and I have seen interpreters sharing signs that they had seen on the previous night's *News*.

Most of the newscasters have been hearing interpreters themselves. The JFD's concern has been that hearing people are creating new signs at the *News* without the feedback of the deaf community. Of course, because the news must go on, the *Sign News* is in a tough position. That is why a central goal of the JFD's Japanese Sign research group has been creating new signs for terms used in the media, but they will always inherently be behind the *News*.

15. Of the fifteen–minute program, only about five minutes are dedicated to headline news. You would be better off scanning the newspaper headlines for information. There is a complex politics as to why the *News* exists. Basically NHK was pressured into it because of the international decade of the disabled.

In 1995, NHK hired a native signer for the *News*. Born in 1967 in Yamagata Prefecture, Nasu Hideaki lost his hearing when he was two years
old from a high fever. He went to deaf schools for his entire elementary
and secondary education, as well as learning sign from an older deaf
person in his neighborhood. D-Pro would say he signs pure JSL, since he
does not use a Japanese grammar system and certainly does not voice.
When he signs the news, he uses very visual-spatial language with lots
of classifiers rather than discrete words to make his point. NHK has an
interpreter voice what he is saying as well as open-captioning the news
script. The reaction to him has been mixed.[16]

Research by Yoshizawa Shōzō at the Tochigi School for the Deaf casts
some light on this complex situation. He ran a study (1996) of deaf viewers in Tochigi where he showed two clips from the *Sign News*. One was a
hearing interpreter who used a sequential sign form, while the other was
Nasu-san who used spatial-sign. Yoshizawa analyzed their comprehension and retention rates.

The results are interesting.[17] For the interpreter who signed in sequential signs (using Japanese grammar), the deaf subjects were better able to
explain in written Japanese what she had signed. In contrast, they had
trouble writing down in Japanese sentences the content of Nasu-san's
segment. However, they better understood what Nasu-san was talking
about, even if they could not write it in Japanese. Yoshizawa's interpretation of these results are that most Japanese deaf people have had many
years of contact with sequential Japanese signing in many settings, including high school and the workplace. They are used to seeing these
signs and immediately transliterating them in their heads, so that they
can write them down. But they have very little comprehension of material presented in this fashion, especially if it is complex or at a fast pace,
as during a news segment.

They are used to seeing Nasu-san's type of sign, because it is the informal
type used among deaf people themselves, but they rarely have seen it used
in a formal setting such as the news. So they have more trouble explaining
(in written Japanese) what was said, even if they have better comprehension at a deeper level. Thus the issue is one of translation and bilingualism.

---

16. He would be described as using "*dentōteki-shuwa*" (traditional sign language) or
"*rōashateki shuwa*" (deaf-person's sign language) in contrast to *gendai no shuwa* (contemporary sign).

17. There is an added complication that he conducted his research in Tochigi Prefecture, where the graduates of the Tochigi School for the Deaf sign with a dialect distinct
from other signers in Japan and one that is grammatically closer to spoken Japanese.

This is indeed a complicated situation, for many older deaf people will tell you that they prefer the sequential form, especially when used by hearing people, even if they do not fully understand it. Situations like this are often referred to as diglossic, the existence of high and low forms of a language, especially in the context of colonialism and literacy (cf. Ferguson 1964[1959]; Aucamp 1978; Alrabaa 1986; Errington 1991, 1992). The political terrain of diglossia is just starting to emerge in Japan, but it is rapidly solidifying along territorial lines.[18]

The Fifth Column: The Students

A new source of language change has emerged in Japan: the new cadre of deaf students in colleges, especially students at the Tsukuba Technical College for the Deaf, the school that Yamashita-san, discussed in the previous chapter, attended. TCT and an organization called the National Association of Deaf Students both bring together a new generation of mainstreamed kids. One of the fascinating things about this generation is their playfulness toward signing. Signing is a fun area of exploration and experimentation for them, and they mix visual and verbal puns in a complex fashion not found with their elders.

For example, one common signing behavior that I noticed among the college students was fingerspelling interjectives. In English, we say "oh . . . yeah . . . ," "hmmm . . . ," "phew" or "wow . . . ," and so on. Spoken Japanese has a huge vocabulary of these types of quasi-onomatopoeic utterances, expanded even more by the popularity of manga comics. In older signers, one might show puzzlement by a quizzical look, but younger signers will actually sign (using fingerspelling): "HO~~~~~" which is the Japanese phrase for being bemused (like "hmmm . . ."). Or they will sign, "HEH HEH HEH HEH HEH" for a confident laugh, or "SA~~~~~" when they are puzzled. These are all simple fingerspelled forms that they drag across the body, just like dialogue imposed on a manga comic frame. There are also complex utterances such as "O-YA?" or "A-RE?" for surprise.[19]

Verbal puns in signs are another new form. For example, one that was

18. James Woodward (1980) has written on a similar diglossic situation within the American deaf community vis-à-vis bilingualism with spoken English and signed ASL.
19. There are at least two equivalent forms in ASL: HA-HA-HA-HA for laughing, and N-O for NO. And then there is a whole area of ASL puns that I don't have space to get into.

apparently popular at TCT is to make a P sign on your knee (which is *hiza* in Japanese). That's the sign for "pizza." Get it? P+*hiza* = *pizza*. This combinational form is totally unlike any other sign use that I saw in Japan.[20]

Middle-aged signers might use fingerspelling to sign conjunctions (such as "DE" which means "AND/BUT"),[21] but I did not see this playfulness. This type of verbal punning really came from those who were born into a mainstream experience, were well acclimated into hearing culture, and applied their deep knowledge of spoken Japanese in a new subculture of playful punning of spoken Japanese and Japanese Sign.

Left-Wing and Right-Wing: Assimilation and Discrimination

The JFD employs what I would call a pragmatic Marxist strategic orientation to the situation of the deaf in Japan in regard to the question of equality and discrimination. The Marxist root of their philosophy comes out most when JFD leaders, staff, and members talk about the *Undō* or Movement. Although the JFD is careful not to couch any of its movement philosophy in the overt language of party politics, the *Movement* is emphasized at all levels of the organization.[22]

Popular with housewives, the signing circles led by the JFD at the bottom tier have at least four purposes. The first is to introduce normal citizens to signing. The second is the hope that at least some of them will follow up with sign interpreter seminars and become sign interpreters. The third is *kōryū* or social interaction/intermingling, the importance of non-deaf building relationships with deaf persons on a one-to-one basis. The fourth aspect is building supporters of the Movement. Signing circle members are funneled into a system where they become Movement supporters, of which their sign interpreting services are just one component.

The JFD sees the interpreters as important allies in the Movement. But

20. It's quite common in ASL, however. For example, the sign for El Paso (Texas) is the L sign held on one hand while the other hand makes an O sign that passes by the L. L pass O. El Paso. Get it? Hyuck hyuck hyuck. There are myriad other examples of these types of puns. What's unclear is whether the students in Japan knew about the ASL punning tradition or came up with it autochthonously.

21. This is regionally specific. Tochigi signers will use this type of conjunctive fingerspelling a lot, but other regions use it much less or not at all.

22. See Patricia Steinhoff (1989:734) on the functioning of the *undō* (movement) in Japanese radical leftist student organizations.

as allies, they are expected to contribute equally. Thus, the JFD is unique in asking their signing circle members, interpreters, hearing employees, and other hearing allies to contribute to the Movement on an equal basis with deaf persons. One direct example would be that interpreters and staff who work/volunteer at the various meetings of the JFD (such as the national and prefectural deaf meetings) are usually asked to pay the meeting's admission fees, just like the deaf participants. They also have to pay for or bring their own lunches. They receive a transportation stipend and are paid around ¥1,000 (~$10) an hour while they are actually interpreting. However, after registration fees and lunch, at times they have a net loss. While they are there, they are also often asked to subscribe to the JFD newspaper.

This is in stark contrast to volunteers for the blind in Japan. "Guide helpers" do not pay for registration at conferences at which they are volunteering, they are provided with lunch, and they are thanked profusely, according to one sign interpreter whose friend was a volunteer for the blind. Her friend could not understand why she would "let the JFD treat her so poorly." This was the basis for this interpreter's conversation with me about how the JFD felt it was important to make the interpreters feel equal within the Movement. They pay for their own lunch, they register out of pocket, and they are not particularly thanked for their help since it all should be coming out of their feelings for the Movement (*undō no seishin*).

Conclusion: The Middle Road

The JFD is clearly in a difficult position. On the one hand, the group's previous strategy of blurring the difference between Japanese Sign and the Japanese language has been very successful. It has allowed for the use of signing in the classroom, brought in interpreter-volunteers who might have been scared away by an emphasis on grammar, and allowed the organization to get grants from the government to build up lexical parity with spoken Japanese.

But on the other hand, newer groups such as D-Pro that emphasize Japanese Sign Language's fundamental grammatical difference from spoken Japanese have appealed to a younger generation of deaf youth who have grown up without much sense of identity or belonging. Language becomes their marker of difference. And the JFD is at risk of losing this younger generation permanently. If that were not bad enough, the public television network, NHK, and its newscasters now threaten the JFD's singular control over the lexicon of Japanese Sign.

The era when the JFD had the ability to control language through its interpreter-training programs and lexicon-building projects is at an end. The situation in Japan may ultimately end up resembling that in the United States and many European nations, where there is no single authority controlling the future direction of signing within a country. Although language politics often lie at the heart of our national and regional identities, languages themselves have a natural tendency to develop and change at the ground level. Linguistic hegemony requires political power in the form of social institutions such as schools or broadcast media; in most situations, national associations of the deaf do not have that type of power, and national governments are insufficiently interested in the future of the deaf community to exercise theirs. In the next and last chapter, we will reflect on the intertwining of identity, language, and nationalism in this book.

CHAPTER TWELVE

Conclusions

Japanese person: A person who has Japanese nationality (and
speaks Japanese as their native language).
                    —*Shinmeikai Kokugo Dictionary*

This definition of being Japanese, from a major Japanese dictionary, crys-
tallizes the issues of language, nationalism, and identity that face the
deaf community in Japan.[1] The community is in the midst of a severe
generational conflict that reveals itself through language and identity.
Up to now, the middle-generation deaf persons represented by the JFD
have articulated themselves as being Japanese. This can be seen (and
heard) through the type of language they use in public, signing using
spoken Japanese grammatical forms. This strategy has allowed the Japanese Federation of the Deaf, led by well-educated elites, to blur the difference between Japanese Sign and spoken Japanese, claim control over
what they call a "participatory welfare" (*sanka fukushi*) system, and use
Japanese Sign in the schools for the deaf. The result has been a number of
tangible benefits that have improved the quality of life for many Japanese deaf persons. But achieving these gains has taken a middle-of-the-
road assimilationist strategy, deemphasizing the differences between
deaf people and the mainstream.

As we have seen, the irony is that the JFD has been almost too success-

1. I thank Ai Nagakawa for bringing this dictionary entry to my attention. Although I
encountered the same social attitude (that a Japanese person must be able to speak Japanese) when I "returned" to Japan at the age of ten, I was still surprised to see it spelled
out so explicitly in a dictionary. Many people (including most of my relatives) believe
that since I *am* Japanese (at a physical-biological level, through my parents), this imbues
me with a natural linguistic predestiny or ability to learn Japanese (as well as to use
chopsticks). Conversely, there is something seen as deeply unsettling about a foreigner
who is absolutely fluent in spoken Japanese (and chopsticks).

ful in arguing for the inclusion of the deaf community within the Japanese national body. The result was that starting in the 1970s, parents of deaf children no longer felt that they had to withhold their children from all of the benefits that the larger society offered. Deaf children began attending regular schools, and there was an erasure of the stigma surrounding deafness; the children learned how to speak Japanese and did not learn how to sign. This new generation of deaf youth grew up not identifying as deaf, preferring euphemisms such as "not being able to hear well." As they entered the more competitive middle school and high school environments in Japan, some of these students U-turned or L-turned back into the schools for the deaf. Others went through the system, entering regular colleges and earning four-year degrees. But at some point, many encountered what has been called "deaf shock," the sudden realization that they were deaf and that signing could replace speech as a primary form of communication. Influenced by American identity politics, they became deaf cultural activists. Generational difference begets language difference begets identity difference, which begets a new form of deaf nationalism as seen in the new radical group D-Pro.

Role of the Ethnographer

"How do we reconcile the post-structuralist project to displace identity with the feminist project to reclaim it?" asked the feminist scholar Diana Fuss in 1989 (cited in Calhoun 1994:19). I felt in much the same sort of bind as I encountered some of the reactions to my own work. "You didn't work with real Deaf people in Japan," was the response of a culturally Deaf individual in the United States to an early presentation of my research findings. Involved in the American Deaf community as both an activist and an academic, she felt in no uncertain terms that I had made fundamental mistakes during my fieldwork and subsequent analysis. The brunt of her criticism was that in the years of my fieldwork experience in Japan, I had not come into contact with what she considered to be the "real Deaf" community in Japan. This individual felt that I was not sensitive enough to the distinction to understand that the members of the middle generation of deaf individuals (namely the JFD leadership) that I primarily worked with were not "really deaf" but actually "hard of hearing" or "late-deafened." That they called themselves deaf and bridled at the latter terms meant little to her.

This is of course the contention of the younger-generation members of

D-Pro, who are using the same critique to challenge the authority of the JFD to define the bounds of deafness and Japanese Sign. I am in a classic anthropological dilemma: caught between two groups, both of whom contest the category of identity under research. I confess that I have kept an intellectual distance from the American cultural Deaf position during this project.[2] I am concerned that by allowing teleological language definitions to bias my research categories (for example, the only "real deaf" are those who use only sign without voicing), I would be seeking to use cross-cultural evidence to reify rather than challenge the political bounds of being deaf/Deaf. The inaudible difference between "deaf" and "Deaf" when both spoken and signed[3] only further blurs the slippage between these categories; the only deafness is Deafness.

Since I approach the study of deaf communities from a background in gender and sexuality studies, I have been very hesitant to engage in the search for a "true Deafness," no matter how appealing the concept of a culturally distinct minority may be in my current profession as a cultural anthropologist. Instead, I have sought to deconstruct the politics of deafness in Japan and tried to be careful in balancing the arguments presented by both sides, showing their historical specificity.

Two people with very different backgrounds and orientations can go to Japan and see very different things. I worked mainly with the Japanese Federation of the Deaf and saw an inclusive organization that avoided the deaf/Deaf divide (anyone who cannot hear is considered deaf by the JFD) and had a pragmatic approach to signing (any sign communication form used by a deaf person in Japan is considered Japanese sign). My critic, a Deaf woman from the United States, interacted with D-Pro while she was in Japan. The American cultural Deaf position and D-Pro are in close philosophical agreement: only those who have signed from birth and are fully engaged in "Deaf culture" can be consid-

2. There are critiques emerging from Deaf Studies of American cultural Deaf politics. Most notably, Donald Grushkin (2003) criticizes its separatist and radical aspects which result in the alienation of the hard of hearing and anyone else who does not sign pure ASL.

3. When speaking or signing, you have to mark Deafness/deafness as "cultural Deafness" or "Big-D" deafness as there is no way to pronounce the capital-D in spoken English or ASL. In ASL, there is a strong assumption that the sign DEAF refers only to cultural Deafness, as the category of HARD-OF-HEARING is available to those who are merely deaf, but do not sign. Merely pronouncing the word "DEAF" in English/ASL leaves an ambiguity as to whether it indicates being deaf or being Deaf. "Hearing impaired" is rarely used in America as a category encompassing both deaf and hard of hearing, as the Deaf community views it as derogatory (one quip is that "deaf people are not hearing impaired, hearing people are deaf impaired").

ered deaf/Deaf, and Japanese Sign Language is a language wholly and absolutely independent of, as well as incompatible with, spoken Japanese. Any sign form that is not pure Japanese Sign Language is not signing. In my opinion, this is a linguistic social determinism just as rigid as that previously used to define only spoken languages as natural human languages and condemned signing as mere mimicry of language.

None of the people within the JFD that I met would deny that they were deaf. This would be nonsense since they *were* deaf (in a biological sense, at least). But how and what that deafness meant changed and shifted based on the context they found themselves in. I sensed no overwhelming need or desire to reconcile those various forms of deafness and deaf identity. This could be seen most visually in language use: they might sign without voicing with deaf friends, vocalize while signing while chatting with hearing friends who knew a little sign, and then voice without signing to sign-ignorant co-workers. They would use whatever was appropriate for the contextual situation. In politics, the JFD was the same way. If arguing a social welfare perspective meant a better life for deaf individuals at the bottom of the social ladder, then disability welfare pensions were justified, even if they went against the JFD's fundamental belief that deaf persons were just as capable as hearing persons.

In the United States, many minority activists have pushed to define, essentialize, and constrain identity. To take an extreme example, the recent broadening of the U.S. Census's ethnic and racial categories to allow for multiplicity can be seen as acknowledging that there are slippages in our identity constructions. But even though we now have 126 possible ethnic/racial categories and 604 ancestry codes (our micro-nationalisms keep getting smaller and smaller), the nature of the effort is similar to a fractal pattern: the closer we get, the more forms of identity appear.[4] So while being Non-Hispanic-Asian-White is possible, that opens up the question of what is someone like me, who was born in Indonesia to Japanese parents, grew up in Australia and Japan, and has spent most of her adult life in the United States. Focusing on the results of strategic maneuvering rather than trying to stabilize the inherently unstable base of identity politics seems more useful in the long term.

There is certainly a great divide between these two positions. I would make no argument that the JFD or the members whom I worked with

---

4. See for example a newspaper article on the conflict between Assyrians, Chaldeans, and the U.S. Census Bureau (Kulish 2001).

represent "Deaf Culture" in Japan, as the term is understood in the United States with all its implications of identity and ethnic minority politics. The JFD has never sought to present itself as culturally Deaf, in this sense. But they do strongly feel that they are *rōa* (deaf) and that the term *shuwa* (signing) should not be restricted to just one particular form ("pure Japanese Sign Language"). And this is where the two ideologies conflict.

Modernization and Fragmentation

Cultural Deaf consciousness in the United States did not arise naturally or individually. As the linguistic theorist Mikhail Bakhtin notes, "signs can arise only on interindividual territory. . . . The individual consciousness is a social-ideological fact" (1994:52)." To put it another way, the current form of identity politics in the United States is the result of one particular historical trajectory, within which ethnic minority politics (especially the Black civil rights movement) has played a crucial role. Without the ethnic minority frame, gay and lesbian as well as Deaf culture movements would have had to frame their sense of themselves in very different terms.

Debate about the meaning of deafness and signing are occurring in many places throughout Japan, and no single site or diagnostic event can explore the entire configuration. My research into broader deaf identities would have been difficult to accomplish in the United States because the trope of ethnic or cultural minority is largely unquestioned and identity politics has until recently been seen as an efficacious political strategy. Neither of these assumptions holds true in Japan, and the analyses of such may contribute to social theory. Within the field of Deaf Studies, Japan bridges the gap between nascent deaf societies such as Nicaragua (Senghas and Kegl 1994) where deaf identity is just starting to emerge, and established deaf cultures such as those in the United States or Western Europe (cf. Le Master 2003, Monaghan 2003a).

In Japan, the trajectory that today lands us with D-Pro, the JFD, and the whole panoply of identities is the result of the historical forces delineated in this book. However, although many within the cultural Deaf community see Deaf culture as a teleological finality, being "deaf" (as well as culturally Deaf) as a social identity is a process that involves elements of both sociohistorical construction and individual choice. In Japan, it was the fracturing of deaf (*rōa*) identity caused by mass mainstreaming and the generally increased affluence and accessibility for the deaf that led to a loss of core identity within many younger Japanese who could not hear. Many have found the American model of a total- ized, essentialized Deaf identity to be appealing, to be a means of recen- tering their existence within a system that currently is lacking meaning not only for them, but for many other Japanese youths. But this new Deaf identity politics is by no means a stable one.

The Movement's Future

In a 1995 article, "Must identity movements self-destruct?," the Ameri- can sociologist Joshua Gamson drew our attention toward the destabiliz- ing forces within contemporary identity movements in the United States. His particular focus was gay and lesbian movements and their desire to create a collective identity. There is considerable contention within these movements, and every time the definition of *gay* or *lesbian* is stabilized, it is undercut by forces coming from both within and without (for example, transgendered gay men, lesbians who sleep with men, bi- sexuals, Log Cabin Republicans). This has led in part to an attempt to es- sentialize the gay or lesbian body (leading, for example, to the relentless search for the "gay brain" or the "gay gene").

Although there is a clear physical basis to deafness caused by various physical and sociological factors, being "culturally Deaf" is a social con- struction (Foucault 1990) maintained through cultural performance (Butler 1993; Morris 1995), practice (Bourdieu 1972; Kondo 1990), and language (Bakhtin 1981; Hall and Bucholtz 1995; Ryang 1997). Although it is tempting to go unilinearly from the physical to the social (audiolog- ical deafness leads naturally to being culturally Deaf), the reality is more dialectic than simply causative since social forms, material conditions, and cultural practice are often intimately interlinked. Social, institu- tional, and economic factors are not enough and in order to understand deaf identity in Japan, a close ethnographic approach to culture and identity is necessary.

Within deaf communities, there is no question that there is a biological physicality that underlies deafness. But as I have shown in this work, this has not led to a concomitant stabilization of identities. Deaf bodies do not lead deterministically to one form of deaf brain, one form of deaf signing, or one form of deaf politics. The middle generation of the JFD has adopted a politics that draws strongly from prior social movements in Japan, arguing for equal rights as part of the Japanese nation. But as discrimination and social inequality faced by deaf individuals in Japan are alleviated by the actions of the JFD, the need for the organization ironically dissipates. Classic social movement–type organizations are faced with the dilemma that their primary goal is the elimination of their own *raison d'être*, discrimination.

That is not to say that new identity-based, social movement–type organizations, such as those founded by the youth generation of deaf in Japan are any less stable. Their appeal is that they provide identity to those who have previously felt identity-less. But as each individual comes into their identity in a very personal way (the feminist phrase "the personal is political" comes to mind), these types of movements tend to be acephalous or leaderless at best, fractured at worst. Simply being Deaf (signing, not voicing, upholding cultural Deaf values) indicates membership in these new social movements. But who controls what it means to be Deaf itself? As Gamson indicates, new social movements tend to fragment and self-destruct over these issues of identity and control.

This is not only a generational conflict but a class conflict as well, in certain ways. The JFD of the sixties and seventies was led by a group of intellectually and politically savvy elite men who went to the best universities of Japan well before anyone else in their cohort had that opportunity. In Marxist terms, they provided the intellectual vanguard of the Japanese deaf liberation movement. In contrast, the younger movement represented by D-Pro is anti-establishment. The leadership is not the elite educated, but came to their identities through grassroots organizing.

At a cultural level, the current leaders of the new youth-based cultural deaf movement in Japan appropriate American discourses on deafness highlighting minority status. But such models of ethnic status cannot be simply transposed (or imported) into Japan; they must be remade (Tobin 1992) or reconfigured for Japanese consumption. The American movement draws on Black and feminist civil rights frames that are simply not available in Japan (cf. Upham 1987)—at least not in the same way, with the same connotations. Thus, cultural deaf leaders such as Kimura Harumi quoted earlier describe the deaf as a "linguistic minority," but differentiate themselves from those other ethnic minorities, Korean, Ainu, or Burakumin.

Within the younger deaf activists in Japan, there is a research project under way into finding a native deaf culture (*rō bunka* or *defu karuchā*). We can read this against a similar concern in mainstream (hearing) Japan for the location of the traditional (Hobsbawm and Ranger 1983; Ivy 1988), native (Robertson 1991), national history movements, reclaiming of the Pacific War, or a sense of nostalgia for the past (Kelly 1986), and we can similarly politicize this search as a form of cultural legitimization and the interplay of power and history. Meanwhile, the hearing community (and their politicians) appear largely sympathetic only to the disability side of the rhetorical debate, and Japanese deaf leaders must carefully articulate that aspect as well without short-circuiting their own politics.

Epilogue: A New Hope for the JFD

The JFD faces many problems as it enters the twenty-first century. The younger generation has fragmented, with half attracted to radical forms of identity politics, while the other half reject the notion of a deaf identity altogether and assimilate. As the middle generation that previously made up the organization's strength ages, the JFD will have to take their needs into account, while not losing the younger generation to cultural Deafness or apathy. The board of directors and membership has gradually been getting older and older with little new blood invigorating the system. Membership in the JFD has dropped almost every year since its peak in 1997.

Furthermore, its own political and social success has weakened the need for organizations such as itself. Deaf individuals can now receive a monthly stipend because of the disability; getting jobs is easy with the Disabled Persons' Employment Promotion Act and its mandatory hiring quotas; more television shows and news programs are being captioned; and interpreter dispatch services are well established. There is almost no need to belong to a local association of the deaf anymore.

Some changes are happening within the JFD to counteract these forces. In July 2000, I visited the Tokyo head office to pay respects to the new director who replaced the feisty Ohtsuki-san, who had just retired. I had known Dr. Osugi Yutaka for quite a long time. We first met in 1996 when I was just beginning my research into deaf communities in the United States and Japan. He was then a doctoral student at the University of Rochester specializing in the linguistics of ASL and JSL. After receiving his Ph.D. in 1997, he continued to teach ASL and JSL linguistics at Rochester.

I had heard his name being bandied about in the JFD upper echelons, but most of the rumors seemed to indicate that he was being nominated to head the newly proposed Japan Sign Interpreter Research Institute. I was a bit surprised when I learned that he had instead been selected to become the director of the JFD's Tokyo head office because the job hardly required his Ph.D. in sign linguistics. In his late thirties, he was very much junior in age to the full-time staff at the JFD, many of whom had been in the deaf movement for over thirty years.

However, Dr. Osugi had other qualifications and his placement could be seen as extremely strategic. Because he was a well-educated professional with a doctoral degree in linguistics, he appealed to the meritocratic upper-middle-class tendencies of the JFD leadership, while at the same time, his deep knowledge of American deaf politics and ASL linguistics gave him considerable cachet among the populist, antiestablishment supporters of D-Pro.

In 2001, the JFD publishing branch inaugurated a new series of books on Japanese Sign Language linguistics. The first volume, titled *A practical sign language grammar*, was written by Matsumoto Masayuki, the pioneering deaf lawyer discussed in chapter 7. The JFD, after having ceded ground to the D-Pro for almost a decade, was moving rapidly to establish itself as the central authority on Japanese Sign Language grammar. In his first chapter, Matsumoto wrote about the four key characteristics of Japanese *shuwa* as the "communication method of Japanese deaf persons" (2001:12):

1. It is a language (*kotoba*) communicated physically, primarily using the hands.
2. The words carry meaning, but not through sounds. If signers wish to relay how a word sounds out loud, they can use fingerspelling to spell out the foreign loan words (*gairaigo*), or they can also use mouth movements at the same time as they sign to indicate the spoken Japanese equivalent.
3. It is a visual communication system or language (*shikaku gengo*).
4. It is a conversational language (there is no writing system yet for it).

When I returned to Japan during the summer of 2004, I was not surprised that Dr. Osugi was becoming more publicly visible. He gave several guest lectures on the University of the Air's television network, explaining Japanese Sign linguistics using facial grammatical markers. The public television network NHK was also emphasizing grammar—its television program *Minna no Shuwa* was now stressing that Japanese

Sign Language was a separate language from spoken Japanese. The JFD was also beginning to promote itself as more of an *information* organization—a central repository of resources for people who were deaf—and not as a social welfare organization. At the other end of the spectrum, D-Pro's Web site appears to be politically softer. They are no longer using the loanword *defu* but have adopted a variation of the traditional term *rōsha* to indicate deaf people.

If we take Dr. Osugi, the NHK, and D-Pro as indicators of changes within the internal politics of deaf communities in Japan, then perhaps there will be a *rapprochement* between the cultural Deaf perspective advocated by D-Pro and others and the inclusive political/strategic deafness that the JFD has traditionally used.[5] Sign linguistics research can be conducted in ways that do not divide the community into "true" JSL signers and "corrupt" JSL signers. Each individual can come to terms with the meaning of his or her deafness and the forms of language he or she uses without concern about rejection by the deaf community or greater social community.

There are many ways to be deaf. Perhaps that message will be the lasting contribution of deaf politics in Japan.

5. Indeed, just as this book was going to press, the latest volume of the JFD's research journal, *Sign Language Communication Studies*, featured an article on JSL phonology by Ichida Yasuhiro (2005), co-author of D-Pro's controversial "Declaration of Deaf Culture" (Kimura and Ichida 1995).

Glossary

Japanese Terms

aidentitī   アイデンティティー   Identity. A loan word from English.

Ainu   アイヌ   The aboriginal inhabitants of the islands of northern Honshu, Hokkaido, and Sakhalins. Distinct from the Japanese (Yamato) people. Colonized in the late 1800s.

amakudari   天下り   Lit. *descending from heaven*. The practice by which retiring government bureaucrats take management, consulting, or board positions with companies or nonprofit organizations in the areas where they previously had oversight responsibilities.

Ampo   安保   The Japanese abbreviation for the Treaty of Mutual Cooperation and Security between Japan and the United States of America, signed in 1960 and renewed in 1970. Both signings were preceded by massive social protest by leftists and students.

burakumin   部落民   Lit. *People of the local village community*. A euphemism referring to the former outcaste members of Japanese society.

		The outcaste groups were restricted to ritually impure occupations (tanning, butchering, executions, etc.) and forced to live in certain areas of villages. They were technically freed by the 1868 Meiji Restoration, yet former burakumin are still discriminated against in employment and marriage in Japan.
Chōkaku shōgaisha	聴覚障害者	Lit. *person with hearing impediments.* Hearing impaired.
dankai no sedai	団塊の世代	Lit. *Clump generation.* The generation born after the Pacific War during the baby boom of 1947–1949.
Defu	デフ	"Deaf" in Japanese katakana glyphs and pronunciation. Used by members of D-Pro to indicate cultural Deafness in the 1990s against the older *rōasha* of the JFD.
dentōteki shuwa	伝統的手話	Lit. *Traditional signing.* A neologism referring to older forms of sign that do not use spoken Japanese grammar or vocalizations. Used only in the context of battles over signing purity.
dōjihō	同時法	A method of simultaneous signing and speech invented in 1968 at the Tochigi School for the Deaf.
dōwa	同和	Lit. *Equivalent harmony.* A set of educational and social policy changes enacted to reduce discrimination against the former burakumin.
dōwa mondai	同和問題	The problems that the former burakumin face with discrimination.
fukushi	福祉	Social welfare.
gaiatsu	外圧	Political pressure applied from outside Japan, as through the United Nations or international treaties. Comp. *naiatsu.*
hai'shichi	廃疾	The middle category of disability in the Nara era.

Heian jidai	平安時代	The period 794–1185 C.E. when the capital of Japan was located in the city of Heian (modern-day Kyoto).
Heisei	平成	The Heisei era of the reign of Emperor Akihito (1989~).
hōjin	法人	Legally incorporated nonprofit entity (corporation). Incorporation allows nonprofit organizations in Japan to sign leases and contracts in the NPO's name rather than the personal names of the leaders and to receive government *itaku* contracts. Until the NPO reforms of 1998, *hōjin* status was very difficult for NPOs in Japan to attain.
hōjin-ka	法人化	The process of incorporation. Legally registering as a nonprofit corporation under the tutelage of a relevant government ministry.
integurē shon	インテグレーション	Mainstreaming. The practice of placing deaf children in regular schools with individual support, rather than at specialized schools for the deaf.
itaku	委託	Government contracts given to companies or nonprofits.
jikaku	自覚	Lit. *seeing yourself.* Self-awareness. In a limited sense, self-identity.
jinken	人権	Human rights.
kikokushijo	帰国子女	Lit. *returnee children.* Children of Japanese citizens who were raised abroad and returned to Japan in adolescence. Many *kikokushijo* such as the author returned knowing little spoken or written Japanese and had to be reeducated in the national language.
kōreikas hakai mondai	高齢化社会問題	Lit. *the aging society problem.* Japanese society is now demographically top-heavy, with more older people than younger. This will create enormous social and economic problems when the baby boomers retire, without

		enough younger people to support them.
koseki	戸籍	Family registry system. The birth, marriage, and death of each individual in Japan is registered in a family registry located at the local government office. Theoretically, the family registry ties all Japanese into the kinship system of the emperor. The imperial family is not registered. The family registry system is opposed by feminists (who dislike the patriarchical nature of marriage embodied in it); communists and Catholics (who dislike the emperor system embodied in it); Burakumin (who dislike its former use in marking outcaste status); and others.
L-tān	L ターン	L-turning, the phenomenon of children with disabilities who began their education in regular integrated kindergartens or elementary schools, but later decided to switch to segregated special education schools because of social isolation or particular educational needs. Comp. *U-tān.*
madoguchi ippō	窓口一方	*"The one window"* policy of the government in dividing the Burakumin Liberation League and Zenkairen by funneling social welfare resources through only one organization in any given district (usually the BLL). This had the effect of weakening the other organization (usually Zenkairen).
Meiji Ishin	明治維新	Meiji Restoration, also called the Meiji Revolution. The overthrow of the feudal shogunate government in 1868 by modernist reformers, often used as the marker to indicate Japan's entry into the modern world. The Meiji period is the reign of Emperor Mutsuhito, September 8, 1868–July 30, 1912.

mimi ga kikoenai	耳が聞こえない	Lit. *ears that cannot hear.* Often used as a gentle way to refer to people who are deaf or hard of hearing.
naiatsu	内圧	Domestic pressure placed on the government through lobbying, legal challenges, or petition drives. Comp. *gaiatsu.*
nanchōsha	難聴者	Hard-of-hearing person. May have enough residual hearing to speak and speechread.
nanchōsha gakkyū	難聴者学級	Special education classes in regular school systems for mainstreamed hard-of-hearing students, a "school within a school."
Nara jidai	奈良时代	The period 710–794 C.E. when the capital of Japan was located in the city of Nara (near modern-day Kyoto).
Nihongo taiō shuwa	日本語対応手話	Lit. *signing that complies to Japanese.* Signing using the grammatical structure of spoken Japanese, often while vocalizing at the same time.
Nikkei	日系	Those descended from Japanese stock. Usually refers to *Nikkei-Brazilians,* the descendants of Japanese who emigrated to Brazil around the turn of the last century. The *Nikkei* were allowed into Japan as temporary foreign workers in the 1990s to solve the manual labor shortage. Because of their Japanese blood, *Nikkei* were believed by the government to be more compliant and cause fewer problems than other foreigners.
rō	聾/ろう	Deaf.
rō bunka	ろう文化	Deaf culture.
rōa	聾唖/ろうあ	Deaf-mute. Most translators render this as "deaf" because of the stigma of "deaf-mute" in English.
rōasha	ろうあ者	Deaf person. Variant: *rōsha.*
sanka fukushi	参加福祉	The JFD's strategy of "participatory welfare" or collaboratively working with the government to provide welfare services to JFD members.

shōgaisha	障害者	Disabled person/person with disabilities. Lit. *person with impediments.*
shōgaisha techō	障害者手帳	Disability ID card.
shōsūminzoku	少数民族	Ethnic minority.
Shōwa	昭和	The Shōwa reign of Emperor Hirohito, from December 25, 1926 to January 7, 1989.
shuwa	手話	Signing, sign language. Lit. *hand-communication.*
sutomai	ストマイ	Streptomycin, a powerful antibiotic introduced after the war that had the side effect of causing deafness in children.
Taishō	大正時代	The Taisho reign of Emperor Yoshihito, from July 30, 1912 to December 25, 1926.
terakoya	寺子屋	Lit. *temple schools.* Small private schools on temple grounds (often nonreligious) used to educate the masses before the reforms of the Meiji Restoration (1868).
Tokugawa	徳川	The Tokugawa period of military rule, from 1600 to 1868.
toku'shichi	篤疾	The most serious form of disability in the Nara era.
tsumbo	ツンボ	An informal way of referring to deaf persons. Now considered archaic and derogatory.
undō	運動	Lit. *The Movement.* The deaf political movement, esp. that of the JFD.
U-tān	U ターン	U-turning, the phenomenon of children with disabilities who began their education in special needs schools, later mainstreamed into regular schools, and then returned to the special needs schools when they reached middle or high school. This is often because they found themselves socially isolated in the regular school system or had particular educational needs which were not met in an integrated environment. Comp. *L-tān.*

zainichi	在日	Lit. *residing in Japan*. Often used as short form of *zainichi-chōsenjin*, below, but can also be used for *zainichi-Chūgokujin* (resident Chinese), *zainichi-korian* (resident Korean), etc.
zainichi chōsenjin	在日朝鮮人	North Korean in Japan, often second, third, or even fourth generation.
zan'shichi	残疾	The most minor form of disability in the Nara era.

English Terms

ASL	American Sign Language.
DPN	Deaf President Now student protests at Gallaudet University in 1988.
fingerspelling	A way of spelling out words letter by letter while signing, used mostly for proper nouns and loan words. E.g., "O-C-O-N-N-E-R" (ASL) or "SHA-N-HA-I" (JSL).
hagiography	The biographies or stories of the saints. By extension, the tendency of literature on minority social movements to focus on the elite leadership rather than the regular membership.
Hard of hearing (HoH)	Hearing impaired enough that spoken conversation is difficult but not impossible. Some HoH identify as deaf, others as hearing.
JFD	Japanese Federation of the Deaf.
JSL	Japanese Sign Language.
late-deafened	Deafened in adolescence or adulthood.
lipreading	See *speechreading*.
L-turn	See Japanese glossary: *L-tān*.
mainstream	The practice of integrating children with disabilities into regular school systems.
manual method	Teaching in the classroom using sign. Comp. *oral method*.
NAD	National Association of the Deaf, the national organization of the deaf in the United States.
NGO	Nongovernmental organization. In Japanese usage, NGOs are nonprofit organizations that do aid work primarily overseas.
NPO	Nonprofit organization. In Japanese usage, NPOs are nonprofits that do volunteer work primarily in Japan.

oral method	Teaching in the classroom using only speech and speechreading. Comp. *manual method.*
ototoxic	*Medical.* Damaging to hearing. Streptomycin has ototoxic side effects in children, causing them to become deaf or hard of hearing.
post-lingual deaf	Deafened in childhood after the acquisition of a spoken language (usually 3–4 years old).
pre-lingual deaf	Deafened *in utero,* soon after birth, or otherwise before the acquisition of a spoken language.
speechreading	Making out the import of speech by observing lip and mouth movements and using context and residual hearing. Also known colloquially as *lipreading.*
terp	Colloquial form of interpreter.
TTY	Real-time teletype machines for the deaf used in the United States. Connected to a regular telephone line, they allow real-time chatting between two deaf persons or, using a TTY relay operator, between a deaf person and a hearing person on a regular phone.
U-turn	See Japanese glossary: *U-tān.*

Bibliography

English Sources

Alcoff, Linda. 1988. Cultural feminism versus post-structuralism: the identity crisis in feminist theory. *Signs: Journal of Women in Culture and Society* 13 (3).

Allison, Anne. 1994. *Nightwork: sexuality, pleasure, and corporate masculinity in a Tokyo hostess club.* Chicago: University of Chicago Press.

Alrabaa, Sami. 1986. Diglossia in the classroom: the Arabic case. *Anthropological Linguistics* 28 (1):73–79.

Anderson, Benedict. 1991 [1983]. *Imagined communities: reflections on the origin and spread of nationalism.* Rev. ed. London: Verso.

Aramburo, Anthony J. 1995. Sociolinguistic aspects of the Black Deaf community. In *Linguistics of American Sign Language,* edited by C. Valli and C. Lucas, 367–379. Washington: Gallaudet University Press.

Aronson, Josh. 2000. *Sound and fury.* New York: New Video Group.

Aucamp, Anna Jacoba. 1978. *Bilingual education and nationalism with special reference to South Africa.* New York: Arno.

Austin, John L. 1975. *How to do things with words.* Cambridge: Harvard University Press.

Baker-Shenk, Charlotte, and Dennis Cokely. 1980/1991. *American Sign Language: a teacher's resource text on grammar and culture.* Washington: Gallaudet University Press.

Bakhtin, Mikhail. 1981. *The dialogic imagination.* Austin: University of Texas Press.

———. 1994 *The Bakhtin reader.* Edited by Pam Morris. London: Arnold.

Bakhtin, Mikhail, Caryl Emerson, and Michael Holquist. 1986. *Speech genres and other late essays.* University of Texas Press Slavic series 8. Austin: University of Texas Press.

Barnartt, Sharon N., and Richard K. Scotch. 2001. *Disability protests: contentious politics 1970–1999.* Washington: Gallaudet University Press.

Battison, Robbin. 1995. Signs have parts: a simple idea. In *Linguistics of American Sign Language,* edited by C. Valli and C. Lucas, 215–225. Washington: Gallaudet University Press.

Baynton, Douglas C. 1996. *Forbidden signs: American culture and the campaign against sign language.* Chicago: University of Chicago Press.

BBC TV. 1997. *Horizon: silent children, new language.* Broadcast on March 4. London: British Broadcasting Corporation.

Bell, Alexander Graham. 1883. *Memoir upon the formation of a deaf variety of the human race.* New Haven, CT: National Academy of Sciences.

Bem, Sandra Lipsitz. 1993. *The lenses of gender: transforming the debate on sexual inequality.* New Haven: Yale University Press.

Berenz, Norine. 2003. Surdos venceremos: the rise of the Brazilian deaf community. In *Many ways to be deaf: international linguistic and sociocultural variation,* edited by L. F. Monaghan, C. Schmaling, K. Nakamura, and G. Turner,173–193. Washington: Gallaudet University Press.

Bertram, Bodo. 1996. An integrated rehabilitation concept for cochlear implant children. In *Cochlear implant rehabilitation in children and adults,* edited by D. J. Allum, 22–30. San Diego: Singular Publishing Group.

Bourdieu, Pierre. 1972. *Outline of a theory of practice.* Translated by Richard Nice. Cambridge: Cambridge University Press.

———. 1991. *Language and symbolic power.* Translated by Gino Raymond and Matthew Adamson. Cambridge: Harvard University Press.

Braman, Donald. 2000. Of race and immutability. *UCLA Law Review* 45 (5):1375–1463.

Brand, David. 1988. This is the Selma of the deaf: Gallaudet students demonstrate for a deaf college president. *Time,* March 21, 64.

Brusky, Amy Elizabeth. 1995. Making decisions for deaf children regarding cochlear implants: the legal ramifications of recognizing deafness as a culture rather than a disability. *Wisconsin Law Review:* 235–270.

Butler, Judith. 1993. *Bodies that matter: on the discursive limits of "sex."* New York: Routledge.

Calhoun, Craig, ed. 1994. *Social theory and the politics of identity.* Oxford: Blackwell.

Campbell, John Creighton. 1992. *How policies change: the Japanese government and the aging society.* Princeton: Princeton University Press.

———. 1996. Media and policy change in Japan. In *Media and politics in Japan,* edited by S. J. Pharr and E. S. Krauss, 187–212. Honolulu: University of Hawaii Press.

Campbell, John Creighton, and Naoki Ikegami, eds. 1998. *The art of balance in health policy: maintaining Japan's low-cost, egalitarian system.* Cambridge: Cambridge University Press.

———. 1999. *Long-term care for frail older people: reaching for the ideal system.* Keio University Symposia for Life Science and Medicine. New York: Springer.

Carmel, Simon J., and Leila F. Monaghan. 1991. Studying Deaf culture: an introduction to ethnographic work in Deaf communities. *Sign Language Studies* 73:411–420.

Christiansen, John B., and Sharon M. Barnartt. 1995. *Deaf president now!: the 1988 revolution at Gallaudet University.* Washington: Gallaudet University Press.

Cohen, Jean L. 1985. Strategy or identity: new theoretical paradigms and contemporary social movements. *Social Research* 52 (4):663–716.

Condry, Ian. 1999. Japanese rap music: an ethnography of globalization in popular culture. Ph.D. diss., Yale University.

Cornell, John B. 1970. "Caste" in Japanese social stratification: a theory and a case. *Monumenta Nipponica* 25 (1–2):107–135.

Cripps, Denise. 1996. Flags and fanfares: the Hinomaru flag and Kimigayo anthem. In *Case studies on human rights in Japan,* edited by R. Goodman and I. Neary, 76–108. Richmond, Surrey: Japan Library.

D-Pro. n.d. What is D-Pro? Photocopied undated manuscript distributed in 1995. Tokyo.

D'Emilio, John. 1983a. Capitalism and gay identity. In *Powers of desire: the politics of sexuality*, edited by A. Snitow, C. Stansell, and S. Thompson, 100–113. New York: Monthly Review Press.

———. 1983b. *Sexual politics, sexual communities: the making of a homosexual minority in the United States, 1940–1970*. Chicago: University of Chicago Press.

Devos, G. A., and H. Wagatsuma, eds. 1967. *Japan's invisible race: caste in culture and personality*. Berkeley: University of California Press.

Donoghue, John D. 1957. An eta community in Japan: the social persistence of out-caste groups. *American Anthropologist* 59:1000–1017.

———. 1978. *Pariah persistence in changing Japan: a case study*. Washington: University Press of America.

Dwyer, Kevin, and Faqir Muhammad. 1982. *Moroccan dialogues: anthropology in question*. Baltimore: Johns Hopkins University Press.

Embree, John F. 1939 [1964]. *Suye mura: a Japanese village*. Chicago: University of Chicago Press.

Errington, J. Joseph. 1991. A muddle for the model: diglossia and the case of Javanese. *Southwest Journal of Linguistics* 10(1):189–213.

———. 1992. On the ideology of Indonesian language development: the state of a language of a state. *Pragmatics* 2 (3):417–426.

Esposito, John L., and John Obert Voll. 1996. *Islam and democracy*. New York: Oxford University Press.

Farnell, Brenda M. 1995. *Do you see what I mean?: Plains Indian sign talk and the embodiment of action*. Austin: University of Texas Press.

Fausto-Sterling, Anne. 1992. *Myths of gender: biological theories and women and men*. 2nd ed. New York: Basic Books.

———. 1993. The five sexes: why male and female are not enough. *Sciences* (March/April): 20–25.

Ferguson, Charles. 1964 [1959]. Diglossia. In *Language in culture and society*, edited by D. Hymes. New York: Harper & Row. Originally published in *Word* [1959] 15:325–340.

Fisher, Robert. 1992. Organizing in the modern metropolis: considering new social movement theory. *Journal of Urban History* 18:222–237.

Fishman, Joshua A. 1982. Bilingualism and biculturalism as individual and as societal phenomena. In *Bilingual education for Hispanic students in the United States*, edited by J. A. Fishman and G. D. Keller, 23–36. New York: Teachers College Press.

Fitzhugh, William W., and Chisato O. Dubreuil, eds. 2000. *Ainu: spirit of a northern people*. Seattle: University of Washington Press.

Foucault, Michel. 1990. *The history of sexuality*. Vol. 1. *An introduction*. Translated by Robert Hurley. New York: Vintage Books.

Fowler, Edward. 2000. The Buraku in modern Japanese literature: texts and contexts. *Journal of Japanese Studies* 26 (1):1–39.

Friedman, Thomas B., Yong Liang, James L. Weber, John T. Hinnant, Thomas D. Barberr, Sunaryana Winata, I. Nyomen Arhya, and James H. Asher Jr. 1995. A gene for congenital, recessive deafness *DFNB3* maps to the pericentromeric region of chromosome 17. *Nature Genetics* 9:86–91.

Fukuoka, Yasunori. 2000. *Lives of young Koreans in Japan*. Translated by Tom Gill. Melbourne: Trans Pacific Press.

Fuss, Diana. 1989. *Essentially speaking: feminism, nature, and difference*. New York: Routledge.

Gamson, Joshua. 1989. Silence, death, and the invisible enemy: AIDS activism and social movement "newness." *Social Problems* 36 (4):351–366.

———. 1995. Must identity movements self-destruct?: a queer dilemma. *Social Problems* 42 (3):390–407.

Gamson, William. 1990. *The strategy of social protest*. Belmont, CA: Wadsworth.

Garon, Sheldon. 1997. *Molding Japanese minds: the state in everyday life*. Princeton: Princeton University Press.

Gitlin, Todd. 1980. *The whole world is watching: mass media in the making and unmaking of the new left*. Berkeley: University of California Press.

Goffman, Erving. 1956. *The presentation of self in everyday life*. Edinburgh: University of Edinburgh Social Sciences Research Centre.

———. 1974. *Frame analysis: an essay on the organization of experience*. New York: Harper & Row.

———. 1986 [1963]. *Stigma: notes on the management of spoiled identity*. 1st Touchstone ed. New York: Touchstone.

Goodman, Roger. 1990. *Japan's "international youth": the emergence of a new class of schoolchildren*. New York: Clarendon Press.

Goodman, Roger, and Ian Neary. 1996. *Case studies on human rights in Japan*. Richmond, Surrey: Japan Library.

Gordon, Andrew. 1993. *Postwar Japan as history*. Berkeley: University of California Press.

Gottlieb, Nanette. 1998. Discriminatory language in Japan: burakumin, the disabled, and women. *Asian Studies Review* (Canberra, Australia) 22 (2):157–173.

Groce, Nora Ellen. 1985. *Everyone here spoke sign language: hereditary deafness on Martha's Vineyard*. Cambridge: Harvard University Press.

Grushkin, Donald A. 2003. The dilemma of the hard-of-hearing within the United States deaf community. In *Many ways to be deaf: international linguistic and sociocultural variation*, edited by L. F. Monaghan, C. Schmaling, K. Nakamura, and G. Turner, 114–140. Washington: Gallaudet University Press.

Hairston, Ernest, and Linwood Smith. 1983. *Black and deaf in America: are we that different?* Silver Spring, MD: T.J. Publishers.

Hall, John A. 1995. *Civil society: theory, history, comparison*. Cambridge, U.K.: Polity Press.

Hall, Kira, and Mary Bucholtz, eds. 1995. *Gender articulated: language and the socially constructed self*. New York: Routledge.

Hall, Stephanie Aileen. 1989. "The deaf club is like a second home": an ethnography of folklore communication in American Sign Language. Ph.D. diss., University of Pennsylvania.

Halley, Janet E. 1994. Sexual orientation and the politics of biology: a critique of the argument from immutability. *Stanford Law Review* 46:503–506.

Hardacre, Helen. 1984. *The religion of Japan's Korean minority: the preservation of ethnic identity*. Berkeley: University of California Institute of East Asian Studies.

Hareven, Tamara K. 1991a. The history of the family and the complexity of social change. *American Historical Review* 96 (1):95–124.

———. 1991b. Synchronizing individual time, family time, historical time. In *Chronotypes: the construction of time*, edited by J. B. Bender and D. E. Wellbery, 167–182. Stanford: Stanford University Press.

Harris, Jennifer. 1995. *The cultural meaning of deafness*. Brookfield, VT: Avebury.

Higgins, Paul C. 1979. Deviance within a disabled community. *Pacific Sociological Review* 22 (1):96–114.

———. 1992. *Making disability: exploring the social transformation of human variation*. Springfield, IL: C. C. Thomas.

Hingwan, Kathianne. 1996. Identity, otherness, and migrant labour in Japan. In *Case studies on human rights in Japan*, edited by R. Goodman and I. Neary, 51–75. Richmond, Surrey: Japan Library.

Hobsbawm, Eric, and Terrence Ranger. 1983. *The invention of tradition*. London: Cambridge University Press.

Horgan, John. 1995. A sign is born: language unfolds among deaf Nicaraguan children. *Scientific American*, December, 18–19.

Hunt, Scott A., Robert D. Benford, and David A. Snow. 1994. Identity fields: framing processes and the social construction of movement identities. In *New social movements: from ideology to identity*, edited by E. Laraña, H. Johnston, and J. R. Gusfield, 185–208. Philadelphia: Temple University Press.

Israelite, Neita, Carolyn Ewoldt, and Robert Hoffmeister. 1992. *Bilingual/bicultural education for deaf and hard-of-hearing students: a review of the literature on the effects of native sign language acquisition on majority language acquisition*. A research study commissioned by the Ontario Ministry of Education, Ontario, Canada: Ministry of Education.

Ivy, Marilyn. 1988. Tradition and difference in the Japanese mass media. *Public Culture Bulletin* 1:21–29.

Jacobs, Leo. 1969. *A deaf adult speaks out*. Washington: Gallaudet College Press.

Japanese Federation of the Deaf. 1991. *The hearing impaired peoples in Japan*. XI World Congress of the World Federation of the Deaf (July 5–11, 1991). Tokyo: Japanese Federation of the Deaf.

——. 1997. *Our 50 year history and future*. English translation of *50nen no Ayumi Soshite Mirai he*. Translated by Karen Nakamura. Tokyo: Japanese Federation of the Deaf.

Japanese Society for Rehabilitation of Disabled Persons. 1995. *Rehabilitation in Japan*. Tokyo: Japanese Society for Rehabilitation of Disabled Persons.

Johnston, Hank, Enrique Laraña, and Joseph R. Gusfield. 1994. Identities, grievances, and new social movements. In *New social movements: from ideology to identity*, edited by E. Laraña, H. Johnston, and J. R. Gusfield, 3–35. Philadelphia: Temple University Press.

Jolivet, Muriel. 1997. *Japan: the childless society*. New York: Routledge.

Karchmer, Michael A., and Ross E. Mitchell. 2003. Demographic and achievement characteristics of deaf and hard-of-hearing students. In *Oxford handbook of deaf studies, language, and education*, edited by M. Marschark and P. E. Spencer, 21–37. Oxford: Oxford University Press.

Kegl, Judy. 1994. The Nicaraguan sign language project: an overview. *Signpost* 7 (1):24–31.

Kelly, William Wright. 1986. Rationalization and nostalgia: cultural dynamics of new middle-class Japan. *American Ethnologist* 13 (4):603–618.

——. 1993. Japan's debates about an aging society: the later years in the land of the rising sun. In *Justice across generations: what does it mean?*, edited by Lee Cohen, 153–168. Washington: Public Policy Institute, American Association of Retired Persons.

Kohno, Masaru. 1997. *Japan's postwar party politics*. Princeton: Princeton University Press.

Kondo, Dorinne K. 1990. *Crafting selves: power, gender, and discourses of identity in a Japanese workplace*. Chicago: University of Chicago Press.

Krauss, Ellis S., Thomas P. Rohlen, and Patricia G. Steinhoff, eds. 1984. *Conflict in Japan*. Honolulu: University of Hawaii Press.

Kulish, Nicholas. 2001. Wrong pigeonhole? Chaldeans, Assyrians are vexed with census. *Wall Street Journal*, March 12, A1, A10.

Lane, Harlan. 1976. *When the mind hears: a history of the deaf.* New York: Random House.

———. 1992. *The mask of benevolence: disabling the deaf community.* New York: Knopf.

———. 1993. Cochlear implants: their cultural and historical meaning. In *Deaf history unveiled: interpretations from the new scholarship,* edited by J. V. Van Cleve. Washington: Gallaudet University Press.

———. 1997. Constructions of deafness. In *Disability studies reader,* edited by Lennard J. Davis, 153–171. New York: Routledge.

Lane, Harlan, Robert Hoffmeister, and Ben Bahan, eds. 1996. *A journey into the Deaf-World.* San Diego: DawnSign Press.

Laraña, Enrique, Hank Johnston, and Joseph R. Gusfield, eds. 1994. *New social movements: from ideology to identity.* Philadelphia: Temple University Press.

Lee, C., and G. A. DeVos, eds. 1981. *Koreans in Japan: ethnic conflict and accommodation.* Berkeley: University of California Press.

Le Master, Barbara. 2003. Local meanings of Irish deaf identity. In *Many ways to be deaf: international linguistic and sociocultural variation,* edited by L. F. Monaghan, C. Schmaling, K. Nakamura, and G. Turner, 153–172. Washington: Gallaudet University Press.

Lo, Jeannie. 1990. *Office ladies, factory women: life and work at a Japanese company.* Armonk, NY: M. E. Sharpe.

Maeda, Daisuke. 1997. The religious situation of the "Aum generation." *Japanese Religions* 22 (1):87–91.

McAdam, Doug. 1994. Culture and social movements. In *New social movements: from ideology to identity,* edited by E. Laraña, H. Johnston, and J. R. Gusfield, 36–57. Philadelphia: Temple University Press.

———. 1996. *Comparative perspectives on social movements: political opportunities, mobilizing structures, and cultural framings.* Cambridge studies in comparative politics. Cambridge: Cambridge University Press.

McAdam, Doug, John D. McCarthy, and Mayer N. Zald. 1988. Social movements. In *Handbook of sociology,* edited by Neil J. Smelser, 695–738. Newberry Park, CA: Sage.

Melucci, Alberto. 1980. The new social movements: a theoretical approach. *Social Science Information* 19 (2):199–226.

———. 1989. *Nomads of the present.* Philadelphia: Temple University Press.

———. 1994. A strange kind of newness: what's "new" in new social movements. In *New social movements: from ideology to identity,* edited by E. Laraña, H. Johnston, and J. R. Gusfield, 101–132. Philadelphia: Temple University Press.

Metraux, Daniel A. 1998. Aum Shinrikyo and Japanese Youth. *Japan Studies Review* 2:69–79.

Mihashi, Osamu. 1987. The symbolism of social discrimination: a decoding of discriminatory language. *Current Anthropology* 28 (4):S19–S29.

Ministry of Health, Labor, and Welfare (MHLW). 2003. *Vital statistics occurring in Japan including foreigners.* Tokyo: Minister's Secretariat.

Miyai, Rika. 1997. A voice from the Aum generation. *Japanese Religions* 22 (1):91–96.

Monaghan, Leila F. 1996. *Signing, oralism, and the development of the New Zealand deaf community: an ethnography and history of language ideologies.* Ph.D. diss., UCLA.

———. 2003a. A world's eye view: deaf cultures in global perspective. In *Many ways to be deaf: international linguistic and sociocultural variation,* edited by L. Monaghan, C. Schmaling, K. Nakamura, and G. Turner, 1–24. Washington: Gallaudet University Press.

———. 2003b. The development of the New Zealand Deaf community. *Deaf Worlds* 19(1):36–63.

———. 2004. Personal communication by telephone, December 8.

Morell, Robert, Yong Liang, James H. Asher Jr., James L. Weber, John T. Hinnant, Sunaryana Winata, I. Nyomen Arhya, and Thomas B. Friedman. 1995. Analysis of short tandem repeat (STR) allele frequency distributions in a Balinese population. *Human Molecular Genetics* 4:85–91.

Morford, Jill P. 1996. Insights to language from the study of gesture: a review of research on the gestural communication of non-signing deaf people. *Language & Communication* 16 (2):165–178.

Morris, Aldon D., and Carol McClurg Mueller, eds. 1992. *Frontiers in social movement theory*. New Haven: Yale University Press.

Morris, Rosalind C. 1995. All made up: performance theory and the new anthropology of sex and gender. *Annual Review of Anthropology* 24:567–592.

Najita, Tetsuo, and J. Victor Koschmann, eds. 1982. *Conflict in modern Japanese history: the neglected tradition*. Princeton: Princeton University Press.

Nakamura, Karen. 2002. Resistance and co-optation: the Japanese Federation of the Deaf and its relations with state power. *Social Science Japan Journal* 5, No. 1 (April):17–35. Oxford: Oxford University Press.

———. 2003. U-turns, "deaf shock," and the hard-of-hearing: Japanese deaf identities at the borderlands. In *Many ways to be deaf: international linguistic and sociocultural variation*, edited by L. Monaghan, C. Schmaling, K. Nakamura, and G. Turner, 211–229. Washington: Gallaudet University Press.

Napier, Susan J. 1996. Panic sites: the Japanese imagination from Godzilla to Akira. In *Contemporary Japan and popular culture*, edited by J. W. Treat, 235–262. Honolulu: University of Hawaii Press.

Neary, Ian. 1997. Burakumin in contemporary Japan. In *Japan's minorities: the illusion of homogeneity*, edited by M. Weiner, 50–78. New York: Routledge.

Ninomiya, Akiie Henry. 1986. Japanese attitudes towards disabled people. *Japan Christian Quarterly (Tokyo)* 52 (4):202–206.

Ogasawara, Yuko. 1998. *Office ladies and salaried men: power, gender, and work in Japanese companies*. Berkeley: University of California Press.

Okamoto, Masazumi. 1989. A position paper on Japanese Sign Language: its place in higher education in Japan. M.A. Project, California State University—Northridge.

Ooms, Herman. 1996. *Tokugawa village practice: class, status, power, law*. Berkeley: University of California Press.

Osugi, Yutaka. 1997. In search of the phonological representation in ASL (signed languages, articulatory clusters). Ph.D. diss., University of Rochester.

Padden, Carol. 1980. The deaf community and culture of deaf people. In *Sign language and the deaf community*, edited by C. Baker and R. Battison. Silver Spring, MD: National Association of the Deaf.

Padden, Carol, and Tom Humphries. 1988. *Deaf in America: voices from a culture*. Cambridge: Harvard University Press.

Pekkanen, Robert. 2002. Japan's dual civil society: members without advocates. Ph.D. diss., Harvard University.

———. 2004a. Molding Japanese civil society: state structure incentives and the patterning of civil society. In *The state of civil society in Japan*, edited by Frank Schwartz and Susan Pharr. Cambridge: Cambridge University Press.

———. 2004b. Personal communication, October 6.

Pharr, Susan J. 1990. *Losing face: status politics in Japan*. Berkeley: University of California Press.

Pharr, Susan J., and Ellis S. Krauss, eds. 1996. *Media and politics in Japan*. Honolulu: University of Hawaii Press.

Preston, Paul Michael. 1994. *Mother father deaf: living between sound and silence.* Cambridge: Harvard University Press.

Reber, Emily. 1999. Buraku mondai in Japan: historical and modern perspectives and directions for the future. *Harvard Human Rights Journal* 12 (Spring): 297–359.

Reilly, Judy S., and Martina McIntire. 1980. ASL and PSE: what's the difference? In *American Sign Language in a bilingual, bicultural context*, edited by F. Caccamise and D. Hicks, 85–113. Washington: National Association of the Deaf.

Rich, Adrienne Cecile. 1980. Compulsory heterosexuality and lesbian existence. *Signs: Journal of Women in Culture and Society* 5:631–660.

Richie, Donald. 1992. *A lateral view: essays on culture and style in contemporary Japan.* Berkeley, CA: Stone Bridge Press.

Robertson, Jennifer Ellen. 1991. *Native and newcomer: making and remaking a Japanese city.* Berkeley: University of California Press.

Rohlen, Thomas P. 1974. *For harmony and strength.* Berkeley: University of California Press.

———. 1983. *Japan's high schools.* Berkeley: University of California Press.

Roper Center for Public Opinion Research. 1995. NHK Broadcasting Culture Research Department Poll conducted January 6, 1995. Storrs, CT: University of Connecticut Roper Center.

———. 1998. NHK Broadcasting Culture Research Department Poll conducted May 1, 1998. Storrs, CT: University of Connecticut Roper Center.

Ryang, Sonia. 1992. Indoctrination or rationalization?: the anthropology of "North Koreans" in Japan. *Critique of Anthropology* 12 (2):101–132.

———. 1993. Poverty of language and the reproduction of ideology: Korean language for Chongryun. *Journal of Asian and African Studies* 28 (3–4):230–242.

———. 1997. *North Koreans in Japan: language, ideology, and identity.* Boulder, CO: Westview.

Schmaling, Constanze. 2003. A for apple: the impact of western education and ASL on the deaf community in Kano State, Northern Nigeria. In *Many ways to be deaf: international linguistic and sociocultural variation*, edited by L. F. Monaghan, C. Schmaling, K. Nakamura, and G. Turner. Washington: Gallaudet University Press.

Scott, James C. 1976. *The moral economy of the peasant: rebellion and subsistence in Southeast Asia.* New Haven: Yale University Press.

———. 1985. *Weapons of the weak: everyday forms of peasant resistance.* New Haven: Yale University Press.

———. 1990. *Domination and the arts of resistance: hidden transcripts.* New Haven: Yale University Press.

———. 1998. *Seeing like a state: how certain schemes to improve the human condition have failed.* New Haven: Yale University Press.

Sellek, Yoko. 1997. Nikkeijin: the phenomenon of return migration. In *Japan's minorities: the illusion of homogeneity*, edited by Michael Weiner, 178–210. New York: Routledge.

Senghas, Ann. 1994. Nicaragua's lessons for language acquisition. *Signpost* 7 (1):32–39.

Senghas, Richard J. 2003. New ways to be deaf in Nicaragua: individual and community development. In *Many ways to be deaf: international linguistic and sociocultural variation*, edited by L. F. Monaghan, C. Schmaling, K. Nakamura, and G. Turner. 260–301. Washington: Gallaudet University Press.

Senghas, Richard J., and Judy Kegl. 1994. Social considerations in the emergence of idioma de signos nicaraguense (Nicaraguan Sign Language). *Signpost* 7 (1):40–46.

Senghas, Richard J., and Leila Monaghan. 2002. Signs of their times: deaf communities and the culture of language. *Annual Review of Anthropology* 31:69–97.

Siddle, Richard. 1996. *Race, resistance, and the Ainu of Japan.* Sheffield Centre for Japanese Studies/Routledge series. New York: Routledge.

——. 1997. Ainu: Japan's indigenous people. In *Japan's minorities: the illusion of homogeneity*, edited by Michael Weiner, 17–49. New York: Routledge.

Snow, David A., and Robert D. Benford. 1992. Master frames and cycles of protest. In *Frontiers in social movement theory*, edited by A. D. Morris and C. McClurg Mueller, 133–155.New Haven: Yale University Press.

Snow, David A., and E. Burke Rochford, Jr. 1986. Frame alignment processes, micromobilization, and movement participation. *American Sociological Review* 51 (August):464–481.

Steinhoff, Patricia G. 1989. Hijackers, bombers, and bank robbers: managerial style in the Japanese Red Army. *Journal of Asian Studies* 48 (4):724–40.

Sterngold, James. 1994. Fear of phrases: When *Hage shokuba no hana=?%¥*#! New York Times*, December 18, E1, E6.

Stokoe, William C. 1960. Sign language structure. *Studies in linguistics: occasional papers* 8.

——. 1970. *The study of sign language.* Washington: ERIC Clearinghouse for Linguistics, Center for Applied Linguistics.

——. 1993. *Sign language structure: an outline of visual communication systems of the American deaf.* Silver Spring, MD: Linstok Press.

——. 1994. Discovering a neglected language. *Sign Language Studies* (85):377–382.

Stokoe, William C., ed. 1980. *Sign and culture: a reader for students of American Sign Language.* Silver Spring, MD: Linstok Press.

Stokoe, William C., Jr., Dorothy C. Casterline, and Carl G. Croneberg. 1965. *A dictionary of American Sign Language on linguistic principles.* Washington: Gallaudet College Press.

Sutton-Spence, Rachel. 2003. British manual alphabets in the education of deaf people since the seventeenth century. In *Many ways to be deaf: international linguistic and sociocultural variation*, edited by L. F. Monaghan, C. Schmaling, K. Nakamura, and G. Turner. Washington: Gallaudet University Press.

Taira, Koji. 1971. Japan's invisible race made visible? *Economic Development and Cultural Change* 19:663–668.

——. 1997. Troubled national identity: the Ryukyuans/Okinawans. In *Japan's minorities: the illusion of homogeneity*, edited by M. Weiner, 140–177. New York: Routledge.

Tobin, Joseph J., ed. 1992. *Re-made in Japan: everyday life and consumer taste in a changing society.* New Haven: Yale University Press.

Treat, John Whittier. 1995. *Writing ground zero: Japanese literature and the atomic bomb.* Chicago: University of Chicago Press.

Tsuda, Takeyuki (Gaku). 1998. The stigma of ethnic difference: the structure of prejudice and "discrimination" towards Japan's new immigrant minority. *Journal of Japanese Studies* 24 (2):317–359.

——. 1999. The permanence of "temporary" migration: the "structural embeddedness" of Japanese-Brazilian migrant workers in Japan. *Journal of Asian Studies* 58 (3).

——. 2000. Acting Brazilian in Japan: ethnic resistance among return migrants. *Ethnology* 39 (1):55–71.

Tsurushima, Setsure. 1984. Human rights issues and the status of Burakumin and Koreans in Japan. In *Institutions for change in Japanese society*, edited by G. A. DeVos. Berkeley: Institute of East Asian Studies, University of California.

Upham, Frank. 1987. Toward a new perspective on Japanese law. In *Law and social change in postwar Japan*, edited by F. Upham, 205–227. Cambridge: Harvard University Press.

——. 1993. Unplaced persons and movements for place. In *Postwar Japan as history*, edited by A. Gordon, 325–346. Berkeley: University of California Press.

Valli, Clayton, and Ceil Lucas, eds. 1995. *Linguistics of American Sign Language*. Washington: Gallaudet University Press.

Van Cleve, John Vickrey, and Barry A. Crouch. 1989. *A place of their own: creating the deaf community in America*. Washington: Gallaudet University Press.

Wetherall, William. 1993. The Ainu Nation. *Japan Times Weekly*, January 2:1, 3–5. Accessed article online at http://members.jcom.home.ne.jp/yosha/minorities/ainunation.html, August 21, 2004.

White, James W. 1995. *Ikki: social conflict and political protest in early modern Japan*. Ithaca: Cornell University Press.

Wiley, Norbert. 1994. The politics of identity in American history. In *Social theory and the politics of identity*, edited by C. Calhoun, 130–149. Oxford: Blackwell.

Williams, Rhys H. 1995. Constructing the public good: social movements and cultural resources. *Social Problems* 42 (1):301–321.

Winata, Sunaryana, I. Nyoman Arhya, Sukarti Moeljopawiro, John T. Hinnant, Yong Liang, Thomas B. Friedman, and James H. Asher Jr.. 1995. Congenital nonsyndromal autosomal recessive deafness in Bengkala, an isolated Balinese village. *Journal of Medical Genetics* 32:336–343.

Woodward, James. 1972. Implications for sociolinguistic research among the Deaf. *Sign Language Studies* 1:1–7.

——. 1980. Sociolinguistic research on American Sign Language: an historical perspective. In *Sign language and the deaf community: essays in honor of William C. Stokoe*, ed. Charlotte Baker and Robbin Battison, 117–134. Silver Spring, MD: National Association of the Deaf.

Woolard, Kathryn A., and Bambi B. Schieffelin. 1994. Language ideology. *Annual Review of Anthropology* 23:55–82.

Wrigley, Owen. 1996. *The politics of deafness*. Washington: Gallaudet University Press.

Yazbak, F. Edward, and Kathy L. Lang-Radosh. 2001. Adverse outcomes associated with postpartum rubella or MMR Vaccine. *Medical Sentinel* 6 (3):95–99, 108.

Japanese Sources

PERIODICALS

D = D (the newsletter of D-Pro). Tokyo: Japan.

JDN = Japanese Deaf News is the monthly newspaper of the Japanese Federation of the Deaf, Tokyo. Although the Japanese title of the newspaper has changed through the years, I use the *JDN* abbreviation in citations to reduce confusion:
1931– *Rōa Geppō* (Deaf Monthly Report; pre-JFD).
1948– *Nippon Rōa Shinbun* (Japanese Deaf Newspaper).
1949– *Nippon Rōa Nyūsu* (Japanese Deaf News).
1952– *Nihon Chōryoku-shōgai Shinbun* (Japanese Hearing Impairment Newspaper).

　　The *JDN* is available in bound, archival editions through the JFD Publishing Office. Currently there are 7 editions, spanning 1931–1995. This is a key primary source of information regarding the changes in the deaf community in the modern period.

SLCS = Sign Language Communication Studies: Quarterly [Journal] of the Japan Institute for Sign Language Studies [Shuwa Komyunikeeshon Kenkyū]. Tokyo: Japan.

BOOKS AND ARTICLES

Note: I have tried to use the official English names of publishing committees and organizations where possible. Otherwise, the translations are my own.

All Japan Sign Interpreter Research Center (AJSIRC) [Zenkoku Shuwa Tsūyaku Mondai Kenkyūkai]. 1994. *Kakebita Zentsūken: 20nen no ayumi* [Keep flying Zentsuken (All Japan Sign Language Interpreter Research Center)]. Kyoto: Zenkoku Shuwatsūyaku Mondai Kenkyūkai.

Asahi Shimbun. 2005. Ōsaka-shi, 66 dantai ni OB 3500 nin [Osaka City finds 66 groups with 3,500 Old Boys]. *Asahi Shimbun* (Kyoto ed.). March 17:1.

Association of Cochlear Implant Transmitted Audition (ACITA). 2002. Jinkō naiji sōyōshasū [Number of people using cochlear implants]. Web page: http://www.normanet.ne.jp/~acita/info/statistics.html. Accessed March 25, 2005.

Cabinet Office [Naikakufu], ed. 2003. *Shōgaisha hakusho* [Disability white paper]. Tokyo: Government Publishing Office.

Culture and Information Center for Hearing Impaired Persons [Chōryoku Shōgaisha Jōhō Bunka Sentaa]. 1995. Jigyō gaiyō: Heisen 7nen 6gatsu [An outline of the Center's projects]. Tokyo: Shakai Fukushi Hōjin Chōryoku Shōgaisha Jōhō Bunka Sentaa.

———. 1998. Shuwa Tsūyakushi Nintei Shiken Seido no Arikata Kentō Iinkai Hōkokusho [A report from the Committee to Analyze the Sign Interpreter Qualification Exam]. Tokyo: Shakai Fukushi Hōjin Chōryoku Shōgaisha Jōhō Bunka Center.

D Editorial Board [D Henshūshitsu]. 1993. *D 11/1/1991–10/1/1993.* Tokyo: *D* Editorial Board.

Editorial Board for the 100th Anniversary of Deaf and Blind Education [Mōrō Kyōiku Kaigaku Hyakushūnen Kinen Jigyō Jikkō Iinkai Henshūbukai], ed. 1978. *Kyōtofu mōrō kyōiku hyakunenshi* [The 100–year history of blind-deaf education in Kyoto Prefecture]. Kyoto: Editorial Board for the 100th Commemoration of the Opening of the Kyoto School for the Deaf and Blind.

Ichida Yasuhiro. 1998. Nihon Shuwa no bunpō [The grammar of Japanese Sign]. *Gekkan Gengo [Monthly Language]* 27 (4): 44–63.

———. 2005. Nihon shuwa no on'inron to sūshi taikei [The phonology and numerical structure of Japanese Sign]. *Sign Language Communication Studies* 57:8–17.

Ikoinomura Central Welfare Facility for Hearing and Language Impairment [Ikoinomura Chōkaku Gengo Shōgaisha Sōgō Fukushi Shisetsu]. 1993. *Ningen to shite* [As human beings]. Vols. 1–3. Kyoto: Chōkaku Gengo Shōgaisha Sōgō Fukushi Shisetsu.

Itabashi Masakuni. 1991. Rōa undō no rekishi [The history of deaf movements]. In *Atarashii chōkaku shōgaishazō wo motomete* [In the search for a new image of deaf people]. Tokyo: Japanese Federation of the Deaf.

Itō Masao. 1998. *Rekishino nakano rōasha* [Deaf within history]. Tokyo: Kindai Shuppan.

Itō Shun'ichi. 1940. *Iwanu hana: Nihon rōa hishi* [The flower that doesn't speak: Japan's hidden deaf history]. Tokyo: Kyōiku Kenkyūkai.

Iwabuchi Norio. 1991. *Jiritsu he no jōken: mimi no fujiyū na hito no fukushi* [The requirements for self-independence: an introduction to the welfare issues of the hearing impaired]. Tokyo: NHK Publications.

Japanese Federation of the Deaf (JFD). 1994. *Ajia no shuwa jijō* [A report on Asian sign languages]. Tokyo: Japanese Federation of the Deaf, Japan Sign Language Research Institute.

———. 1996. *Renmei no genzei* [The structure of the federation]. Tokyo: Japanese Federation of the Deaf.

———. 1997. *Heisei 9–nendo Hyōjun Shuwa Kenkyūjo Jigyō hōkokusho* [New signs: a report of the 1997 Sign Standardization Committee]. Tokyo: Japanese Federation of the Deaf.

———. 1998a. *Kikoenaitte donna koto* [What is it like to not be able to hear?]. Tokyo: Hitotsubashi Shuppan.

———. 1998b. Shuwa ni kansuru FAQ [Frequently asked questions about signing]. *Sign Language Communication Studies* 28:2.

———. 2004. Dai 55kai Hyōgi'inkai sankō shiryō [55th Annual Board Meeting reference material]. Tokyo: Japanese Federation of the Deaf.

Kanda Kazuyuki. 1989. Shuwa no hensen [Changes in sign language]. *Nihon Shuwa Gakujutsu* 10:30–43.

———. 1998. Shuwa toha dōiu gengoka [What type of language is Japanese signing?]. *Gekkan Gengo* 27 (4): 26–33.

Kawai Yohsuke. 1991. Chōkakushōgaisha Undō [Deaf movements]. In *Atarashii chōkaku shōgaishazō wo motomete* [In the search for a new image of deaf people]. Tokyo: Japanese Federation of the Deaf.

Kimura Harumi and Ichida Yasuhiro. 1995. Rō bunka sengen: gengoteki shōsūha to shite no rōsha [A declaration of deaf culture: deaf people as a linguistic minority]. *Gendai Shisō* 23 (3):354–399.

Kimura Harumi. 1998. Shuwa nyūmon: hajime no ippo [An introduction to signing: some first steps]. *Gekkan Gengo* 27 (4):34–42.

Kindaichi Kyōsuke. 1995. *Shinmeikai kokugo jiten dai 4 ban* [The Shinmeikai Japanese dictionary, 4th ed.]. Tokyo: Sanseidō.

Kyoto City Signing Circle Mimizuku 20th Anniversary Publication Committee [Kyōto-shi Shuwa Gakushūkai Mimizuku 20–shūnen Kinen Shuppan Jigyō Henshū Iinkai]. 1983. *Kyōto-shi Shuwa Gakushūkai Mimizuku: 20–shūnen no ayumi* [The 20-year history of the Kyoto City Signing Circle Mimizuku[1]]. Kyoto: Kyōto-shi Shuwa Gakushūkai Mimizuku.

Kyoto Forum on Deaf Education [Chōkaku Shōgai Kyōiku Kyōto Fōramu]. 1996. *Kyōtorō 'Jugyō Kyohi' sonogo: kōtōbu no kyōiku wo chūshinni* [After the "school strike" at Kyoto School for the Deaf: focusing on education at the high school level]. Kyoto: Kyoto Forum on Deaf Education.

Kyoto Prefectural Association for the Hearing Impaired. 1996 [1968]. *Jugyō Kyohi: 3.3 Seimei ni kansuru shiryōshū* [Student strikes: background material on the "3.3 Proclamation"]. Kyoto: Kyoto Prefectural Association for the Hearing Impaired.

Kyoto Prefectural School for the Deaf. 1998. *Heisei 10–nendo gakkō yōran* [1998 Annual report on the school]. Kyoto: Kyoto Prefectural School for the Deaf.

Matsumoto Masayuki. 1991. Hōritsu-mondai wo chūshin ni [Focusing on legal issues]. In *Atarashii Chōkaku shōgaishazō wo motomete* [In the search for a new image of deaf people]. Tokyo: Japanese Federation of the Deaf.

1. A *mimizuku* is a Japanese owl with large ears that look like horns, thus the English name, "Horned Owl." The name is a triple-entendre. First, the circle met late at night, just like owls. Second, an owl has big eyes, prominent ears, and good hearing, just like the students. The third level is a bad pun: *mimizuku* sounds like *mimi-tsuku*—to have or put on ears—as well as *mi-ni-tsuku*—to become good at something.

——. 1997a. *Rōasha, shuwa, shuwa tsūyaku* [Deaf persons, signing, sign interpreters]. Kyoto: Bunrikaku.

——. 1997b. Jikkanteki shuwa bunpō shiron I [A practical sign language grammar (unit 1)]. *Sign Language Communication Studies* 27:4.

——. 2001. *Jikkanteki shuwa bunpō shiron* [A practical sign language grammar]. Sign Language Communication Library 1. Tokyo: Japanese Federation of the Deaf.

Ministry of Education (MOE). 1992. *Tokushu kyōiku shogakkō gakushū shidōyōryō kaisetsu: rō gakkōhen* [Explanation of the guidelines for special education schools: schools for the deaf]. Tokyo: Kaibundō.

——. 1993. Chōkakushōgaiji no Komyunikeeshon Shudan ni Kansuru Chōsakenkyūkyōrokusha Kaigi Hōkoku [A report on the findings of the Research Committee on Communication Techniques for Hearing-Impaired Children]. *TC Kenkyūhō [TC Research Reports]* 53 (addendum).

——. 1995. *Chōkakushōgai kyōiku no tebiki: tayōna komyunikēshon shudan to sore wo katsuyō shita shidō [A handbook of hearing-impaired education: implementing guidelines for communication methods]*. Tokyo: Kaibundo.

Ministry of Health and Welfare Institute of Population Problems (MHWIPP). 1995. *Jinkō tōkei shiryōshū* [Latest demographic statistics 1995]. Tokyo: Ministry of Health and Welfare.

Ministry of Health and Welfare Disability Health and Welfare Division [Kōseishō Shōgai Hoken Fukushibu]. 1998. *Heisei 10nen shintai shōgaiji jittai chōsa oyobi shintai shōgaisha jittai chōsa no gaiyō ni tsuite* [1998 report on the status of disabled children and adults]. White paper dated July 2. Tokyo: Ministry of Health and Welfare.

Minoura Yasuko. 1991. *Kodomo no ibunka taiken* [The cross-cultural experience of children]. Tokyo: Shisakusha.

Miura Sangendō, ed. 1922. *Yokihino tameni* [Toward a better day]. Kyoto: Dōbōsha.

Murayama Miwa. 1995. *Andōnatsu: 'Hitoridekurasuyo'* [Bean filled donuts: I'm going to live by myself.] Tokyo: Nanananasha.

Nakamura, Karen. 1999a. Gengo bunka jinruigaku kara mita Nichibei rō shakai to kyōiku [A cross-cultural comparison of deaf society and education in Japan and the U.S. from a linguistic and cultural anthropological perspective]. *TC Kenkyūhō* 79:24–39.

——. 1999b. Nichibei no rō undō: hikakukenkyū no shiten kara [Deaf movements in Japan and the United States: a comparative approach]. *Sign Language Communication Studies* 33:45–54.

National Council of the Disability Liberation Movement (NCDLM)—Kansai Block [Zenkoku Shōgaisha Kaihō Undō Renrakukaigi Kansai-burokku], ed. 1998. *Shitteimasuka? Shōgaisha mondai ichimon ittō* [Do you know? the problems facing people with disabilities: one question, one answer]. Osaka: Kaihō Shuppansha.

National Institute for Population and Social Security Research [Kokuritsu Shakai Hoshō Jinkō Mondai Kenkyūjo]. 2002. *Social security annual report [Shakai hoshō tōkei nenpō]*. Tokyo: National Institute for Population and Social Security Research.

Ogura Takeo. 1997. *Yamanashi-ken chōkaku shōgaisha jōhō teikyō shisetu kensetsu undō ni torikonde* [A report on the movement to build a deaf information center in Yamanashi Prefecture]. Yamanashi: Yamanashi Association of the Hearing Impaired.

Ōhara Shōzō. 1987. *Shuwa no chie: sono gogen wo chūshin ni* [The wisdom of sign language: toward understanding its roots]. Tokyo: Japanese Federation of the Deaf.

Okamoto Inamaru. 1999a. Furukawa Tashirō no mōrō kyōiku no sōshi to kon'nichiteki igi [The contemporary significance of the foundation of blind-deaf education by Furukawa Tashirō]. *Kyōiku* 34:14–35.

——. 1999b. Furukawa Tashirō no gengo kyōikukan to hōhōron: Rōkyōiku Gakkai Dai 40kai Taikai shōto rekuchā [The linguistic pedagogy and methodology of Furukawa Tashirō: a short lecture in commemoration of the 40th meeting of the Association for the Study of Deaf Education]. *Rōkyōikugaku* 40 (4):203–212.

——. 2000. *Shuwa no hajimari* [The beginning of sign language]. August 4. Tokyo: NHK Texts.

Ono Takushi. 1991. *Haikō no natsu: nanchōjitachi no Kōshien* [The summer that school closed: Koshien Stadium for the hearing-impaired children]. Tokyo: Kodansha Bunko.

Ototake Hirotada. 1998. *Gotai fumanzoku* [Imperfect limbs]. Tokyo: Kodansha.

Ototake Iwazō. 1929. *Nihon shomin kyōiku shi* [The history of the education of the masses in Japan]. Tokyo: Meguro Publishing.

Ōya Zen'ichirō. 1995. *Kaisō* [Thoughts]. Tokyo: Japanese Federation of the Deaf.

Prime Minister's Office [Sōrifu], ed. 1995, 1996, 1999, 2003. *Shōgaisha hakusho* [Disability white paper]. Tokyo: Ministry of Finance Publishing.

Sakaiya, Taichi. 1980. *Dankai no sedai.* Tokyo: Bungei Shunju.

Sakata Keiko. 1990. Chōkaku shōgaisha no jigadōitusei nitsuite I, II [Report I & II: on the self-identity of the hearing impaired]. *Rōkyōiku Kagaku* 32:61–81, 109–125.

Shinoda Saburō and Japanese Federation of the Deaf. 1993. *Shuwa no handbook* [A signing handbook]. Tokyo: Sainseidō.

Suzuki Yasuyuki. 2001. *Shuwa no tame no gengogaku no jōshiki* (A general knowledge of linguistics for sign language). Sign Language Communication Library 2. Tokyo: Japanese Federation of the Deaf.

Takamura Mariko. 1993. *Amerika shuwa ryūgakuki* [Diary of an American Sign exchange student]. Tokyo: Keishobō.

Tamura Tomoko. 1994. *Hāfu taimu: nijūgosai no kiseki* [Half time: my 25-year life history]. Utsunomiya: Takita Publishing.

Terajima Ryōan. 1713 [1715]. *Wa-Kan sansai zue* [An illustrated Japanese-Chinese encyclopedia]. Naniwa [Osaka, Japan]: Shōtoku Itsumi.

Tobe Yoshinari. 1987. *Harukanaru Kōshien* [Kōshien Stadium, ever so far away]. Tokyo: Futabasha.

Tokyo Shakujii School for the Deaf. 1995. *Sotsugyōsei shinrosaki* [Post-graduation tracking of alumni]. Tokyo: Shakujii School for the Deaf.

Tsukuba College of Technology Public Relations Committee. 1998. *Tsukuba Gijutsu Tankidaigaku gaiyō* [Outline of Tsukuba College of Technology]. Tsukuba City: Tsukuba College Printing Department.

Tsukuba University School for the Deaf Alumni Association. 1991. *Tsukuba Daigaku Fuzoku Rōgakkō Dōsōkai hyakunenshi* [The 100-year history of the Tsukuba University School for the Deaf Alumni Association]. Chiba: Tsukuba University School for the Deaf Alumni Association.

Uenō Seigō. 1996. Rōsha to wa dareka / Shuwa to wa dare no mono ka? [Who is deaf? Who does signing belong to?]. *Gendai Shisō* 24 (05):110–136.

Yamamoto Osamu. 1988. *Harukanaru Kōshien* [Kōshien Stadium, ever so far away]. Original story by Tobe Yoshinari. Serialized 1988–1990 in *Weekly Manga Action.* Tokyo: Futabasha.

——. 1998. *"Donguri no Ie" no dessan* [Rough sketches of "Donguri no Ie"]. Tokyo: Iwanami.

Yasuragi, the Ibaraki Prefectural Center for the Hearing Impaired [Ibaraki-kenritsu Chōkakushōgaisha Fukushi Sentaa Yasuragi]. 1992. *Ibaraki-kenritsu Chōkakushōgaisha Fukushi Sentā Yasuragi* [Yasuragi, the Ibaraki Prefectural Center for the Hearing Impaired]. Mito City, Ibaragi Prefecture: Ibaragi Association for the Hearing Impaired.

Yazawa Kuniteru. 1996. Dōkateki sōgō kara tayōsei wo mitometa kyōsei he: rōky-ōiku kara mita "rō bunka sengen" [From assimilation towards a symbiotic recognition of diversity: "a deaf declaration" from the perspective of deaf education]. *Gendai Shisō* 24 (5):23–31.

Yoneyama Akihiko. 1998. Korekara shuwa wo manabu hito no tameni [For those who are about to learn signing]. *Gekkan Gengo* 27 (4):20–25.

Yonekawa Akihiko, ed. 1997. *Nihongo-Shuwa jiten* [Japanese Language Signing dictionary]. Tokyo: Japanese Federation of the Deaf.

Yoshizawa Shōzō. 1996. Bairingaru kyōiku, bairingarizumu wo kangaeru tokino shuwa ya gengo no shosokumen ni tsuite [Thoughts on signing and language in bilingualism and bilingual education from the reader's perspective]. Unpublished manuscript dated April 14, 1996.

SERIALIZED TELEVISION DRAMAS, MOVIES, AND ANIMATIONS WITH DEAF THEMES

Karube Junko. 1997. *Kimi no te ga sasayaiteiru* [Your whispering hands]. Serialized television drama. Original story by Karube Junko. Directed by Shinjō Takehiko. Tokyo: Asahi Television.

Kitagawa Eriko. 1995. *Aishiteiru to ittekure* [Tell me that you love me]. Original screenplay by Kitagawa Eriko. Directed by Kijima Seiichiro. Serialized television drama. Tokyo: Tokyo Broadcasting Station.

Matsuyama Shōzō. 1951. *Namonaku mazushiku utsukushiku*. Released in the U.S. as *Happiness of us alone*. Motion Picture. Tokyo: Tōhō Pictures.

Osawa Yutaka. 1990. *Harukanaru Kōshien* [Kōshien Stadium, ever so far away]. Original story by Ono Takushi, Tobe Yoshinari, and Yamamoto Osamu. Directed by Osawa Yutaka. Motion Picture. Tokyo: Toho Pictures.

Tatsui Yukari. 1995. *Hoshi no kinka (Die sterntaler)* [Gold coins in the sky]. Original screenplay by Tatsui Yukari. Directed by Yoshino Hiroshi et al. Serialized television drama. Tokyo: Nippon Television.

Yamamoto Osamu. 1997. *Donguri no Ie* [Acorn House]. Original screenplay by Yamamoto Osamu. Animated motion film. Tokyo: Donguri no Ie Seisaku Iinkai.

Index